Microsoft® SQL Server™ 2005:

Database Essentials
Step by Step

Solid Quality Learning

PUBLISHED BY
Microsoft Press
A Division of Microsoft Corporation
One Microsoft Way
Redmond, Washington 98052-6399

Library of Congress Control Number 2006921727

Printed and bound in the United States of America.

1 2 3 4 5 6 7 8 9   QWT   1 0 9 8 7 6

Distributed in Canada by H.B. Fenn and Company Ltd.

A CIP catalogue record for this book is available from the British Library.

Microsoft Press books are available through booksellers and distributors worldwide. For further information about international editions, contact your local Microsoft Corporation office or contact Microsoft Press International directly at fax (425) 936-7329. Visit our Web site at www.microsoft.com/mspress. Send comments to mspinput@microsoft.com.

Acquisitions Editor: Ben Ryan
Project Editors: Valerie Woolley and Rosemary Caperton
Technical Editor: Kurt Meyer
Editorial and Production: Custom Editorial Productions, Inc.

Body Part No. X11-50510

Table of Contents

**What do you think
of this book?
We want to hear from you!**
Microsoft is interested in hearing your feedback about this
publication so we can continually improve our books and learning
resources for you. To participate in a brief online survey, please visit:
www.microsoft.com/learning/booksurvey/

Part II   How to Create a Microsoft SQL Server 2005 Database

**4   Gathering and Understanding Business Requirements
before Creating Database Objects** **73**

5   Designing a Database to Solve Business Needs **91**

Part III   How to Query Data from Microsoft SQL Server 2005

Part IV   How to Modify Data in Microsoft SQL Server 2005

Introduction

Database solutions are integral to every organization that needs to store, analyze, and report on data. Microsoft SQL Server 2005 provides a robust platform for implementing your database solutions. SQL Server 2005 is packed with easy-to-use features that make it an ideal environment. In particular, this latest version of SQL Server is more secure, more scalable, and easier to use and manage than previous versions.

Microsoft SQL Server 2005: Database Essentials Step by Step is the first book in a series of two designed to help you build skills in a number of essential SQL Server areas. You can use this book if you are new to programming databases or if you are switching from another information storage system, such as Microsoft Office Access, or from a file-based storage system, such as .dbf or .txt files.

Inside, you'll find information on which installation options to use in both a development and a production environment; which tools to use during your database design, database creation, and database objects definition; and what steps to take to retrieve and update data. The hands-on presentation of database skills will prepare you to move to the next level of SQL Server database management and to start applying the tools you've practiced in these chapters to your own work.

The second book in the series, *Microsoft SQL Server 2005: Applied Techniques Step by Step*, builds on the material presented in this book, with more extensive coverage of retrieving and analyzing data and of many features that make SQL Server 2005 such a comprehensive solution to your database needs.

Who This Book Is For

Microsoft SQL Server 2005: Database Essentials Step by Step is intended for developers and database administrators who want to begin using SQL Server 2005 as their main data repository and to use it not only as another file storage method, but also to enhance and speed their applications. By following the step-by-step procedures in each chapter, you will obtain a comprehensive, hands-on introduction to the most important options needed to program your database solutions using SQL Server 2005. Your skill level, job function, and familiarity with SQL Server will determine how this book will best serve you. See the chart in "Finding Your Best Starting Point in This Book" to determine how you can get what you need from this book.

How This Book Is Organized

Part I of this book describes why you need a database system, what tools you need to easily create database solutions, and how to utilize the different applications and tools that accompany SQL Server 2005. Part II provides the step-by-step procedures needed to both design and create a database and its objects. Part III explains how to retrieve information. Part IV details the steps and various methods used to update information in a database.

Finding Your Best Starting Point in This Book

If you are:	Follow these steps:
New to Relational Databases	1. Install the sample files as described in the "Sample Files" section of this Introduction.
	2. Start at the beginning and work through the entire book for a quick introduction to the many capabilities of SQL Server 2005.
Planning to Set Up a Database in Your Shop	1. Install the sample files as described in the "Sample Files" section of this Introduction.
	2. Pay particular attention to Chapter 4, which will guide you through some of the analysis you'll need before beginning to design your system.
Familiar with Relational Databases or Migrating from an Earlier Version of SQL Server	1. Install the sample files as described in the "Sample Files" section of this Introduction.
	2. Skim Chapter 2 as necessary and then work through Chapter 3. Skim the remainder of the book to find the areas that might be new to you.
Migrating to SQL Server from Another Database Platform	1. Install the sample files as described in the "Sample Files" section of this Introduction.
	2. Work carefully through Chapters 2 and 3, skip (or skim) Chapters 4 and 5, and then work through the remainder of the book.
Familiar with SQL Server and Want to Enhance Your Understanding of the Capabilities in SQL Server 2005	1. Install the sample files as described in the "Sample Files" section of this Introduction.
	2. Focus on Chapters 3, 4, and 5 and work through the rest of the book depending on your areas of interest.
Wanting to Deepen Your Level of Expertise in Coding Database Applications	1. Install the sample files as described in the "Sample Files" section of this Introduction.
	2. Skim Chapters 3, 4, and 5, then work carefully through the remaining chapters.
Referencing the Book after Working Through the Exercises	1. Use the index or the table of contents to find information about particular subjects.
	2. Read the Quick Reference sections at the end of each chapter to find a brief review of the syntax and techniques presented in the chapter.
Interested in Learning More about Applying the Techniques Covered in This Book	See *Microsoft SQL Server 2005: Applied Techniques Step by Step*, Microsoft Press, 2006 (ISBN 0-7356-2316-3).

Conventions and Features in This Book

This book presents information using conventions designed to make the information readable and easy to follow. Before you start the book, read the following list, which explains conventions you will see throughout the book and points out helpful features in the book that you might want to use.

Conventions

- Each chapter gives you a background explanation as well as a set of procedures for learning by doing. Each procedure is presented as a series of numbered steps (1, 2, and so on).

- Notes labeled "Tip" provide additional information or alternative methods for completing a step successfully.

- Notes labeled "Important" alert you to information you need to check before continuing.

- Text that you type appears in bold.

- SQL keywords appear in uppercase.

- Visual Basic programming elements appear in italics.

- A series of menu commands are shown separated by the pipe character (|).

- A plus sign (+) between two key names means that you must press those keys at the same time. For example, "Press Alt+Tab" means that you hold down the Alt key while you press the Tab key.

Other Features

- Sidebars throughout the book provide more in-depth information about the topic. The sidebars might contain background information, design tips, or features related to the information being discussed.

- Each chapter ends with a Quick Reference section. The Quick Reference section contains quick reminders of how to perform the tasks you learned in the chapter.

System Requirements

You will need the following hardware and software to complete the practice exercises in this book.

> **Note**   Microsoft SQL Server 2005 and Microsoft Visual Studio 2005 software are **not** included with this book! The CD-ROM packaged in the back of this book contains the code samples needed to complete the exercises. SQL Server 2005 and Visual Studio 2005 software must both be purchased separately.

- Microsoft Windows XP with Service Pack 2, Microsoft Windows Server 2003 with Service Pack 1, or Microsoft Windows 2000 with Service Pack 4

- Microsoft Visual Studio 2005 Standard Edition or Microsoft Visual Studio 2005 Professional Edition. For Chapter 5, you will need Microsoft Visio 2003, which is included with Visual Studio 2005 Professional with MSDN Premium. Alternatively, you can execute most of the code in this book using Microsoft Visual Basic 2005 Express Edition, which is available as a free download from *www.microsoft.com.*

- Microsoft SQL Server 2005 Express (included with Visual Studio 2005) or Microsoft SQL Server 2005 Developer Edition

- 600 MHz Pentium or compatible processor (1 GHz Pentium recommended)

- 256 MB RAM (512 MB or more recommended)

- Video monitor (800 × 600 or higher resolution) with at least 256 colors (1024 × 768 high-color 16-bit recommended)

- CD-ROM or DVD-ROM drive

- Microsoft mouse or compatible pointing device

Sample Files

The companion CD inside this book contains the sample files that you will use as you perform the exercises in the book. The files and step-by-step instructions in the chapters allow you to learn by doing, which is an easy and effective way to acquire and remember new skills.

Installing the Sample Files

Follow these steps to install the sample files on your computer so that you can use them with the exercises in this book.

1. Remove the companion CD from the package inside this book and insert it into your CD-ROM drive.

> **Note** An end user license agreement should open automatically. If this agreement does not appear, open My Computer on the desktop or Start menu, double-click the icon for your CD-ROM drive, and then double-click StartCD.exe.

2. Review the end user license agreement. If you accept the terms, select the accept option and then click Next.

   A menu will appear with options related to the book.

3. Click Install Sample Files.

4. Follow the instructions that appear.

   The sample files are installed to the following location on your computer:

   My Documents\Microsoft Press\SQL DB Essentials SBS

Using the Sample Files

Each chapter in this book explains when and how to use any sample files for that chapter. When it's time to use a sample file, the book will point you to the appropriate file or folder. The chapters are built around scenarios that simulate real programming projects so that you can easily apply the skills you learn to your own work. For SQL Script samples, you will typically open the file in SQL Server Management Studio, highlight the relevant portion of the script, and execute only that portion before proceeding. For Visual Studio projects, you will double-click the .sln file to open the project and navigate within Visual Studio to the relevant code.

Project	Description
Chapter 3	Scripts to learn how to create traces, to study how different actions against the database alter its performance, and to create some deadlock troubleshooting.
Chapter 6	Samples allow you to test each of the different ways to access database information using the different technologies that can be used.
Chapter 7	Samples show you how to perform select operations against the database to obtain different results.
Chapter 8	Samples demonstrate how to create and work with views.
Chapter 9	Samples demonstrate how to use programmable objects to retrieve information.
Chapter 10	AdoNet Samples folder: Shows you how to insert information using ADO.NET objects.
	Sample Codes folder: Includes different T-SQL scripts to insert information.
	SSIS folder: Contains samples about how to insert data using Integration Services.
Chapter 11	Samples to learn how to perform delete operations.
Chapter 11-Completed	Contains the final version after performance of all step-by-step operations in the chapter.
Chapter 12	Shows how to perform update operations against the database.
Chapter 12-Completed	Contains the final version after performance of all step-by-step operations in the chapter.

Uninstalling the Sample Files

Follow these steps to remove the sample files from your computer.

1. In the Control Panel, open Add Or Remove Programs.

2. From the list of Currently Installed Programs, select Microsoft SQL Server 2005 Database Essentials Step by Step.

3. Click Remove.

4. Follow the instructions that appear to remove the sample files.

Note   Sample files for this book are on the companion CD.

Support for This Book

Every effort has been made to ensure the accuracy of this book and the contents of the companion CD. As corrections or changes are collected, they will be added to a Microsoft Knowledge Base article. To view the list of known corrections for this book, visit the following site:

http://support.microsoft.com/kb/

Microsoft Learning provides support for books and companion CDs at the following address:

http://www.microsoft.com/learning/support/search.asp

Questions and Comments

If you have comments, questions, or ideas regarding the book or the companion CD or have questions that are not answered by visiting the sites listed above, please send them to Microsoft Press via e-mail to

mspinput@microsoft.com

Or via postal mail to

Microsoft Press
Attn: Microsoft SQL Server 2005: Database Essentials Step by Step Editor
One Microsoft Way
Redmond, WA 98052-6399

Please note that Microsoft software product support is not offered through the above addresses.

Acknowledgments

Authors

Miguel Egea

Fernando Guerrero

Javier Loria

Eladio Rincón

Mauro Sant'Anna

Daniel Seara

Antonio Soto

Technical Editor

Kurt Meyer

Part I
Introduction to Database Development with Microsoft SQL Server 2005

Chapter 1

Introducing Database Development with Microsoft SQL Server 2005

The world around you is full of data. Your brain is constantly processing this data even if you do not realize it. Your eyes capture light of different intensities and colors, and your brain translates this data into images that you can identify. Your ears capture some sounds, and your brain analyzes their nature and highlights whatever you should pay attention to. All of your senses are continuously capturing data, which flows to your brain and is analyzed, filtered, highlighted for instant attention, or discarded as unimportant.

Some of this data also gets stored for future use. You remember a certain smell, but perhaps you do not remember why. Why do you recognize a certain face or a particular song? This happens because your brain is capable not only of storing an immense amount of data, but also of processing this data in such a way that you can break down complex objects into individual units of information stored in your brain. This book will help you to use a computer system to store and retrieve data in a way that is sensible and practical for business purposes.

The Process of Storing and Managing Data

Your brain is not well designed to deal with vast amounts of unnatural data, such as numbers and business information. You might know someone who has memorized an entire telephone book by heart (my mother had that power when our hometown contained only 100 telephone numbers). However, your brain has been designed for more specific purposes such as protecting you against natural enemies, finding food, and perpetuating your family tree. In your personal life, do you remember the telephone numbers of all of your contacts? You might need a good way to store and retrieve them when necessary, just as the database within your cell phone is capable of doing.

My grandfather operated his own little convenience store, and he kept all of his important information in several notebooks. He kept these notebooks current by writing down the amount owed to him each time someone bought something they could not immediately afford. These books were for his own personal use, and whether the debts were repaid concerned no one but him.

However, in any organization, you need to share information. This information could involve contacts, sales, finances, or any important data required to run the business. You could hire someone to keep all of this business information current and refer everyone to this person for any information, but this solution is not practical. A better solution is to store your data in a location where other people can easily access it. The information must be stored in a format that other people can understand. It must be presented within a structure whereby the required information can easily be found and the confidentiality and integrity of the data can be ensured to protect your business needs.

What kind of data would you need to store, maintain, and share? In business terms, you might need to keep records of purchase orders, invoices, and payment receipts. However, businesses of all sizes and functions need to store and share increasingly different types of data. Some of it might be fully structured, but some of it might lack any obvious structure. For example, important business information may exist only as text or attachments in e-mail messages.

And what about images? Live feeds are captured on security cameras. Temperature, sound, and pressure data are captured in highly secure rooms. Music, films, or even business meetings can be recorded from any angle and point of view and then analyzed at a later date.

What should you do with this information? Is it worthwhile to spend time analyzing and cataloging whatever data this information may contain? What if this data changes over time? How do you deal with the changes, and should you store the original data as well as the changes? Do you need to analyze how the data changed over time?

In summary, we all need to store data. However, the format and purpose of this data will differ depending on the particular business, its current situation, its past performance, and how it wishes to operate in the future. Whatever data you decide to store needs to be captured, structured, and processed so as to answer your specific needs for information.

Introducing Database Systems

There has always existed a need to store information. To this end, people through the ages have written down information on papyrus, wood, stones, and paper—anything they could use to ensure that the knowledge they had struggled to obtain would not be lost.

These knowledge gatherers were creating raw files of unstructured data, even if they did not understand the concept of a database. Searching for information stored in this way required reading a huge amount of information, and very few people were able to devote their lives to analyzing these documents. Some of these chosen few disseminated their information verbally, but vbase (verbal-based) data was not capable of spreading knowledge to all who may have needed it.

Simply storing data is not enough. A structure is needed to help you search for necessary information. In addition, a technique is needed that can help you navigate through this established structure.

With this in mind, there are three main components to a database system:

1. The data
2. The structure of the data
3. The technology to store and retrieve the data

An example of a simple database would be a dictionary. It stores words and their meanings. However, it stores the words alphabetically so that the reader can use a searching technique to quickly find a specific word among tens of thousands of other unwanted words.

A more sophisticated database would be a telephone book. It can be considered as a sequential list of contacts (people or businesses) for which some key attributes are listed: name, address, and telephone number. Again, you can apply well known manual techniques to search for any contact by name, for this is the way the telephone book is structured. Once you find the name, you can discover the other attributes. However, if you want to search for all contacts that live in the same building, this telephone book would be useless. You would need to read the entire telephone book to obtain this information.

So far, only databases built on paper whose information must be processed manually using simple binary searching techniques have been discussed. When people built the first database systems, they were designed to store all data in flat files. Indexes were built on top of the system to find answers to specific questions. These database systems evolved over time to result in modern relational database systems, other types of database systems (object-oriented database systems), or even hybrid object-relational database systems. This book will focus on relational database systems, which is the basis for the way that Microsoft SQL Server 2005 structures data.

Understanding the Requirements of a Database System

From a purely relational point of view, data is organized around entities and the relationship between these entities. A database designer must identify the following:

- The entities that describe the reality of the business
- The attributes of these entities
- The roles that each one of these attributes play in the business
- The relationship between entities and the nature of these relationships
- The behavior of these entities and attributes when the data changes

The importance of the analysis above cannot be over-emphasized regardless of which type of database system you will be using. Your first and primary objective is to know your business and to design a model that appropriately describes your business data and procedures. Your database system will be limited by your design and will inherit any problems built into this design that are caused by a lack of understanding of your business needs.

With this design, you could build some sequential or random files (such as the old xBase files), or you could use something a little more sophisticated, such as Microsoft Access. This book will not cover these technologies. You might decide to build your own relational database system from this logical design. In this case, you would need to build tables containing columns and indexes, as well as constraints. You might perhaps need to add some behavior to them through programmable objects that would perform complex actions on this data.

However, designing a database in this way is not enough. You also need to take care of simple but important things, such as:

- Authenticating the users who access the data

- Authorizing or denying access to the data

- Writing data to disk

- Reading data from disk

- Keeping indexes current so they can be used to search for the data needed

- Checking data against business rules to ensure the quality of the data

- Ensuring that relations between data are maintained, thereby avoiding disconnections between related objects

- Isolating actions from concurrent users so that they cannot interfere with each other

- Ensuring the durability of the data against system failures

- Providing system information so as to monitor the system and take corrective action when necessary

This list can be lengthened, but the key point is that you need an intelligent system that can handle all of these tasks, regardless of the way the data is accessed. In the past, the database engine stored the data while the user application was responsible for performing the additional tasks listed above. However, it was impossible to guarantee that data was always managed through the user application, thereby leading to chances for data corruption.

This is why you can benefit from a server application that can both own and manage your data and perform all of these tasks to your advantage. This type of management is precisely the role of SQL Server 2005.

Having a system that can store and manage your data is important, but how should you read this data? How should you search for answers to your business questions? Relational database systems would be useless without a well defined query language that could help you write questions in a way that the system could understand, analyze, and execute. Most modern relational database systems use Structured Query Language (SQL) as the language of choice to interact with database systems. SQL Server 2005 uses a dialect of this language called Transact SQL, or T-SQL, as it is commonly called.

T-SQL is not only a query language, but also a programming language designed to interact with relational database systems. It might not be as sophisticated as other programming languages for procedural tasks, but it is extremely rich for database operations. In fact, it is an extremely difficult language to analyze by a computer system. Consider this fact: most programming languages are very predictive. In Visual Basic, if you write the keyword FOR, the system knows the exact structure of whatever you are going to write after it. However, when you write the keyword SELECT in T-SQL, it is difficult for the system to know what type of statement you are trying to write.

T-SQL possesses a complex and rich grammar that makes it extremely efficient for data access. However, this grammar would be useless without an intelligent query processor that was able to convert human-written T-SQL sentences into machine-executable instructions. In other languages, this is the role of the compiler. Yet a database needs an intermediary agent that makes sure that the code produced is optimum for the specific data it is to manage. This is the role of the Query Optimizer. There are always many ways to access the information you need, and the system should be able to identify the best manner to do it.

Defining the Architecture of a Database Application

In this section, the structure of a database application will be explained gradually, from the least sophisticated application to the most complex.

Using a Monolithic Application with Data Embedded in the Application Code

A database application can be as simple as a computer program managing its own internal data. This was the way that most FORTRAN applications were written, with a block of data at the beginning of the code and the logic to deal with this data coded immediately below. This type of application can be called a *single-tier* database application, as shown in Figure 1-1.

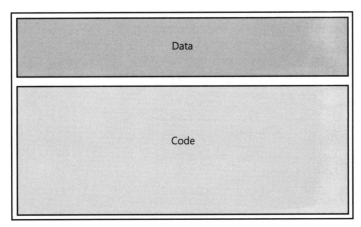

Figure 1-1   Monolithic application containing data and logic inside the application itself.

Using a Monolithic Application with Data Stored in an External File

The problem with a single-tier structure is that, each time the size or format of the data changes, you must modify the code and recompile the application. The solution to this problem would be to store the data in a different file and then access this file in a generic way from the application. In this way, you can keep the application untouched and edit only the data file. Still, the logic for data access is inside the application itself, which could then access data sequentially or randomly. This was the technique used by some early mono-user database applications. For example, some xBase applications were designed in this way, as shown in Figure 1-2.

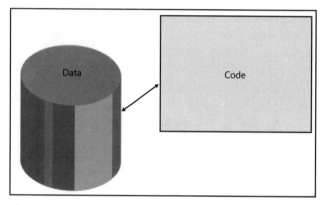

Figure 1-2   Monolithic application accessing external data to improve flexibility.

It is easy to try one of these applications. Click Start | All Programs | Microsoft SQL Server 2005 | SQL Server Management Studio and you will see one of them in action. SQL Server Management Studio is a tool that comes with the SQL Server installation and manages external databases, but it is a monolithic application.

Now that the data is stored in an external file, you can store this file in a shared location where other people can access it, as shown in Figure 1-3. Each application might need to use this data in different ways, but all applications could access the shared information, which is very convenient.

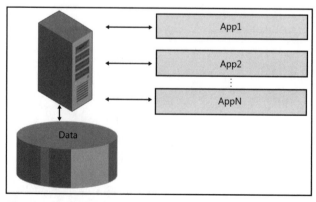

Figure 1-3   Monolithic application accessing shared external data.

A problem arises when some applications need to change some of the data. In this situation, specific transactional rules must be observed to avoid potential conflicts. All applications need to agree on the specific protocol to follow to avoid these problems, but this can be difficult to regulate.

Multi-user xBase applications, such as applications developed with Clipper, were designed in this way. What we call "Access applications" are not drastically different from the model shown in Figure 1-3 because the Access database that is stored in a central location has no logic on its own. The logic is provided by the Jet database engine that is running as part of the Access interface on each client machine.

Using a Database Application with Data Managed by a Database Server

The solution to problems associated with sharing data might be to create a service that owns the data and manages how this data is accessed so that it can avoid conflicts between requests sent from different applications. To make this a workable solution, you need to ensure that all applications access data through this service, which publishes well defined interfaces to the functionality it provides. Early SQL Server applications designed to connect to SQL Server through the DBLib interface were a typical example of this technique. Refer to Figure 1-4 as an example of this process.

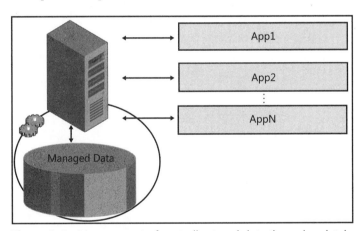

Figure 1-4   Management of centrally stored data through a database management service.

Using an Application with a Generic Data Access Layer

Applications were designed for a specific database system. Consequently, this produced portability problems when the same application had to be redesigned to connect to a different database system. The industry thus agreed on specific interfaces that could provide generic access to database systems from different vendors, thereby giving more flexibility to programmers and making it easier to write database applications (see Figure 1-5). The best known of these interfaces are ODBC (open database connectivity) and OLE DB (object-linking and embedding database), but the managed data providers of ADO.NET could be considered part of the same principle.

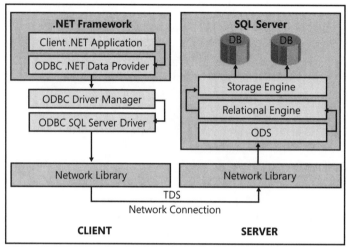

Figure 1-5   Main components of a database application connecting to SQL Server 2005 through ODBC.

As you can see in Figure 1-5, each database system requires a specific ODBC driver, but applications can be designed to connect to ODBC in a generic way. However, ODBC provides a call-level interface that is very efficient for C++ applications, but difficult to use from other languages. This is typically why applications use ODBC through an extra programming layer, such as RDO (remote data object) or ADO (active data object), as shown in Figure 1-6.

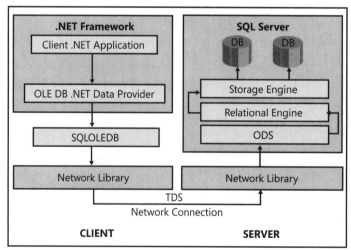

Figure 1-6   Main components of a database application connecting to SQL Server 2005 through OLE DB.

Each database system requires a specific OLE DB provider, but applications can be designed to connect to OLE DB in a generic way. As was mentioned earlier about ODBC, OLE DB exposes a Component Object Model (COM) interface that is designed to be consumed natively from C++ applications, but is difficult to use from other languages. This is why the most common programming layer to use with OLE DB is ADO, which exposes OLE DB functionality as collections of objects with properties and methods in a way that is easier to be consumed from client applications.

ADO.NET changes this situation quite dramatically by providing natively managed data providers to some database systems, such as SQL Server 2005, thus avoiding the need for an external data driver or data provider. This managed native data provider talks directly to the database server without any extra programmable layer, as shown in Figure 1-7.

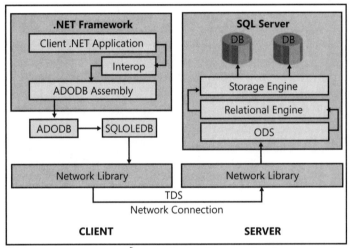

Figure 1-7   Main components of a database application connecting to SQL Server 2005 through the ADO.NET managed data provider.

However, some applications still require extremely fast processing and therefore prefer to avoid the potential overhead that .NET might produce. In the past, these applications might have been designed with C++ and ODBC, but now they can use the SQL Server Native Client, which connects natively to SQL Server 2005 while providing ODBC- and OLE DB-like interfaces to the application. This relationship is shown in Figure 1-8.

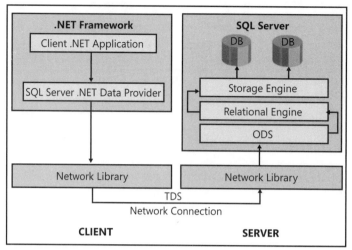

Figure 1-8   Main components of a database application connecting to SQL Server 2005 through the SQL Server Native Client.

Using an Application with Separated Presentation, Business, and Data Access Layers

The next step in an application's architectural design is the *three-tier* application design. This design was used in several standard architectures, such as Windows DNA during the late 20th century, and it is still one of the most popular designs. When attempting to keep the data access problem isolated within a component, this type of application isolates the graphical user interface (GUI) presentation as well. The principle behind this type of design is that the business problem is neither a data problem nor a presentation problem. However, this type of division of components is not always well understood or used.

For example, part of the power of relational databases, such as SQL Server 2005, is their ability to impose some consistency into the database definition with the use of constraints, relationships between tables, default values, and so on. A purist adhering to the three-tier architecture will try to manage all of the business rules in the business layer, foregoing one of the biggest capabilities that the database system possesses—the facility to ensure the integrity of your information.

Using a Complex Application with Multiple Options for Each Layer

Nowadays, many applications rely on Internet connectivity. A recent development in the 21st century is the appearance of a new type of mixed application that can store information in a company database, but that sometimes needs to run disconnected from the main system.

For these applications, a new design appears. Each of the layers can be different, depending on the environmental condition. If the computer is connected to the Enterprise network, the application works against the central database. If not, it stores the information locally and will update the central repository as soon as it can connect again to the central system. To help you develop these applications, SQL Server 2005 contains an Express edition that uses exactly the same database format as the other versions, but which can run locally.

Conclusion

Microsoft SQL Server 2005 is a relational database management system designed to store data organized as entities, with simple and complex attributes as well as business behavior. This functional model matches the conceptual model that you likely use to organize your business information. This book will help you understand how to build useful and efficient databases with SQL Server 2005.

Chapter 2

Installing and Setting Up Your Microsoft SQL Server 2005 Development Environment

After completing this chapter, you will be able to:

- Install Microsoft SQL Server 2005
- Evaluate different versions of Microsoft SQL Server 2005

Using a Virtual PC

The hardware requirements for Microsoft SQL Server 2005 are covered in the Introduction of this book. But as you begin installing and setting up your SQL Server development environment, you might want to consider using a virtual PC. Using virtual machines allows you to define a well-controlled environment without changing your normal configuration. With a vitual PC, you can manage different platforms with different database versions or development environments in a very safe way.

When using a virtual PC, consider at least 400 MB of extra RAM in the host; that is, you need this amount plus the required amount for running the virtual PC machine. Ideally, a good hardware configuration includes at least 2 GB of RAM to allow you to run more than one vitual PC at the same time. Note that you must add this configuration in addition to any other requirements for other tools, such as development tools, or other services, such as the operating system.

Operating System Requirements for Development of SQL Server Database Applications

Once you have the appropriate hardware to run SQL Server 2005, you must choose the proper operating system. SQL Server 2005 Developer Edition will run on Microsoft Windows 2000 Professional or Microsoft Windows Server with Service Pack 4 or higher. Alternatively, you can use Microsoft Windows XP Professional Edition with Service Pack 2 or Microsoft Windows Server 2003 with Service Pack 1. If you are connected to a company network, a SQL Server may already be installed for development purposes. In this case, you only need to install the client tools to manage your development. These client tools can be installed in Microsoft Windows 95 or any other higher operating system version.

Although SQL Server 2005 will work with all of these operating systems, Windows XP Professional provides the most stable and secure environment for developing databases with SQL Server, especially if you plan to use all of the services and technologies SQL Server 2005 offers.

When setting up SQL Server 2005, it may be helpful to join a Windows domain. This will allow you to properly test all of the security implementations you will need for your applications. If your development requires more than one SQL Server, being joined to a domain may be essential for testing server delegation or linked server implementations. However, if you work in an independent workstation, you still can use local integrated security for your development. Moreover, in some cases, having the appropriate hardware will allow you to use virtual machines to define the domain and create a test environment that closely matches the production environment.

Recommended Productivity Tools

Work in database development is not only a SQL Server matter. Besides the proper development tools, you also need evaluation tools that allow you to examine such things as the effectiveness of your application, its reliability, and its fault tolerance. The operating system includes some of these tools, and SQL Server 2005 installation adds others as well.

Using Performance Monitor

Performance Monitor measures resource utilization, such as processor time and memory in use—not only for those resources required by SQL Server 2005, but also for those required by the application. Using Performance Monitor, you can evaluate which part of the entire application uses the most resources and explore execution alternatives to maximize performance.

To launch Performance Monitor, open the Control Panel and double click the Administrative Tools icon. Double-click the Performance icon to launch Performance Monitor.

Using Network Monitor

Usually, database applications run in a network environment. This means that the applications use some network resources to obtain or update information. Network Monitor allows you to analyze what happens "behind the scenes" in the network. It helps you to evaluate which actions consume more network bandwidth and which is the best way to perform a certain task. Evaluating Network Monitor information may be difficult because it provides low-level information dealing with network frames; however, the hard work of examining this information can be rewarding.

> **Note** Network Monitor is not installed by default. You must add it to your operating system. To do this:
>
> 1. Ensure that you have the original operating system setup media ready (in your CD reader or available in a network share).
> 2. On the Control Panel, double-click the Add Or Remove Programs icon.
> 3. Click Add Or Remove Windows Components in the left bar.
> 4. After the Microsoft Windows XP (or Microsoft Windows Server) setup starts, scroll down to select Management And Monitoring Tools, click the Details button, and check Simple Network Management Protocol.
> 5. Click OK, and then click Next.

Using Upgrade Advisor

Upgrade Advisor allows you to assess the impact of a database migration process and recommends actions you may take to better migrate your databases, while pointing out potential problems and corresponding solutions. Since it will be possible to migrate older applications to the new SQL Server version, this tool will be much appreciated.

Recommended Development Tools

SQL Server 2005 includes a limited version of the Visual Studio development environment to create reports, analysis services applications, and so on. In addition, it allows you to create common language runtime (CLR) objects inside your database. However, it is very important to have a full version of Visual Studio 2005 so as to have all of its capabilities available for developing a small set of test projects to evaluate such things as availability and functionality.

Visual Studio allows you to use sample code obtained from many sources, including development communities, where you can discover not only CLR samples, but also management scripts and solutions to common problems. The environment has access to public sites, such as *http://www.gotdotnet.com*, where you can find "workspaces"—that is, areas arranged by interest or some specific functionality where the participants collaborate to create better solutions. The Visual Studio environment also has access to local communities where you can find specific solutions for local problems.

Another useful tool is Microsoft Office. You can use Microsoft Access to generate test sets of data, or you can use Microsoft Excel to obtain and evaluate results and create batch scripts based on pre-existing sets of data by using its string manipulation capabilities.

Microsoft SQL Server 2005 Editions

Depending on the requirements of a particular project, you must choose the proper SQL Server version. For example, a small Web site might use SQL Server Express when, in another situation, availability, reliability, and data protection may require a more robust version. We will briefly review each version and its capabilities.

Microsoft SQL Server Express Edition

SQL Server Express Edition is the smallest version of SQL Server 2005, but enables developers to create a fully functional database locally. This version is the proper choice for local, one-user applications, but also can be used for small Web sites.

SQL Server Express may be the smallest version, but be aware that this is a real SQL Server. SQL Server Express can manage databases up to 4 GB and implements the same security management, auditing capabilities, and encryption as the other versions. It also includes the same programmability features including stored procedures, CLR integration, and XML datatype management. Databases created with SQL Server Express are fully compatible with the other versions of SQL Server 2005 and can be used in them without any modification.

Microsoft SQL Server Workgroup Edition

When implementing applications in small- or medium-sized companies with peer-to-peer networks, SQL Server Workgroup Edition is the appropriate version to choose. SQL Server Workgroup has no database size limit, allows you to create transaction log backups, and includes SQL Server Management Studio as part of its installation. In addition, it supports up to two processors.

Microsoft SQL Server Standard Edition

SQL Server Standard Edition increases the SQL Server Workgroup multiprocessor support to four processors and is the lightest version of the software that supports sixty-four-bit platforms. It also includes basic data transformation services, Web Services support as HTTP Endpoints, and Analysis Services.

Microsoft SQL Server Enterprise Edition

SQL Server Enterprise Edition is the most powerful version of the SQL Server software and supports unlimited multiprocessors. It allows you to create SQL Server clusters to manage availability and fault tolerance environments.

Installing SQL Server 2005

Before you install SQL Server 2005, you must determine whether certain services in your operating system have been installed and install them if necessary. For example, if you want to work with Web Services security, you must have Internet Information Services (IIS) installed. However, if you install SQL Server 2005 over Windows XP with Service Pack 2 or Windows Server 2003 and do not want to manage security-related functions, you can run Web Services without IIS.

Installing SQL Server 2005

1. Launch the software and accept the license agreement.

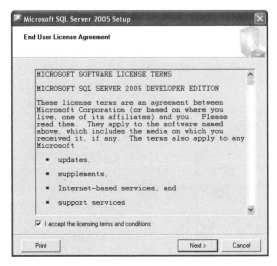

2. The installation process advises that it needs some prerequisites and asks you to install them.

Since SQL Server 2005 has a close relationship with .NET Framework 2.0, it is necessary to install it before any other SQL Server task.

3. When the prerequisites are fully installed, the setup process informs you of this and allows you to continue.

4. After loading the setup components, the Installation Wizard dialog box appears.

The System Configuration Check process begins and progresses through fourteen actions, informing you of any warnings or errors. For example, if you do not have IIS installed, this action will be marked with a warning.

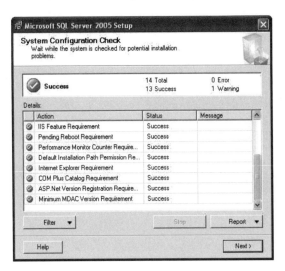

5. The setup program then asks for your identification and product key information.

> **Note**   Depending on the version you are installing, it is possible that another window will prompt you for registration information.

6. The next step involves choosing the components you want to install. The dialog box displays the major components with checkboxes and an Advanced button with more options.

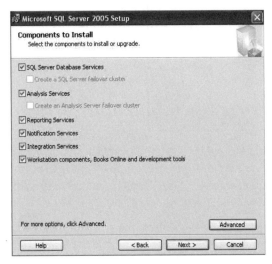

Clicking the Advanced button is the only way to install the code and database samples.

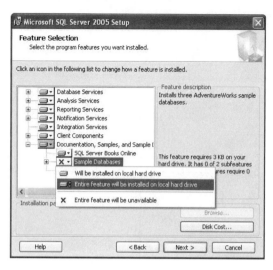

7. After you confirm the components you want to install, the setup process asks you for the instance name.

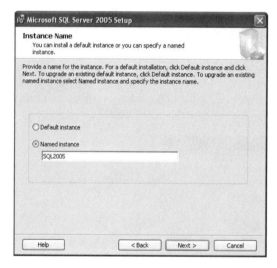

If you choose the Default Instance option, you will be able to access your database server using the "(local)" data server name. However, if you need to preserve your existing SQL Server 2000 installation—for example, if it is a default instance—you will have to assign a new name for the instance you are installing.

8. After the instance name definition is established, the setup process asks you for the account name to be used by the services.

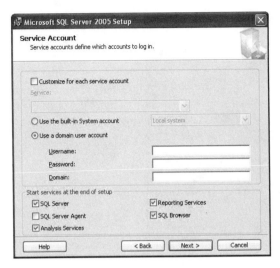

If you are inside a domain, it will be preferable to create an account for your SQL Server's services. This will facilitate some inter-server processes as well as the utilization of other services, such as simple mail transfer protocol (SMTP) e-mail. If you are not inside a domain, you can use a built-in system account, such as Network Services or Local System. This dialog box also allows you to choose which SQL Server services will be configured to start when the operating system starts.

9. The next step is to specify the Authentication Mode.

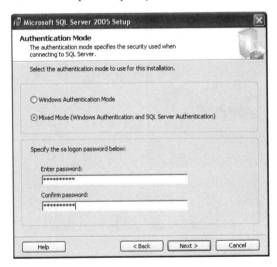

You can simply use Windows Authentication or specify Mixed Mode. In this case, you must define a password for the "sa" account.

10. If you choose to install Reporting Services, the setup process asks you how to install the Web site for this service.

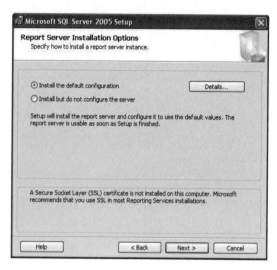

11. The last setup configuration step is to specify the default collation that this instance will use.

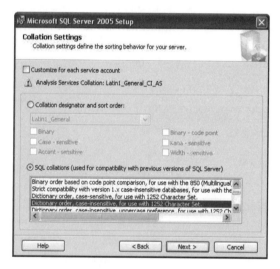

You can typically keep the default configuration, but consider what languages may be necessary in using the databases.

12. Another configuration dialog box appears before the installation process begins, but it is not related to your data server configuration.

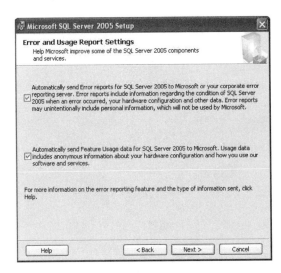

This dialog box allows you to configure what kind of relevant, non-private information the server will send to Microsoft Corporation, such as errors during execution or information about feature use.

13. After starting the setup process, the user interface (UI) displays a summary of your selections.

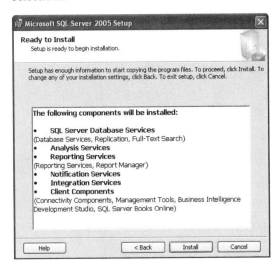

During the installation process, a Setup Progress dialog box lets you know how the installation is progressing.

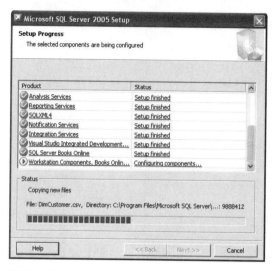

When the setup process is finished, you are informed of the final results.

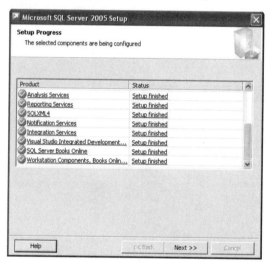

14. The last dialog box provides information about other related tasks that may be necessary to perform if you have a previous installation or it may describe how to configure other services.

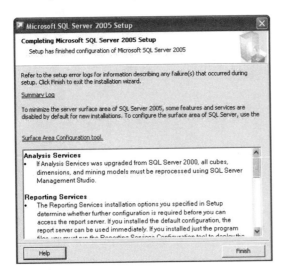

Using the Surface Area Configuration Tool

When the setup process is completed, SQL Server 2005 has implemented all of its default configurations to afford you the most secure and reliable environment. It is up to you to change any of the configuration options to accomplish your own needs. To do this, you must open the Surface Area Configuration Tool. A link to this tool is provided in the final dialog box of the setup process. This tool contains two major parts. The Surface Area Configuration dialog box is shown in Figure 2-1.

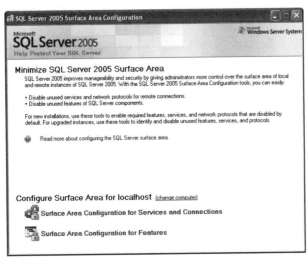

Figure 2-1   SQL Server 2005 Surface Area Configuration dialog box.

Surface Area Configuration For Services And Connections

The Surface Area Configuration For Services And Connections dialog box lists the services for all of the instances and allows you to specify the startup situation for each. This dialog box is shown in Figure 2-2.

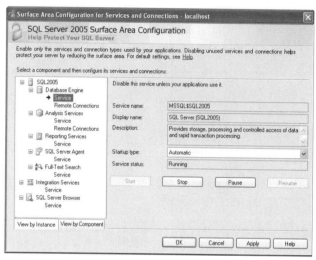

Figure 2-2   Startup options for Services.

In addition, when the service supports them, this tool allows you to specify the Remote Connection behavior for each service (see Figure 2-3).

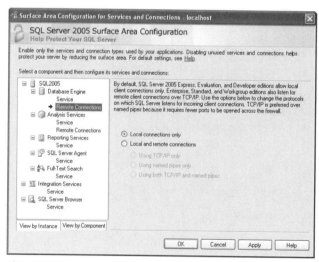

Figure 2-3   Remote Connections configuration.

Surface Area Configuration For Features

The other part of the Surface Area Configuration Tool refers to different features that can be enabled in every service/instance, such as admitting remote queries or CLR integration. As none of these features is enabled by default, you must use this tool to enable them yourself. The Features Configuration dialog box is shown in Figure 2-4.

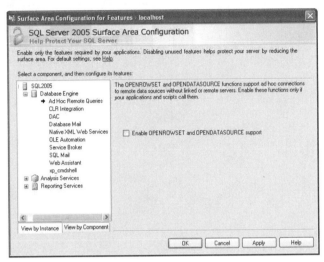

Figure 2-4   Features configuration.

Conclusion

Developing database applications requires not only the SQL Server itself, but also the inclusion of other tools to ensure the quality and reliability of your applications. Moreover, you need to make the proper choice about the SQL Server 2005 version you will use. Remember: you don't need a sophisticated environment to develop applications. In fact, SQL Server Express Edition might meet all of your development needs. However, it is a good idea to have at least the SQL Server Workgroup version of the software to test scalability and perform multi-user testing.

Chapter 2 Quick Reference

To	Do This
Work with security strengths, the Web, and Reporting Services	Previously install IIS.
Work smoothly with database application development	Ensure that you have a 500 MHz processor or higher and have at least 512 MB of memory.
Test different production environments	Use Virtual PC or Virtual Server.

To	Do This
Develop with security in mind	Try to work with a domain controller (Active Directory DC), and use a domain account to run SQL Server Services.
Configure which services to run	Use the Surface Area Configuration Tool.
Enable special features in your database server	Use the Surface Area Configuration Tool.

Chapter 3

Reviewing Microsoft SQL Server 2005 Management Tools

After completing this chapter, you will be able to:

- Use SQL Server Books Online
- Use SQL Server Configuration Manager
- Use SQL Server Surface Area Configuration
- Use SQL Server Management Studio
- Use SQL Server Profiler
- Use Database Engine Tuning Advisor
- Use SQLCmd

Introduction

Using Microsoft SQL Server 2005 does not only involve the creation and development of databases, tables, indexes, and stored procedures. Many tools are available to help you analyze behavior, enable features, and study and enhance the performance of your server. This chapter will acquaint you with all of these tools so that you will discover where to find the exact information you need and achieve the best results during the development and configuration process.

Using SQL Server Books Online

SQL Server Books Online is the SQL Server 2005 product documentation. It covers all of the features of the product such as the Database Engine, Analysis Services, Integration Services, Replication, Reporting Services, Notification Services, Service Broker, and Full-Text Search.

Accessing SQL Server Books Online

1. To open SQL Server Books Online, from the Start menu, select All Programs | Microsoft SQL Server 2005 | Documentation And Tutorials | SQL Server Books Online. You will arrive at the Welcome page, which contains links to the major divisions of the content.

2. Click the Search tab in the upper zone to search for specific information.

3. In the Search tab, type the topic of your search in the empty search string textbox.

4. Under the search string textbox, two expandable links can be used to select either the technology or the type of content that you want to search.

5. The results of your search will appear grouped into four sections on the right side of the Search tab according to the source of the information. These four sections are:

- Local Help

- MSDN Online

- Codezone Community

- Questions

Click one of the four sections to view the list of results from that source.

> **Tip**   You will find the MSDN Online section to be very useful because this is where the most current content is located. The Codezone Community and Questions sections contain solutions from other users and community specialists, such as the MVPs nominated by Microsoft.

Using SQL Server Configuration Manager

SQL Server Configuration Manager is a Microsoft Management Console application that allows you to configure SQL Server 2005's installed services, network configuration, and network protocols. You can perform actions such as starting, pausing, and stopping services as well as defining the SQL Server and SQL Native Client network configuration. SQL Server Configuration Manager uses the Window Management Instrumentation (WMI) provider to interact with the system. For example, if the SQL Server Configuration Manager needs to modify a registry entry, it will use WMI to access the appropriate registry entry instead of accessing the registry directly.

To Open SQL Server Configuration Manager, from the Start menu, choose All Programs | Microsoft SQL Server 2005 | Configuration Tools | SQL Server Configuration Manager. Your screen will appear like that shown in Figure 3-1.

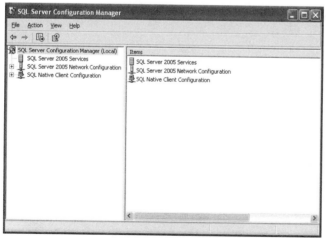

Figure 3-1   SQL Server Configuration Manager.

Using the SQL Server 2005 Services Node

The SQL Server 2005 Services node in SQL Server Configuration Manager allows you to configure SQL Server 2005 services on the local machine, as shown in Figure 3-2.

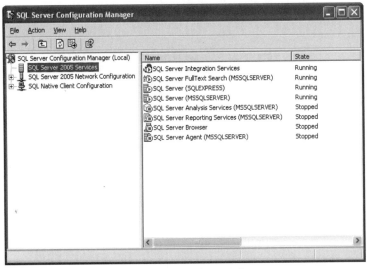

Figure 3-2   The SQL Server 2005 Services node.

You can pause, stop, and start services, change the user account that is running a service, and view the advanced properties of a service. For example, if you double-click on an instance of SQL Server 2005 and then click Advanced, you can view whether the instance is clustered, the startup parameters, and the particular version of the SQL Server instance, as shown in Figure 3-3.

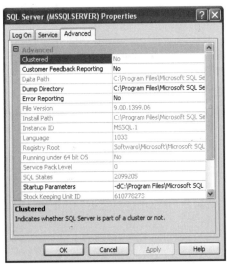

Figure 3-3   Advanced options for an instance of SQL Server 2005.

You may notice that the SQL Server 2005 Services interface is a bit slower than the Windows Services tool. It is slower because the SQL Server Configuration Manager uses the WMI provider to access and configure its services. You should use SQL Server Configuration Manager because it performs registry permission validations when changing the service account. In addition, in some cases, such as password account changes, a service does not need to be restarted as it does when using the Windows Services tool.

Using the SQL Server 2005 Network Configuration Node

The SQL Server 2005 Network Configuration node allows you to configure the network protocols used by each SQL Server instance by enabling or disabling the protocol. Refer to Figure 3-4.

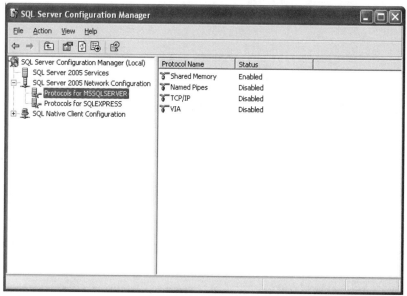

Figure 3-4   The SQL Server 2005 Network Configuration node.

> **Note**   The default installations of SQL Server 2005 Developer and Express Editions do not enable networking protocols. You should use the SQL Server 2005 Network Configuration utility or SQL Server Surface Area Configuration utility to enable networking protocols.

You can configure each protocol property. For example, you can access the Transmission Control Protocol/Internet Protocol (TCP/IP) network configuration properties to configure IP addresses as well as the ports where the SQL Server instance will listen, as shown in Figure 3-5.

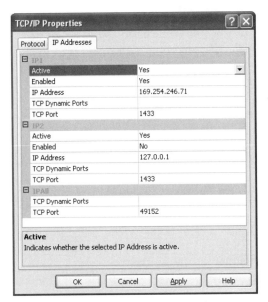

Figure 3-5   TCP/IP Properties dialog box.

Static Ports, Dynamic Ports, and Windows Firewall

By using the SQL Server 2005 Network Configuration tool, you can configure the port that will be used by SQL Server instances to attend to client application requests. You can configure an instance to listen to a specific TCP port, or dynamic port. When configuring an instance by using a static port, the client application can specify the server port in the connection string that will be used to connect to the server. On the other hand, if the server port is configured as dynamic, the server will have to use a mechanism to establish communication with the client application. The following text details an example of each port configuration.

Static ports   Assume that you have configured your SQL Server instance to enable TCP/IP connections, and you have set the TCP/IP port number to 1457. The client application can connect to the SQL Server instance by specifying the server in the connection string as well as the port with which the instance should connect. The client application will then connect to the SQL Server instance through the specified port. For example, in the client application, you can code the connection string to look like the following:

```
' sqlClient Provider Connection String Example
Dim sqlClient_connString As String = _
    "Server=<IP_ADDRESS>,1457;" _
  + "Database=AdventureWorks;Integrated Security=SSPI;"

' sql Native Client Provider Connection String Example
Dim native_connString As String = _
    "Provider=SQLNCLI;" _
  + "Server=<IP_ADDRESS>,1457;" _
  + "Database=AdventureWorks;Integrated Security=SSPI;"
```

If the client application does not specify the port with which the instance should connect in the connection string, then the SQL Server Browser Service is responsible for detecting the port number that the instance is listening to and retrieving it for the client application. The connection string will be similar to the two previous examples, but it will not specify the port number.

```
' sqlClient Provider Connection String Example
Dim sqlClient_connString As String = _
    "Server=server_name\instance_name;" _
  + "Database=AdventureWorks;Integrated Security=SSPI;"

' sql Native Client Provider Connection String Example
Dim native_connString As String = _
    "Provider=SQLNCLI;" _
  + "Server=server_name\instance_name;" _
  + "Database=AdventureWorks;Integrated Security=SSPI;"
```

Dynamic ports   In dynamic port configurations, the client application does not know the SQL Server instance listening port. The SQL Server Browser Service will determine which port number is sent to the client application.

In dynamic port configurations, a port is assigned to an instance when the instance starts. The instance will use the same port number until the service is stopped. When the instance service begins again, the SQL Server Browser Service will assign the same or a different port to the instance.

Windows Firewall   How you configure Windows firewall settings will depend on how the client applications connect to the server instance and how the server protocols are configured. As noted earlier, there are situations when a client application needs to use the SQL Server Browser Service (that listens to the 1434 UDP port). You will also need to allow connections to the TCP port where the SQL Server instance is listening. It is recommended that you create exceptions for the specific client application instead of configuring exceptions for port numbers, as shown in Figure 3-6.

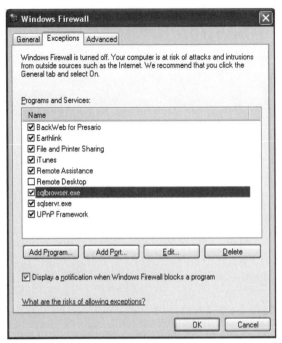

Figure 3-6   Windows Firewall exception configuration.

What is the best configuration?

■ Static ports, with the client application specifying the port number

   In this scenario, the client application knows the port number and does not need the help of the SQL Server Browser Service to resolve the port number of the instance name. The benefit is that you avoid using the SQL Server Browser Service. The drawback is that the application is dependent on the port number.

■ Static ports, with the client application not specifying the port number of the instance, or dynamic ports

   The server is configured with a static port, but the client application does not know the port. The SQL Server Browser Service will resolve the port number for the client application. The benefit is that the server does not depend on specific ports. The drawback is that the client application needs the SQL Server Browser Service to resolve the port number.

Using the SQL Native Client Configuration Node

The SQL Native Client Configuration node allows you to specify how client applications on the local computer will connect to SQL Server instances. You can determine whether a Secure Socket Layer (SSL) will be requested on the server and whether the server certificate must be validated when connecting to the server.

To open the SQL Native Client Configuration Properties dialog box, first select the SQL Native Client Configuration node and then select Properties from the Action menu. The dialog box is shown in Figure 3-7.

Figure 3-7   SQL Native Client Configuration Properties dialog box.

Client Protocols

The Client Protocols option configures the order in which the protocols will be used. When a client application tries to connect to a SQL Server instance without defining the protocol to use, the client application will try to connect using the protocols in the configured order, as shown in Figure 3-8.

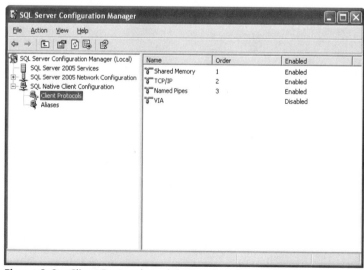

Figure 3-8   Client Protocols and their order of precedence.

> **Tip**   The Microsoft .NET SqlClient data provider does not follow the order configured in the Client Protocols option. The protocol order for .NET SqlClient is first TCP and then named pipes.

Aliases

Aliases are alternate names that can be used to connect to a SQL Server instance. By defining an alias, you associate the alias name with an instance name, a network protocol, and a port number if applicable. For example, you could create an alias such as the one found in Figure 3-9.

Figure 3-9   Alias creation.

SRV2 will be the alias name that maps to the SQL Server instance PROD_SERVER\ INSTANCE1, using the TCP/IP network protocol with port number 1433. If you would rather define a dynamic port, you must leave the port number empty.

Using SQL Server Surface Area Configuration

SQL Server Surface Area Configuration is a tool that helps you enable, disable, start, or stop the features and services of your local and remote SQL Server 2005 installations. *Surface area* refers to the memory and other system resources required to run a program. Stopping and disabling unused services allows you to reduce the surface area and makes your system more secure. The tool uses the WMI provider to access the server configuration. To start SQL Server Surface Area Configuration, from the Start Menu, choose All Programs | Microsoft SQL Server 2005 | Configuration Tools | SQL Server Surface Area Configuration. You will see the initial screen shown in Figure 3-10.

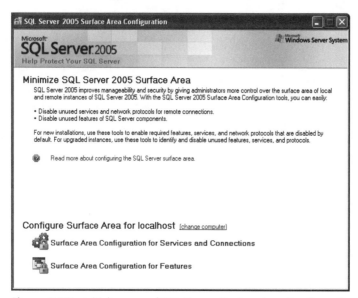

Figure 3-10   Initial screen of SQL Server Surface Area Configuration.

Using Surface Area Configuration For Services And Connections

Surface Area Configuration For Services And Connections allows you to configure the state of SQL Server services. You can stop, pause, resume, and start the SQL Server instance services. Moreover, you are able to configure whether the SQL Server instance will allow remote connections and, if so, which protocols to use. Refer to Figure 3-11.

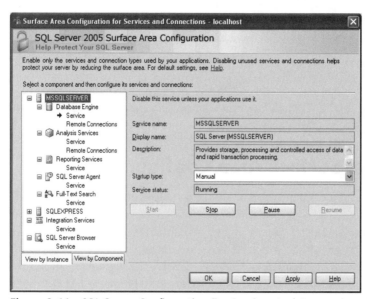

Figure 3-11   SQL Server Configuration For Services And Connections dialog box.

Using Surface Area Configuration For Features

Surface Area Configuration For Features allows you to enable features on your server. For example, you can enable or disable features such as CLR Integration, Database Mail, Service Broker, or Native XML Web Services, as shown in Figure 3-12.

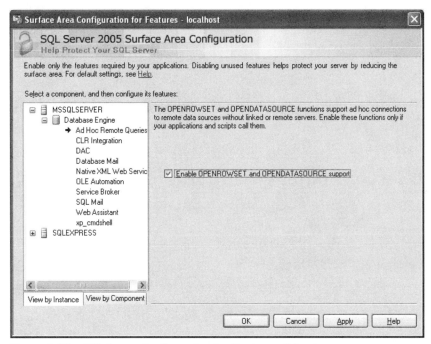

Figure 3-12   SQL Server Configuration For Features dialog box.

Most of these features can also be configured by using system stored procedures, such as sp_configure. For example, if you want to enable CLR Integration, you could run the following script on the SQL Server instance.

```
EXEC sys.sp_configure N'clr enabled', N'1';
RECONFIGURE WITH OVERRIDE;
```

> **Note**   Surface Area Configuration For Features executes the sys.sp_configure system stored procedure behind the scenes to configure most of the features. You could easily verify this by running a SQL Server Profiler trace while running the Surface Area Configuration For Features utility.

Sac Utility

The Sac utility is a command-line tool that helps you configure the surface area in local machines and applies the same setting to remote machines. The tool helps you to easily export the surface area settings in a machine to a configuration file and then use the file for other purposes, such as documenting the server's configuration. In the example below, the following code generates the file config.xml with the surface area setting of the local machine.

```
sac out c:\config.xml
```

The generated file is an xml-type document that can be used to import the surface area settings into a different machine. For example, to apply the configuration in a server named Server2, you would execute the following command-line batch.

```
sac in c:\config.xml -S Server2
```

The Sac utility is located in the Program Files\Microsoft SQL Server\90\Shared directory, and you customize the execution by using the different command line arguments that can be seen by using the argument -?.

Using SQL Server Management Studio

SQL Server Management Studio is a new graphical tool within SQL Server 2005 that combines and extends the features introduced by Enterprise Manager, Analysis Manager, and Query Analyzer in SQL Server 2000. The tool is built on top of a new integrated development environment (IDE), which is shared by Visual Studio 2005 Development Studio, SQL Server Management Studio, and SQL Server Business Intelligence Development Studio.

Administering Servers with SQL Server Management Studio

By using SQL Server Management Studios you can connect to any existing SQL Server system in your network for which you have the appropriate credentials (depending, of course, on the remote connections configured on the servers).

Connecting to a Server

1. Start SQL Server Management Studio from the Start menu by choosing All Programs | Microsoft SQL Server 2005 | SQL Server Management Studio. The application will request the name of the server to which you would like to connect. Select a server from the Server Name drop-down list and click the Connect button.

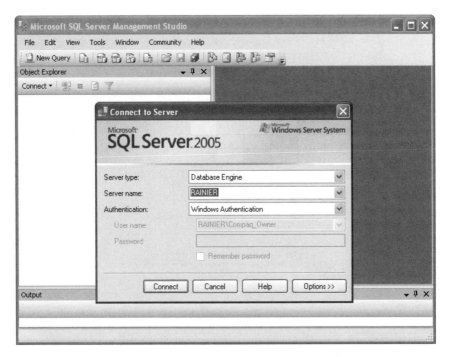

Once you are working within SQL Server Management Studio, you can connect to another server by clicking the Connect toolbar button at the top of the left tree.

2. Select the type of server you want to connect to and enter the appropriate information.

If you typically work with more than one server, it is useful to register them in SQL Server Management Studio.

Registering a Server in SQL Server Management Studio

1. From the View menu, choose Registered Servers, or press Ctrl+Alt+G.

2. Right-click Database Engine and select New | Server Registration from the context menu.

3. Expand the Server Name drop-down list and select <Browse For More...>.

4. Select local or network servers as needed.

5. Expand the Database Engine node and select the server you want to register. Click the OK button.

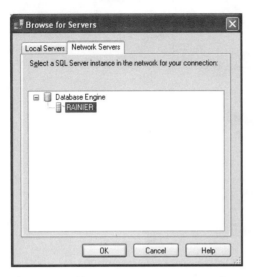

6.   If you would like to connect to a named instance, add a backslash (\) followed by the name of the instance in the Server Name drop-down listbox.

7.   Select the Connection Properties tab to define any special connection attribute that you need.

Using Object Explorer in SQL Server Management Studio

You can use Object Explorer to manage any of the SQL Server objects. Object Explorer presents them in a tree-view fashion, as shown in Figure 3-13.

Figure 3-13   Object Explorer pane in SQL Server Management Studio.

Using the Database Node

You will find all of your databases under the Database node. Databases are divided into three groups:

- System databases, which are those that SQL Server uses internally

- Database snapshots

- User databases, which are implemented as folders that appear directly under the Database node

If you expand one of the User Database nodes, you will obtain a set of Grouping nodes, as shown in Figure 3-14.

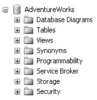

Figure 3-14   Grouping nodes within a User Database node in Object Explorer.

From within a Grouping node, you can access database objects. For example, if you expand the Tables node, you will see all of the tables in the database. You will notice one node that groups the system tables, which are those that SQL Server 2005 uses internally to manage database-related information, including its structure. If you right-click a table, you receive a context menu with several actions that you can perform on that table, as shown in Figure 3-15.

Figure 3-15   Table actions in Object Explorer.

When you select the Modify option from the context menu, you can alter the table structure; add, remove, or rename columns; and perform many other definition tasks using a graphical interface. Moreover, you can perform all of the changes you wish and then generate the Transact-SQL (T-SQL) script to replicate it in other databases (see Figure 3-16). This feature is very important for replicating the changes made during the development process into the production server.

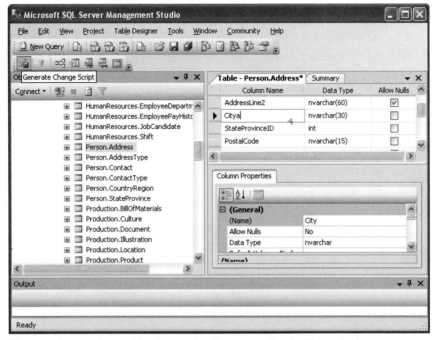

Figure 3-16   Table modification and script generation in Object Explorer.

Another important task that you can perform with tables is to open them.

Creating SELECT Queries

1. Right-click a table and select Open Table from the context menu to view the contents of the entire table.

2. Use the four toolbar buttons in the upper-left corner of the Object Explorer pane to choose which columns in the table to display (Show Diagram Pane toolbar button), filter data in the columns (Show Criteria Pane toolbar button), view the T-SQL sentence used to retrieve information from the table (Show SQL Pane toolbar button), and show or hide the actual information (Show Results Pane toolbar button).

3. You can right-click the Diagram pane to add more tables or views to your query or to define the grouping mode for the query.

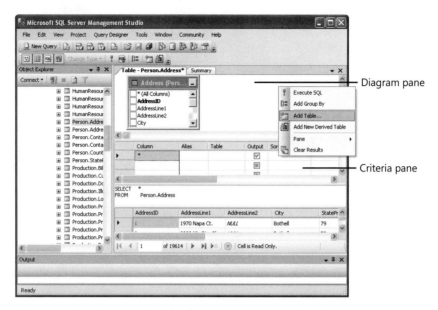

Diagram pane

Criteria pane

4. Select the checkbox to the left of a column name in the Diagram pane to add that column to your query.

> **Important**   By default, the asterisk (*) column (which means "all columns") appears in the Criteria pane. Using the all columns indicator is not a good practice. Right-click the asterisk column in the Criteria pane and choose Delete from the context menu to delete it. You can then choose exactly the columns that you need.

Once you have added a column, you can assign a filter to it by adding the condition in the Filter column.

5. Select the Sort Type and Sort Order values for a column to assign the order that you want for your data.

Querying More than One Table

It is possible to perform complex query operations by using the Open Table context menu.

Creating More Complex SELECT Queries

1. Open SQL Server Management Studio by clicking Start | All Programs | Microsoft SQL Server 2005 | SQL Server Management Studio.

2. Connect to your local server.

> **Note**   The way that you specify your local server may differ depending on your instal-
> lation. If you have a default instance, it can be simply *(local)*. SQL Server Management
> Studio typically offers you the default connection properties.

3. In Object Explorer, expand the Server node, the Database node, the AdventureWorks
    database, and the Tables node.

4. Locate the Production.Product table. Right-click the table and select Open Table from
    the context menu.

5. Click the Show Diagram Pane toolbar button, the Show Criteria Pane toolbar button,
    and the Show SQL Pane toolbar button.

6. Right-click the asterisk (*) in the Criteria pane and choose Delete from the context
    menu.

7. Right-click the blank surface of the Diagram pane and select Add Table from the context
    menu.

8. In the Add Table dialog box, scroll through the list of tables to find the ProductCategory
    (Production) table. Select the table and click the Add button.

    Repeat this step to add the ProductSubcategory (Production) table.

9. Click the Close button to close the Add Table dialog box.

> **Tip**   Because the last two tables added to the diagram are both related to the
> Production table, between them you will see "pipes" demonstrating these relationships.
> You will learn more about relationships in Chapter 5, Designing a Database to Solve
> Business Needs, and Chapter 7, Selecting the Data You Need.

10. In the Diagram pane, check the Name column in both the ProductCategory table and
     the ProductSubcategory table. Check the Name, ProductNumber, ListPrice, and Size
     columns in the Product table.

11. In the Criteria pane, change the alias for the Name column of the ProductCategory table
     to Category Name, the alias for the Name column of the ProductSubcategory table to
     Subcategory Name, and the alias for the Name column of the Product table to Name.

12. In the Sort Type column, select Ascending for the Category Name, Subcategory Name,
     and Name columns in that order. Notice that the Sort Order column is updated auto-
     matically as you set the Sort Type column.

13. In the Filter column for the ListPrice row, type **>10** to display only those rows that con-
     tain a price greater than 10.

14. Right-click the Diagram pane and select Execute SQL to see the results.

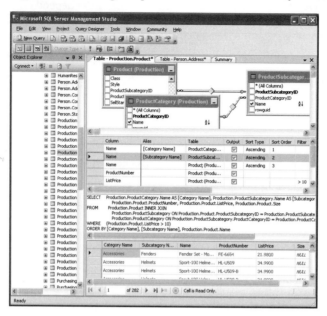

Managing Other Objects

Each object under the Database node has different options in the context menu. The options for stored procedures are shown in Figure 3-17.

Figure 3-17   Stored procedure actions in Object Explorer.

> **Note**   SQL Server Management Studio is a very complex application to explain in just one chapter. You will learn more about this application throughout the rest of this book.

Using Database Diagrams

Another feature included with Object Explorer is the Database Diagrams node. In this node, you can add diagrams representing your tables and their relationships, modify or create table structures, and manage other table-related definitions, such as indexes and triggers. You can use database diagrams to better understand your database implementation and alter it if necessary.

Creating a Database Diagram

1. Right-click the Database Diagram node and choose New Database Diagram from the context menu.

    If this is the first time you have accessed this node, it is possible that SQL Server Management Studio will ask you to add the support objects for the diagrams, as shown in the figure below. Click the Yes button to add the necessary objects.

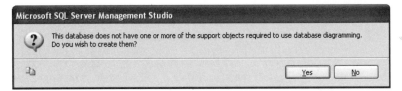

2. In the Add Table dialog box, select all of the tables you want to analyze. For this example, select only the Product (Production) table, click Add, and then click the Close button.

3. Right-click the Title bar, click the Table View context menu, and select another view, which will give you a different perspective. You can experiment here with various views.

4. Right-click the Title bar again and choose Add Related Tables from the context menu. This will add all of the tables related to the Product table, of which there are many.

5. The Arrange Tables toolbar button is located to the left of the Zoom drop-down list. Click it to arrange the tables in the diagram surface.

    You can zoom in or out of the view by selecting another percentage value in the Zoom drop-down list.

Writing Scripts in SQL Server Management Studio

As mentioned earlier, you can create SELECT queries by using the Open Table option in the Table context menu. However, you can create many other T-SQL sentences in SQL Server Management Studio. To facilitate this task, SQL Server Management Studio contains a Query Editor.

Starting a Query Using the New Query Toolbar Button

1. Open SQL Server Management Studio from the Start menu by choosing All Programs | Microsoft SQL Server 2005 | SQL Server Management Studio.

2. Connect to your local server.

3. Click the New Query button in the first toolbar at the left of the screen.

4. In the second toolbar that now appears, expand the Database drop-down list and select the database against which you want to execute the query. Begin to write your query in the New Query window to the right of the Object Explorer pane.

Caution   Make sure you select the appropriate database when creating a query. Since your default database is specified in your user profile, it is a common mistake to execute a query in the default database. If you are working as the admin user or as the sa user, your default database is the master database.

An alternative method of creating a new query is to create it from the Database context menu.

Starting a New Query Using the Database Context Menu

1. In Object Explorer, right-click your destination database and select New Query from the context menu.

2. When the Editor window appears, begin to write your query.

   Your query may contain as much T-SQL language as necessary. As you enter your query in the New Query window, your T-SQL syntax will be examined by SQL Server Management Studio and various syntax elements will be appropriately colored on the screen.

Tip   After creating a query, you may want to use the same query script in the future. To ensure that the query is always executed in the proper database, start your query with USE <databaseName>; GO; to establish a connection to your database.

Retrieving Information about Your Queries

You can obtain information about your queries other than simply receiving the results, such as query statistics and the way in which SQL Server 2005 performs the query.

Obtaining Query Information

1. In the New Query window, write the following T-SQL code (included in the sample files as \Ch03\SQLQuery1.sql).

```
USE AdventureWorks
GO
SELECT
    Production.ProductCategory.Name AS [Category Name],
    Production.ProductSubcategory.Name AS [SubCategory Name],
    Production.Product.Name,
    Production.Product.ListPrice,
    Production.Product.Size
FROM
    Production.Product
    INNER JOIN
        Production.ProductSubcategory
    ON
    Production.Product.ProductSubcategoryID = Production.ProductSubcategory.ProductSub
categoryID
        INNER JOIN
            Production.ProductCategory
        ON Production.ProductSubcategory.ProductCategoryID = Production.ProductCategor
y.ProductCategoryID
WHERE
    (Production.Product.ListPrice > 10)
GO
```

2. Click the Execute button. You will receive the results in the lower pane.

3. Click the Display Estimated Execution Plan button, which is the third button to the right of the Execute button, as shown below.

In the Display pane, you will receive a graphical representation of how SQL Server 2005 decides to execute the query. Each step will be described, and the proportional cost of each task will be listed.

> **More Info**   Estimated execution plans are discussed fully in Chapter 5, Computing Aggregates, in Microsoft® SQL Server™ 2005: Applied Techniques Step by Step.

Retrieving Statistics

By clicking the Include Client Statistics button shown in Figure 3-18 and re-executing the query, you will obtain another tab in the Results pane that contains statistical information about times and resources utilized.

Figure 3-18   Include Client Statistics button in Object Explorer.

Writing Solutions and Projects in SQL Server Management Studio

You may need to create a group of queries, modifications, and other actions for one or more databases. SQL Server Management Studio allows you to create projects to manage all scripts, connections, and other files that you may need.

Creating a Project in SQL Server Management Studio

1. Open SQL Server Management Studio from the Start menu by choosing All Programs | Microsoft SQL Server 2005 | SQL Server Management Studio.

2. When SQL Server Management Studio prompts you for a connection, click Cancel.

3. From the File menu, choose New | Project. A dialog box will appear like that shown in the following figure, where you can create several types of projects.

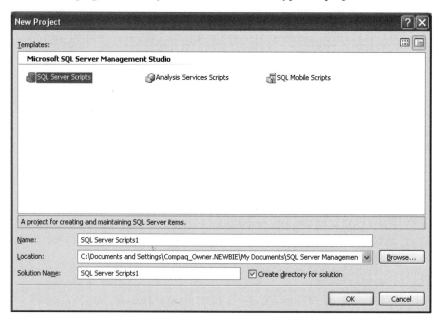

4. Select the SQL Server Scripts template and type a name for the solution in the Name textbox.

5. From the View menu, choose Solution Explorer, or press Ctrl+Alt+L to display Solution Explorer.

6. In the Server Explorer pane, right-click the Connections folder and choose New Connection from the context menu.

7. Accept the default values for your local server, or choose another server if desired.

8. In the Server Explorer pane, right-click the Queries folder and select New Query.

9. Click the Connect button in the Connect To Database Engine dialog box.

10. Write your desired query and close the window. When prompted, click Yes to save the query.

11. In the Server Explorer pane, right-click SQLQuery1.sql and select Rename to type a clearer name for the query.

12. Repeat Steps 8–11 to add additional queries.

13. Close SQL Server Management Studio. When you do so, you will be asked to save the project. You will be prompted to save the project file (with the *.ssmssqlproj* extension) and the solution file (with the *.ssmssln* extension).

Using SQL Server Management Studio Templates

Another available feature in SQL Server Management Studio is the Template Explorer. By using templates, you can accelerate many standard tasks within your databases.

Performing Actions with Templates

1. From the View menu, choose Template Explorer, or press Ctrl+Alt+T.

2. Expand the folder of the particular template that you want to use. For example, expand the Database folder.

3. Right-click the desired template (e.g., Create Database), and choose Open from the context menu. Click the Connect button in the Connect To Database Engine dialog box.

4. Click the Specify Values For Template Parameters button or, from the Query menu, choose Specify Values For Template Parameters. Alternatively, you can press Ctrl+Shift+M.

5.   In the Specify Values For Template Parameters dialog box, complete the values to fill in the template and click OK.

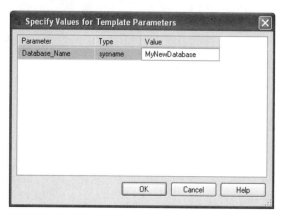

You will receive something similar to the following script.

```
-- =================================================
-- Create database template
-- =================================================
USE master
GO

-- Drop the database if it already exists
IF  EXISTS (
    SELECT name
        FROM sys.databases
        WHERE name = N'MyNewDatabase'
)
DROP DATABASE MyNewDatabase
GO

CREATE DATABASE MyNewDatabase
GO
```

Using SQL Server Management Studio Express

SQL Server Management Studio Express is a reduced version of SQL Server Management Studio that can be obtained as a free download with the SQL Server 2005 Express Edition, Service Pack 1. It allows you to manage the Express version of SQL Server 2005 just as you would using SQL Server Management Studio, but it has disabled all of the actions and operations that the SQL Server Express Edition does not support. If you are already familiar with SQL Server Management Studio, then you are already acquainted with SQL Server Management Studio Express as well.

Using SQL Server Profiler

SQL Server Profiler is a tool that captures events that occur in the SQL Server 2005 server. This feature allows you to know exactly what is contained in all of the sentences that your applications send to the server. This section will help you to:

- Understand how the tool works.

- Define traces and capture events.

- Understand the different types of events that can be captured.

- Cross-check traces with Performance Monitor.

More Info   SQL Server Profiler is also discussed in Chapter 4, Gathering and Understanding Business Requirements before Creating Database Objects.

Using the SQL Server Profiler Tool and Creating a Trace

SQL Server Profiler contains two parts: one is a client application and the other is part of the server.

- The client application is a graphical user interface (GUI) that helps you create traces, use templates, configure the tool based on templates, select columns and events to be audited, and file and trace schedules.

- The server part is the kernel of SQL Server Profiler. It listens for the events subscribed to by the GUI or by other traces. Any trace definition uses some system stored procedures to configure the trace in the server side of the SQL Server Profiler. The server component will synchronize with the client application to bring it the information audited by the trace.

Creating a Trace with the GUI

1. From the Start menu, choose All Programs | Microsoft SQL Server 2005 | Performance Tools | SQL Server Profiler.

2. Once the application is running, select New Trace from the File menu.

3. Connect to your SQL Server instance. You will see a screen resembling the following image.

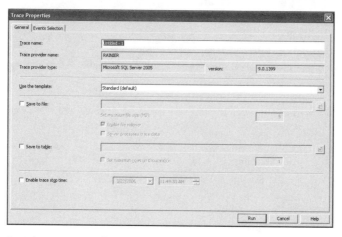

Besides generic information about the trace, such as the name, template, and SQL Server instance, you can configure other SQL Server Profiler trace general properties in the Trace Properties dialog box.

4. To save the trace into a file (with a .trc extension):

   4.1. Select the Save To File option in the Trace Properties dialog box.

   4.2. Choose the file's location and name.

   4.3. Once you have specified the file location and name, you can edit other options in the Trace Properties dialog box:

      ❏ Maximum size for the trace

      ❏ Enable File Rollover—Allows the Profiler to re-create the file when it reaches the maximum size

      ❏ Server Processes Trace Data—Indicates whether the server is responsible for saving the trace data. If you do not configure this option, the client application must save the data.

5. To save the trace in a SQL Server data table instead of a file:

   5.1. Select the Save To Table option.

   5.2. Connect to the desired SQL Server instance.

   5.3. Choose both the database and the table in which to save the information.

   5.4. Once you have specified the database and table, you can specify a maximum number of rows to which the table can grow.

6. Regardless of whether and where you save your trace, you can select the Enable Trace Stop Time option, which allows you to choose precisely the time to stop the trace.

> **Tip**   We do not recommend saving the trace either in a file or a data table, for this uses more resources and jeopardizes the measurements.

7. On the Trace Events tab of the Trace Properties dialog box, you can specify which events you want to audit, which columns will be registered, and which filters will be applied.

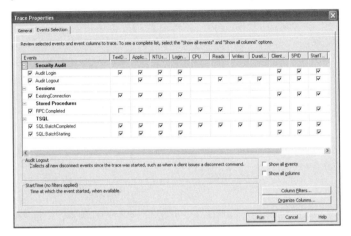

8. To define filters, click the Column Filters button. A new window will appear in which you can apply filters to every audited column.

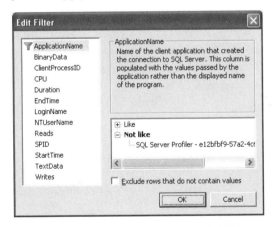

> **Note**   In SQL Profiler for SQL Server 2000, it was a complex process to determine which columns retrieved information in which events. In the SQL Server 2005 version, columns and events appear in a matrix where you can easily identify them. For that reason, it is recommended that you also use SQL Server Profiler 2005 with SQL Server 2000.

9. When the trace has been properly configured, click the Run button in the Trace Properties dialog box to begin capturing the events. SQL Server Profiler will show you each event sequentially.

When Should You Use SQL Server Profiler?

SQL Server Profiler is useful for:

- Analyzing how applications use the SQL Server instance.

- Detecting which stored procedures are used most often, which means obtaining a standard initial utilization point benchmark.

- Debugging stored procedures and T-SQL sentences. You can evaluate values, such as reads, writes, and central processing unit utilization, for each operation that a stored procedure or T-SQL sentence performs.

- Recording the trace for specific processes to optimize their design and replaying the trace once the processes are modified.

- Analyzing queries by storing the query plan in traces.

- Analyzing the performance of the database engine, Analysis Services, and the security audit of Integration Services.

- Locating deadlocks graphically.

Accessing Event Types

SQL Server Profiler events are grouped into event categories such as Broker, Security Audit, Performance, Cursors, and Locks. Each of these categories includes a set of event classes to obtain information about the specific events. Depending on their nature and style, you must select the information to capture in each event class by using the corresponding data columns.

Selecting Data in Event Classes

1. In SQL Server Profiler, stop the trace if it is running by choosing Stop Trace from the File menu. It is not possible to modify event class selections while the trace is running.

2. Choose Properties from the File menu, or click the Properties toolbar button.

3. Select the Events Selection tab. Note that only the selected event classes and columns are displayed by default. Check the Show All Events and Show All Columns checkboxes.

4. Navigate through the events columns, and check the event classes and related columns of your choice. You can change the order of displayed columns by clicking the Organize Columns button.

5. Click the Run button to start the SQL Server Profiler trace with the new event selection.

Running SQL Server Profiler and Performance Monitor Together

One of the new SQL Server Profiler features is the ability to run Performance Monitor and SQL Server Profiler side by side. This option provides you with detailed information about performance counters related to SQL Server activity. To run SQL Server Profiler and Performance Monitor side by side, perform the following steps.

Running SQL Server Profiler and Performance Monitor Side by Side

1. Start Performance Monitor by choosing Performance Monitor from the Tools menu in SQL Server Profiler. Alternatively, from the Start menu, choose All Programs | Control Panel. Double-click the Administrative Tools icon and then double-click the Performance icon.

2. Expand the Performance Logs And Alerts node in the Console Root tree and select Counter Logs to create a new counter log.

3. Right-click the Details pane (to the right of the tree pane) and select New Log Settings from the context menu. In the Name textbox, type **TestLog** and click OK.

4. Click the Add Objects button and add the following objects (select them in the list and click the Add button):

   - Memory
   - Processor
   - SQLServer:Databases
   - SQLServer:General Statistics

   Click the Close button to close the Add Objects dialog box.

5. Click OK. If the Perflog folder is not yet created, you will receive a warning message. Accept it. The counter log will start automatically.

6. Switch to SQL Server Profiler and create a new trace.

7. In the Trace Name textbox, type **TestTrace**.

8. Click the Save To File checkbox, and navigate to the C:\Perflogs folder to store the trace.

9. Click the Run button.

   To generate some activity, in SQL Server Management Studio, open the \Ch03\TestTrace.sql file included in the sample files and execute it while the counter log and trace are running. Wait until the script ends, which will take a few minutes.

10. Switch to SQL Server Profiler and stop the trace. Close the trace.

11. Switch to Performance Monitor and stop the counter log by right-clicking it in the Details pane and choosing Stop from the context menu.

12. Switch back to SQL Server Profiler. From the File menu, choose Open | Trace File. Navigate to C:\Perflogs and choose the TestTrace.trc file.

13. From the File menu, choose Import Performance Data. Navigate to C:\Perflogs and select the TestLog_000001.blg file. The Performance Counters Limit dialog box appears. Select the following counters:

    ■ Expand the Memory node and select Pages\Sec.

    ■ Expand the Processor node and select % Processor Time.

    ■ Select the SQLServer:Databases node.

    ■ Select the SQLServer:General Statistics node.

14. You will be informed that you have selected too many Performance Monitor counters. Click Yes to the warning message, and then click OK.

You can now view SQL Server Profiler and Performance Monitor data side by side. Note that both data are synchronized; therefore, if you select a trace event, a cursor will be positioned in the performance graphic at the location of that event.

Viewing Deadlocks in SQL Server Profiler

Another new feature of SQL Server Profiler is the ability to view deadlocks graphically. In addition, you can export deadlock information to an .xml file to analyze the deadlock in SQL Server Management Studio. To do so, complete the following steps.

Exporting Deadlock Information

1. Start SQL Server Profiler from the Start menu by choosing All Programs | Microsoft SQL Server 2005 | Performance Tools | SQL Server Profiler.

2. Choose File | New Trace and connect to your server. In the Events Selection tab of the Trace Properties dialog box, select the Show All Events checkbox. Expand the Locks event category and select the following event classes: Deadlock Graph, Lock:Deadlock, and Lock:Deadlock Chain.

3. Click the Run button.

4. In SQL Server Management Studio, open \Ch03\Deadlock1.sql and \Ch03\Deadlock2.sql.

5. Execute both scripts. These scripts will produce a deadlock. When the deadlock is detected, switch to SQL Server Profiler.

6. Stop the trace.

7. In the EventClass column, locate the Deadlock Graph event class.

   The deadlock is displayed graphically in the Details pane. If you move your mouse over the image of the processes, you will see a Tool Tip with the associated T-SQL sentence.

8. Right-click the Deadlock Graph event class and choose Extract Event Data from the context menu.

9. Navigate to \Ch03 and save the deadlock as **deadlock.xdl**.

10. Open Windows Explorer and navigate to \Ch03.

11. Double-click deadlock.xdl. SQL Server Management Studio will open the deadlock file.

Using Database Engine Tuning Advisor

Database Engine Tuning Advisor is a performance tool that allows you to examine workload files, such as trace and .sql files, and advise changes in physical database structures, such as indexes, index views, and partitioning, to achieve your best performance. Database Engine Tuning Advisor can also recommend what statistics should be collected to support physical structures.

Analyzing Database Engine Tuning Advisor

Database Engine Tuning Advisor has several tuning capabilities that are always based on the workload files used as input. It is critical that the workload files include a load representative of the database activity. Database Engine Tuning Advisor can:

- Use the Query Optimizer to propose indexes and indexed views.
- Recommend partitions.
- Analyze the impact of recommended changes.
- Provide information about query distribution and index usage.

You can set all of these options for each session. You will learn about options and sessions in following sections of this chapter.

Working with Database Engine Tuning Advisor

To use Database Engine Tuning Advisor, you should first create a workload file. This workload file can be a trace file created with SQL Server Profiler, T-SQL code that you want to analyze, or an .xml file. Once you have created the workload files, proceed to the following steps.

Starting Database Engine Tuning Advisor

1. Start Database Engine Tuning Advisor from the Start menu by choosing All Programs | Microsoft SQL Server 2005 | Performance Tools | Database Engine Tuning Advisor.

2. Connect to the SQL Server instance.

3. A new Tuning Advisor session appears. You can change the session name in the Session Name textbox, as shown below.

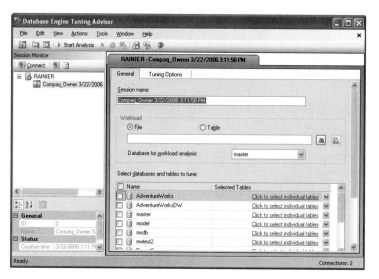

4. In the Workload frame, choose the File option. Click the button to the right of the text-box to browse for a file and navigate to \Ch03\DTATrace.trc in the sample files.

5. In the Database For Workload Analysis drop-down list, select AdventureWorks.

6. In the Databases And Tables To Tune frame, select AdventureWorks. Note that you can click the cell in the Selected Tables column to specify individual tables.

7. Select the Tuning Options tab, which allows you to configure session behavior and recommendation constraints. You will learn more about these options later in the "Managing Tuning Options" section of this chapter.

8. Click the Start Analysis toolbar button.

When the Database Engine Tuning Advisor ends (this will take a few seconds), you will observe two new tabs: Recommendations and Reports. The Recommendations tab presents Tuning Advisor recommendations based on the workload file and tuning options. To view only the recommended changes, you can uncheck the Show Existing Objects checkbox, as shown in Figure 3-19.

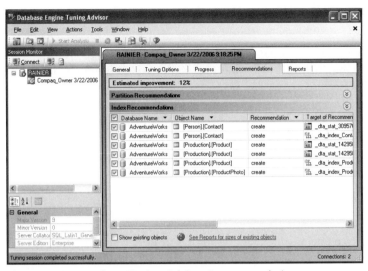

Figure 3-19   Database Tuning Advisor Recommendations.

In the Recommendation column, you see the actions that can be created, altered, or dropped. In the Definition column, you see the T-SQL code used to implement the recommendation. You can also save all of the recommendations by selecting Save Recommendations from the Actions menu. If you select the Reports tab, you can choose a report from the Select Report drop-down list to view detailed information about the analysis, including index usage reports (both before and after the recommendation is implemented) and a statement-index relations report.

Evaluating the Recommendations

One of the most interesting Database Engine Tuning Advisor features is the ability to evaluate the impact of the recommendations.

Evaluating the Impact of Database Engine Tuning Advisor Recommendations

1.   In the Database Engine Tuning Advisor, from the Actions menu, choose Evaluate Recommendations. A new session is created to evaluate the impact.

2.   Click the Start Analysis button.

When the analysis ends, you will receive information concerning how the recommendations would affect the database.

Managing Tuning Options

There are many options available to use for configuration purposes in a Database Engine Tuning Advisor session. You can set the following options on the Tuning Options tab.

■   **Physical Design Structures (PDS) To Use In Database**   Allows you to choose which database objects the Database Engine Tuning Advisor can recommend using to achieve best performance.

- **Partitioning Strategy To Employ** Allows you to choose whether and what kind of partitions Database Engine Tuning Advisor will advise using to optimize the workload.

- **Physical Design Structures (PDS) To Keep In Database** Allows you to choose whether you want to maintain all database objects or will consider recommendations to drop certain objects.

You can configure advanced options by clicking the Advanced Options button. Advanced options include:

- **Define Max Space For Recommendations** Allows you to specify the maximum space used for recommendations.

- **Max Columns Per Index** Allows you to specify the maximum number of columns per index.

- **Online Index Recommendations** Allows you to choose whether index operations will be online or offline.

Managing Database Engine Tuning Advisor Sessions

Database Engine Tuning Advisor uses sessions to manage analysis operations. Earlier in this section, you created two Tuning Advisor sessions: one for the initial analysis and another for the evaluation session. You can create as many sessions as you need, close them, and import and export sessions from the Database Engine Tuning Advisor.

Exporting a Session Definition

1. In Database Engine Tuning Advisor from the File menu, choose Export Session Definition.

2. Navigate to \Ch03. Save the definition as **SessionDefinition.xml**.

Once the definition has been exported, you can import it into another SQL Server instance. These export and import operations allow you to efficiently deploy Database Engine Tuning Advisor sessions in several SQL Server instances.

Session information is stored in the msdb database to allow you to reuse sessions. All Database Engine Tuning Advisor-related tables start with the prefix DTA_ so they can be detected easily.

Using SQLCmd

SQLCmd is a command line tool that allows you to enter T-SQL sentences or script files by connecting to the SQL Server instance using OLE DB. SQLCmd is the replacement for the previous osql command.

Working with the SQLCmd Utility

To start the SQLCmd utility, you should launch SQLCmd from the command line. You can use the default SQL Server instance or connect to a named SQL Server instance.

Connecting to a Default SQL Server Instance

1. From the Start menu, click Run. In the Open textbox, type **cmd** and click OK.

2. In the command prompt, type **sqlcmd** and press Enter.

3. You will enter the SQLCmd shell and observe a 1> prompt.

4. Type **Select name from sys.databases** and press Enter.

5. Type **Go** and press Enter. The result will be displayed.

6. Type **Exit** and press Enter to quit SQLCmd.

If you want to connect to a named instance, you should use the −S input parameter and specify the instance name in the Server\Instance format. You can view all input parameters by executing SQLCmd /?, as shown in Figure 3-20.

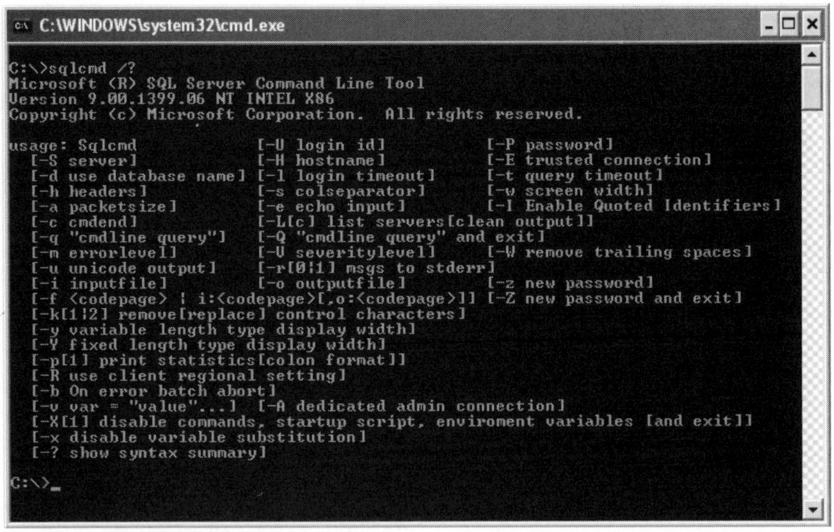

Figure 3-20   SQLCmd input parameters.

Executing Script Files

You can use SQLCmd to execute script files from the command line, which allows you to schedule scripts outside the SQL Server instance.

Executing the DTA.sql Script by Using the SQLCmd Utility

1. From the Start menu, click Run.

2. In the Open textbox, type **cmd** and click OK.

3. In the command prompt, type **sqlcmd −i <path>\Ch03\SQLCmd.sql** (replace <path> with the path in which you installed the sample files).

4. Press Enter. A list of product names is displayed.

Conclusion

You have learned how to configure your SQL Server instance and the security features in SQL Server 2005 by using the new SQL Server Surface Area Configuration tool. You have learned to use the new SQL Server Management Studio and Database Engine Tuning Advisor, as well as the enhanced SQL Server Profiler.

Chapter 3 Quick Reference

To	Do This
Learn about SQL Server 2005 features and search for help	Use SQL Server Books Online.
Configure a SQL Server 2005 instance	Use the SQL Server Configuration Manager tool.
Manage databases and run queries	Use the new SQL Server Management Studio or the SQLCmd tool.
Tune a SQL Server instance	Use the new Database Engine Tuning Advisor.
Analyze your SQL Server query performance and server use	Use SQL Server Profiler and Performance Monitor.

Part II
How to Create a Microsoft SQL Server 2005 Database

In this part:

Chapter 4

Gathering and Understanding Business Requirements before Creating Database Objects

After completing this chapter, you will be able to:

- Gather requirements from the database perspective
- Understand business data and its lifetime
- Pinpoint operating requirements such as performance, scalability, and security
- Estimate capacity planning

In previous lessons, you learned the basics of Microsoft SQL Server 2005: how it may help you, how to install it, and what tools it offers. We will now shift the focus from SQL Server 2005 to your application and explore the way you should capture business requirements to build a solid foundation for your design.

Programmers and project managers frequently underestimate how critical the gathering and comprehension of business requirements are in the software development process—with devastating effects. Industry studies estimate that more than 35% and up to 50% of project failures are related to lack of user input as well as incomplete or changing requirements. The Standish Group International Inc., in their Chaos Report and Extreme Chaos Reports, estimated that only 29% of all projects succeeded (delivered on time, on budget, with required features and functions). If you apply the concepts learned in this lesson, you will avoid much of that risk and increase your development effectiveness.

Understanding Business Processes and User Interaction Requirements

The software development process starts with the gathering of user requirements. Developing a solution based on the collected requirements helps you create applications that satisfy user needs.

Defining the Business Problem

Before writing the first line of code, you should always ask yourself why you are building the solution. The best way to understand your motives is to define a business problem that you will be addressing. The process of identifying the problem will help those affected by the project to make decisions concerning how much money, time, and resources to expend building the solution.

To find sponsors for your project, you may formalize the previous process and write a business case that describes the business need for which you are seeking a solution. Also include such factors as business benefits, expected costs, and risks. If you already have a sponsor, you should still write a business case because it provides justification for the project. Effective business cases convince management that the investment in time and resources is aligned with business strategies and is financially sound.

More Info   For more information about how to create an effective business case, refer to the "Build an Airtight Business Case for New IT Investments" article at http://www.microsoft.com/business/enterprise/value.mspx.

Capturing Requirements

Defining the problem is only the first step in the process of understanding business processes and user requirements. A *requirement* is a description of what a solution should do. Requirements can be described as either functional or operational. *Functional requirements* are attributes that the software solution must contain to be acceptable to stakeholders. The involvement of actual users in the process of defining and validating functional requirements is critical for the survival of the project because they provide business value to users and customers.

Experienced developers rely on domain experts as the main source of business requirements. Domain experts are people who have a clear understanding of specific areas of the business, along with its data and processes. They know how the business operates and how things are accomplished. You may find domain experts in any level of the company hierarchy, but the better experts are typically found in middle management.

Among the techniques used to capture requirements are user surveys, interviewing, and shadowing.

Writing User Surveys

Surveys are written or electronic questionnaires that users answer about what software should or should not do. Surveys help software designers to identify key issues. Some advantages of user surveys are:

- They provide written "evidence."
- They can be used broadly and with remote users.

- They are very cost efficient.

The limitations of user surveys are:

- Users tend to answer ambiguously, thus making it difficult to obtain useful results. Surveys are not always effective.

- They provide a broad view of the software solution, for it is both difficult and expensive to gather detailed information.

- It is a limited communication mechanism—you ask, they answer. It becomes a very slow process because their answers raise new questions, thereby making it difficult to "close the loop."

Surveys are a cost-efficient tool used in identifying key issues that are later detailed with interviews.

Interviewing

The most popular technique for gathering requirements is the interview. The *interview* is a conversation between the software designer and the user. The advantage of the interview is that it allows users to participate in a free and direct way. As a result, the designer will have a better perspective of the users' needs and, if handled properly, the interview may reduce users' stress and resistance to new software solutions.

Interviews bring with them two disadvantages: they are expensive in both time and resource expenditure, and they require interviewing skills. Some advice to keep in mind when interviewing customers and users includes the following:

- Establish an environment of trust; the user must feel that you want to help him. When the user trusts you, he will be more inclined to help you.

- Listen attentively. Take notes. The users will notice if you appear interested.

- Ensure that you and the users have enough time to conduct the interview, and schedule the interview at a convenient time for both participants.

- Use the interview as an observation mechanism, for the user environment is an important source of information for you.

- Interview the right users. Make certain you are interviewing the domain experts who facilitate the process.

- Prepare for the interview.

When interviewing users, it is important to keep in mind that the goal is to find and analyze key issues, not simply to get questions answered. You should use questions as tools to direct the conversation to the subjects of your interest. Software designers also use the interview as a mechanism to observe, identify, and capture user artifacts. *Artifacts* are user objects such as invoices, reports, spreadsheets, paper notes, and so forth.

Shadowing

Shadowing is a requirements-gathering technique in which you observe the user performing daily tasks in the real work environment. The advantage of using this technique is that the information is first hand and is more reliable than other sources. With shadowing, you discover the tasks that the user performs through observation and ask questions only about the reasons why the task is being performed. Shadowing is a good technique for capturing requirements on daily and repetitive tasks.

Writing Requirements

It is important that you explicitly state requirements in a formal document. Some consequences of the writing requirement process are that it helps you to better understand the requirements, find missing requirements, and preview the solution.

The formal requirements document is also an open communication channel with users and stakeholders (people affected by the project), ensuring that the project will satisfy user rather than developer requirements. Finally, formally documented requirements reduce the number of changes after the development process begins.

When capturing requirements, you should make sure they are:

- Customer or user oriented
- Clear and concise
- Necessary and relevant
- Reachable and verifiable
- Complete and validated

> **Tip**   Consider utilizing Unified Modeling Language (UML) use cases to capture and write user requirements.

Understanding Business Data and Its Lifetime

In the previous section, we discussed how to capture functional requirements, but there exists another set of requirements: operational requirements. *Operational requirements* are attributes that a system or solution must possess to be acceptable from the information technology (IT) perspective. Operational requirements include availability, interoperability, manageability, performance, reliability, scalability, and security. Some examples of operational requirements include:

- The payroll calculations should take less than 15 minutes.

- The application will only be available through the intranet to previously authenticated Windows users.
- The application will be available and function properly 99% of the time.

Architecture and Operational Requirements

Possessing a good understanding of operational requirements demands that you have substantial knowledge of the business information that the system will manage and understand the business need that the software will solve. Operational requirements are important because they have a deep impact on the architecture of the solution. For example, if a solution needs to support 500 concurrent users, you will probably want to use SQL Server 2005 Enterprise Edition; if only five concurrent users are needed, a SQL Server 2005 Express Edition may suffice.

One way to evaluate the operational requirements is to analyze the business impact if the requirement is not fulfilled. For example, what will be the business impact if the application is not available for three hours? For three days? These questions can help you measure the benefits of the requirements, especially for requirements that are expensive to fulfill. A good understanding of the operational requirements helps stakeholders perform a cost-benefit analysis.

Well-designed applications use features of the technology to match the operational requirements. SQL Server 2005 offers features such as failover clustering, database mirroring, and database snapshots. If used appropriately, all of these features can help you increase application availability. Good application architecture leverages technology features to satisfy operational requirements.

Availability

Availability refers to the ability of the solution, system, or component to stay operational for the required length of time. Availability can be defined as the time that a solution is available for use. Availability is usually measured as a relative operational level. Perfect availability will be 100 percent and is typically specified in nines notation. For example, 5 nines represent 99.999%, 4 nines represent 99.99%, and so on.

> **More Info**   To learn more about SQL Server 2005 availability technologies, refer to the following SQL Server Books Online topic: Database Mirroring, Failover Clustering, and Log Shipping.

To understand how difficult it is to achieve a certain level of availability, Table 4-1 translates the availability percentage to a time-per-year downtime that will be permitted.

Table 4-1   Availability and Yearly Downtime

Availability	Downtime
99%	3.65 days/year
99.9%	8.76 hours/year
99.99%	52 minutes/year
99.999%	5 minutes 15 sec/year

Interoperability

Interoperability requirements demand that software has the ability to communicate with other programs using common protocols or file formats. Interoperability helps businesses manage the diversity of software products and platforms.

You can achieve interoperability after your solution has been developed. You may add code to read and save files to communicate with other programs, or you may use products such as Biz-Talk Server 2005 to orchestrate messages between different applications. However, if you include interoperability requirements in advance, your design will have built-in interoperability. Built-in interoperability offers better performance and manageability than added interoperability.

SQL Server 2005 is designed to help you create interoperable solutions through support of industry standards such as XML, Web Services, and the .NET Framework. The following SQL Server 2005 technologies may help you interoperate with different platforms.

- **SQL Server Integration Services**   A platform to build data integration solutions. SQL Server Integration Services (SSIS) is a valuable tool to build extraction, transform, and load (ETL) packages for data warehousing. Use SSIS to extract data from heterogeneous sources (including .NET data providers, OLE DB data providers, Microsoft Excel, XML files, flat files, and raw files) and merge that data in a consistent database.

- **SQL Server Replication**   A set of technologies for copying and distributing data between databases. Replication allows you to automate the copy of data to and from other database platforms including Oracle, IBM, and Sybase.

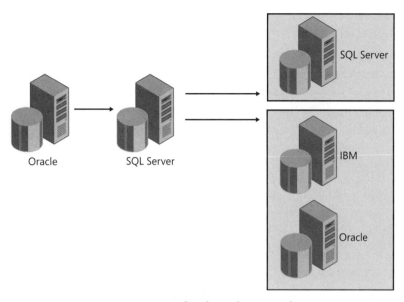

- **SQL Server Service Broker**   A technology that provides message queuing and reliable messaging in an asynchronous programming model. SQL Server Service Broker allows for the creation of messages between applications for interoperability purposes. For example, a sales processing application may send a summarized sales total message to an accounting application.

- **SQL Reporting Services**   A server reporting technology that allows you to create reports from relational and multidimensional data sources. With Reporting Services, you may create reports from .NET, OLE DB, and ODBC (open database connectivity) data providers, allowing your application to interact with a wide range of data sources. Because the SQL Server Report Server (the main component of SQL Server Reporting Services) is offered through a set of XML Web Services, other platforms may consume its services.

Manageability

Manageability refers to the capacity of the software to be managed or controlled. Several industry studies confirm that the cost of managing applications is a major part of the total cost of software ownership. To build a manageable solution, you must provide tools that allow the application to be administered. Manageable solutions include configuration settings, performance counters, application logs, and so on.

To design a manageable solution, you must consider a different type of user—the application administrator. Application administrators usually belong to the IT department. To build a manageable solution, you must provide them with an information and configuration infrastructure. Your application should allow the application administrator to monitor processes, services, and devices. With this information, the application administrator may perform preventive and corrective actions and handle administrative tasks such as installation, configuration, and general software maintenance.

As you learned in Chapter 3, Reviewing Microsoft SQL Server 2005 Management Tools, SQL Server 2005 offers SQL Server Management Studio, an integrated environment for configuring, managing, and administering all components of SQL Server 2005. Because SQL Server Management Studio includes a graphical user interface for all common management tasks, it reduces the amount of time database administrators need to support the database.

If you want to automate even further, thus increasing the manageability of your application, SQL Server 2005 offers Server Management Objects (SMO). SMOs are objects designed to manage SQL Server 2005 programmatically. With SMO, you may satisfy the needs of nontechnical users and reduce their training costs by integrating the server and database management into your application. For example, the following Visual Basic code will back up the AdventureWorks database using SMO.

Database Backup with SMO

```
Imports Microsoft.SqlServer.Management.Smo
Public Class BackDB
    Public Shared Sub BackDB()
        Dim back As New Backup()
    back.Database = "AdventureWorks"
    back.Devices.Add(New BackupDeviceItem( _
                    "C:\Lab\AdventureWorks.bak", DeviceType.File))
        back.Action = BackupActionType.Database
    back.SqlBackup(New Server("ServerName"))
        MessageBox.Show("Backup Complete!")
    End Sub
End Class
```

> **Note**   To use the *SMO* namespace, you must install the Client Tools option in the SQL Server 2005 installation program and add a reference to the *Microsoft.SqlServer.SMO* namespace. Refer to the following SQL Server Books Online topics for detailed instructions: How to Create a Visual C# SMO Project in Visual Studio .NET or How to Create a Visual Basic SMO Project in Visual Studio .NET.

Performance

Performance requirements identify how fast the solution should complete a process under a particular workload. There are two ways to measure performance: throughput and response time. *Throughput* measures how much work an application can perform, and *response time* measures the amount of time between the user request and the outcome of the request. An example of a performance requirement is that a home page should load within five seconds under a 150-user load. You can see that the performance requirement has two measures: five seconds (response time) and an implicit throughput to handle a given amount of data for a 150-user load.

You should design your application with performance in mind because some elements that affect performance are difficult to optimize after a database is in production. The following tips should help you in the designing process.

■ Establish performance requirements to manage user and developer expectations.

■ Develop a testing plan that checks performance requirements.

■ Design your database appropriately, and use normalization to reduce data redundancy (see Chapter 5, Designing a Database to Solve Business Needs).

■ Develop and test your stored procedures while taking performance into consideration (see Chapter 9, Retrieving Data Using Programmable Objects).

■ Optimize the most significant queries and design your indexes appropriately (see Chapter 6, Improving Query Performance in Microsoft® SQL Server™ 2005: Applied Techniques Step by Step).

Several factors affect application performance metrics. In SQL Server 2005, the following factors may affect performance:

■ Hardware (processor, memory, disk input/output (I/O) speed)

■ Windows operating system version and configuration

■ SQL Server 2005 version and configuration

■ Database physical design (file placement, database configuration, indexes, and so on)

■ Database logical design

■ Network (drivers, devices, topology, and so forth)

■ Client application

Some performance issues can be resolved by increasing hardware resources, but applications with serious design flaws will have performance difficulties no matter how much you increase the hardware. Testing should include realistic quantities of data because metrics can change dramatically depending on the size of the input.

Reliability

Reliability requirements establish software quality goals that help you measure how users and applications depend on the solution. Reliability is measured with the mean time between failure (MTBF) metric, meaning the average time between failures. The MTBF formula is:

MTBF = hours of operation/failure count

Reliability and availability are related, but they set requirements quite differently. From a reliability point of view, the causes of failure may include not only the lack of service, but also the provision of inaccurate services. For example, if an application incorrectly calculates the sales tax under certain conditions, it will affect the reliability of the software, but it will not affect the availability. On the other hand, if a hard disk problem causes the application to be unavailable for two or three days, the reliability will be affected with only one failure, but the availability of the software will be greatly affected (1 percent). Software failures are counted only when the software is available and executing.

A well known fact is that about 80 percent of system failures are caused by human errors or flawed processes. That is why industry studies indicate that the reliability of software is only marginally affected by hardware and software technology; it is mainly controlled by the quality of the software engineering process, the emphasis on training, and the commitment to reliability.

Scalability

Scalability is the capacity of the solution to increase the total throughput (quantity of work) when hardware resources are added. In an ideal scalable application, an increase in hardware resources increases the throughput of the application proportionally. Non-scalable applications require increasing quantities of hardware to support additional users.

Performance and scalability are easily confused because performance problems are usually detected when the application is tested with increasing loads, but they are different. Measuring the maximum workload that an application can handle while meeting the minimum response time under varying hardware conditions determines the scalability of the application.

Internet applications and applications that support business models with the possibility of significant economic growth should include scalability requirements. Internet applications frequently demand support to an increasing number of users, as shown in Figure 4-1.

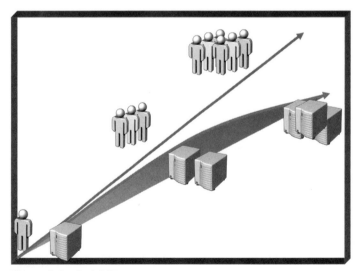

Figure 4-1   Scalability

Security

Security operational requirements determine how to control user access to information. Because new threats arise daily, there is an important difference between security and other operational requirements: the security design process continues even after the solution is developed. A high-quality initial design reduces both the application's exposure to attacks and the impact to the design caused by any new threats. Issues involving some basic principles of database security will be discussed in greater detail in Chapter 6, Reading Microsoft SQL Server 2005 Data from Client Applications.

Predicting the Volume of Information to Store and Manage and Predicting Database Utilization

In software construction, you need to estimate the amount of work that the software and hardware will handle. Similar to an engineer who calculates how much weight a bridge needs to support, software developers forecast and analyze the workload that the application must handle. To estimate this workload, developers use prototypes. *Prototypes* are samples of the software that allow the developer to simulate what the actual version will accomplish.

The process of predicting the volume of information that a server or application will store and manage is called *capacity planning*. Capacity planning measures, forecasts, analyzes, and sets goals for resource utilization and transaction throughput under load. Capacity planning includes things such as estimates of the number of users, user profiles and usage patterns, server loads, and resource utilization. It also provides hardware recommendations and server configurations for different scenarios. To plan for growth and forecast peak application usage involves extensive performance testing and the measurement of resource utilization and transaction throughput under different loads.

Two methodologies documented by the Microsoft Patterns & Practices Development Center may help you predict the volume of information and database utilization: transaction cost analysis and predictive analysis. *Predictive analysis* uses historic data. In this book, we will focus on transaction cost analysis.

Using Transaction Cost Analysis

In *transaction cost analysis*, you calculate the cost of users' operations in terms of the resources consumed by the operation. For example, if a user registers a new order, you will estimate how much CPU (central processing unit), memory, and network resources will be consumed by this event.

More Info   To learn more about transactional cost analysis, read Capacity Model for Internet Transactions at http://www.microsoft.com/technet/archive/mcis/rkcapmit.mspx?mfr=true.

The following steps help you perform a transaction cost analysis.

Step 1: Compiling a Users Profile

In this step, you will document the transactions that users frequently perform in their daily work. For example, in the order scenario, you may know that, on average, the cashier user opens the application, logs on, opens the register, registers forty-five invoices per hour, voids two invoices per hour, closes the register after four hours, and logs off. This set of tasks is repeated during the day by various shifts.

As shown in the previous example, to compile user profiles requires an understanding of business volumes and application usage patterns. Capture usage scenarios based on the information provided by domain experts.

Step 2: Executing Discrete Tests

In this step, the tasks described in the user profile are performed in an isolated environment (lab or development environment) and captured. To capture and save data about events happening in the server, use Microsoft SQL Server Profiler. As you learned in Chapter 3, SQL Server Profiler is a graphical user interface used to monitor an instance of the SQL Server database engine.

Before capturing the test, perform a full database backup to help you replay the test. To learn how to back up the database, refer to Chapter 3, Disaster Recovery Techniques to Protect Your Database in Microsoft® SQL Server™ 2005: Applied Techniques Step by Step.

Creating the Script

1. Open the SQL Server Profiler by selecting Start | Programs | Microsoft SQL Server 2005 | Performance Tools | SQL Server Profiler.

2. Create a new trace by choosing New Trace from the File menu.

3. In the Connect To Server dialog box, log on to the server with an appropriate account.

4. In the Trace Properties dialog box, name the trace and select the TSQL Replay template from the Use The Template drop-down list.

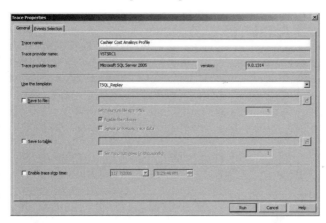

5.   Select the Save To File option. The Save As dialog box will appear.

6.   In the Save As dialog box, browse to a folder in which to save the file, and click the Save button.

7.   In the Trace Properties dialog box, click the Run button.

8.   Start the application and complete all of the required operations. Whenever possible, start multiple instances of the application (5-25 instances) to obtain a better sample of the average user.

9.   After all operations are finished, stop the trace by using the Stop button on the toolbar in the SQL Server Profiler.

Step 3: Measuring the Cost of Each Operation

Measure the cost of each operation in terms of the resources consumed during the test. To capture resource utilization, you will need to create a Windows performance log.

Creating a Windows Performance Log

1.   Open the Performance Monitor by selecting Start | Settings | Control Panel. Open Administrative Tools, and then double-click the Performance icon.

2.   In the left panel under the Console Root folder, expand the Performance Logs And Alerts node and then select the Counter Logs folder.

3.   Right-click the Counter Logs folder and select New Log Settings in the context menu.

4.   When the New Log Settings dialog box opens, name the log setting and click the OK button.

5.   Click the Add Counters button.

6.   Select an object from the Performance Object drop-down list and select the required counter.

7.   Click the Add button.

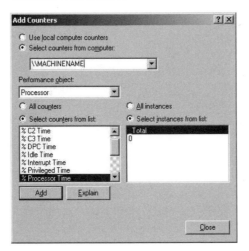

8. Continue to select objects and add counters.

9. When all required counters are added, click the Close button.

10. On the General tab, select a data sample interval. For transaction cost analysis, use a one-second interval.

11. On the Log Files tab, select the appropriate log type and name. For transaction cost analysis, the default (binary file in the C:\PerfLogs path) should suffice.

12. On the Schedule tab, select the appropriate schedule settings. For transaction cost analysis, the best option is to start and stop the log manually.

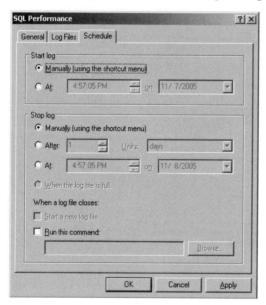

In SQL Server 2005, the following Windows performance counters shown in Table 4-2 will help you to predict the resource usage.

Table 4-2 Windows Performance Counters

Resource	Performance Object	Counter
Processor	Processor	Processor Time
	System	Processor Queue Length
Memory	Memory	Pages/Sec
	SQLServerBufferManager	Buffer Cache Hit Ratio
Disk	PhysicalDisk	% Disk Time
	PhysicalDisk	Avg Disk Queue Length
Network	Network Interface	Bytes Total/Sec

To begin capturing information, right-click the log and select Start from the context menu. To finish capturing information, right-click the log and select Stop from the context menu. Capture one log for each operation, or use a single log and keep track of the beginning and end time for each operation.

Based on the number of instances of the application, user operations, and resource usage information, calculate the cost of the average profile in each resource by dividing the resource usage by the number of instances. Use each of the following counters:

- Processor: Processor Time
- Memory: Pages/Sec
- PhysicalDisk: %Disk Time
- Network Interface: Bytes Total/Sec

Reviewing the Captured Information

1. In the Performance Monitor, select the System Monitor folder.
2. Press the View Log Data button on the toolbar.

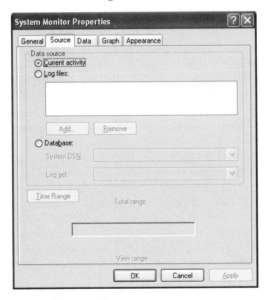

3. Select the Log Files option.
4. Click the Add button.
5. Select the trace file and click the Open button.
6. Click OK.
7. Press the Add button on the toolbar.
8. Add the following counters:
    - Processor: Processor Time
    - Memory: Pages/Sec

- PhysicalDisk: % Disk Time

- Network Interface: Bytes Total/Sec

9. Close the Add Counter dialog box.

As an example, you may have the following metrics in the register invoice task of the cashier profile as shown in Table 4-3.

Table 4-3   Cashier Profile: Register Invoice Task

Resource	Resource Usage	Average User
Processor	15%	0.75%
Memory	5 Pages/Sec	0.25
Disk	3%	0.15%
Network	1530 Bytes/Sec	76.75

The other counters (System: Processor Queue Length, SQLServerBufferManager: Buffer Cache Hit Ratio, and Physical Disk:Avg Disk Queue Length) indicate when the resource is becoming a system bottleneck. A *bottleneck* is any resource, component, or activity that limits performance.

If the counters are consistently above the following threshold, the resource must be considered a bottleneck and will considerably affect the performance of the application. To have small bursts of the counter over the threshold is expected. Only when the resource's counter value is consistently above the threshold is the resource considered to be a bottleneck (refer to Table 4-4).

Table 4-4   Resource Bottleneck Threshold

Counter	Threshold	Resource
Buffer Cache Hit Ratio	<90%	Memory
Processor Queue Length	>2	Processor
Avg Disk Queue Length	>2	Disk

When a bottleneck is reached, not only is performance greatly reduced, but the rest of the counters also change dramatically. For example, assume that the Buffer Cache Hit Ratio indicates a memory bottleneck because the register invoice task produces a persistent 70 percent value. Because memory is scarce, the Windows operating system will likely start swapping pages (saving memory to hard disk in a virtual memory file). This will not only increase the memory counter, but also the disk counter.

Step 4: Calculating the Cost of an Average Profile

Based on the information captured and your understanding of the business volumes and application usage patterns, estimate the average profile by estimating the average resource cost of the profile at the peak usage.

Table 4-5 demonstrates the input and results of the average profile user calculations. In this example, the Logon value (2.5%) would be chosen as the processor resource because experience suggests that most cashiers will log on at the same time. The memory resource would use a weighted average of register and void invoices based on your user profile, in this case (45*.025+2*1.25)/47. The disk and network resources would use a weighted average of register invoice (70%) and close register (30%) because experience indicates that no more than 30 percent of cashiers close simultaneously.

Table 4-5   Cashier Profile

Resource	Logon	Register Invoice	Void Invoice	Close Register	Average Profile
Processor	2.50%	0.75%	0.90%	3.50%	2.50%
Memory	0.02	0.25	1.25	0.25	0.29
Disk	0.06%	0.15%	0.30%	6.28%	1.99%
Network	1776.75	76.75	125.45	5476.75	1696.75

Step 5 : Calculating the Maximum Capacity

With the information collected in the previous step, estimate the maximum server capacity. To calculate this capacity, divide the maximum server capacity between the average profile cost. If you assume that the server will only support cashiers, you may estimate the following maximum capacity as shown in Table 4-6.

Table 4-6   Server Maximum Capacity

Resource	Average Profile	Maximum Capacity	Maximum # of Users
Processor	2.50%	100%	40
Memory	0.29	200	689
Disk	1.99%	100%	50
Network	1697	500,000	294
Server Maximum Capacity			40

Based on the previous example, the maximum number of users that the server supports will be forty users. Select the least of the maximum number of users supported by each resource. When multiple profiles are estimated, create a weighted average of all users and use that as the average profile.

Step 6: Verifying the Maximum Capacity

After making the needed calculations, you may verify the maximum capacity of the server by using the scripts captured with the SQL Server Profiler or other testing tools.

Conclusion

In this chapter, you learned some of the important tasks that developers must perform to help them gather and understand business and operational requirements. Use surveys, interviewing, and shadowing to capture user requirements, for these procedures will help you understand how the business process works and how the user will interact with the software. Also review operational requirements, such as availability, interoperability, manageability, performance, reliability, scalability, and security. This information will ultimately help you decide which SQL Server 2005 technologies your application will use and the hardware your solution will require.

Chapter 4 Quick Reference

To	Do This
Find sponsors for your project	Write a business case that identifies the addressed business problem.
Simplify the gathering of user requirements	Use domain experts that have a clear understanding of business.
Obtain a better perspective of users' needs	Employ user interviews.
Communicate with users and stakeholders	Use a formal document to capture user requirements.
Guarantee the operational viability of the solution	Verify that operational requirements are considered.
Estimate the amount of work that software and hardware will handle	Use transaction cost analysis.

Chapter 5

Designing a Database to Solve Business Needs

After completing this chapter, you will be able to:

- Model business needs
- Validate business requirements through entity-relationship models
- Understand Microsoft SQL Server 2005 datatypes
- Enforce data integrity through table constraints

In this chapter, you will learn how to design and create a database to support business and application requirements. You will learn modeling techniques and practices that will assist in the process of transforming a business requirement document into the Transact-SQL (T-SQL) code required to create the database.

Designing a Database Conceptually

Database design is a critical part of the software development process. To ensure that the design fulfills business and operational requirements, database designers typically create three different database models, as shown in Figure 5-1.

- **Conceptual model**   A high-level representation of user and operational requirements. It helps the formalization process of the requirements and represents how data is perceived by business users.

- **Logical model**   Detailed representation of the software model that will capture the structured data. It helps to eliminate or at least drastically reduce data redundancy and increases data integrity. Logical models represent how the developer sees the data.

- **Physical model**   Detailed specification of all tables and columns of the database. It maps specific vendor technologies in the model. Physical models represent how the server stores the data.

Figure 5-1   Three-Step Database Model

> **Note**   To the untrained eye, this three-step process may seem time consuming, but that is not the case. Modeling the database in three steps offers a better quality control process and is frequently faster than a single-step design process.

Validating Business Requirements through Conceptual Models

To comprehend and validate the business problem, database designers create *conceptual models* that serve as the foundation of logical and physical models. Four modeling techniques can be used to create conceptual models.

- Object-Role Modeling (ORM)
- Unified Modeling Language (UML)
- Object-Oriented Systems Model (OSM)
- Entity-Relationship modeling (ER)

> **Note**   Microsoft Office Visio for Enterprise Architects supports ORM, UML, and ER diagrams.

ER conceptual modeling is used in this book, but you should examine other models to discover a system with which you are comfortable.

Creating the First Model

To create a conceptual model of your application, you will need to examine all of the captured requirements and identify the following components:

- **Entities**   People, places, items, or concepts
- **Attributes**   Properties of an entity
- **Relationships**   Connections between entities

The best way to understand these concepts is by example. As part of the requirement-gathering process, assume that you obtain the following copy of an Adventure Works invoice.

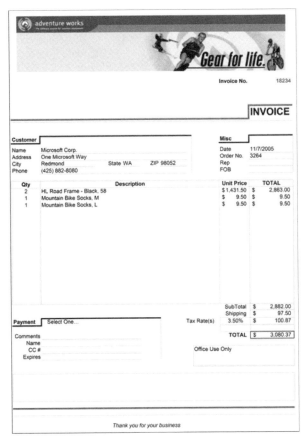

On this invoice, you identify the following entities: Invoice, Invoice Line (Invoice Item), Customer, Order, and Payment. You also identify the following attributes of the Customer entity: Name, Address, City, State, Zip Code, and Phone. Lastly, there is a relationship between Invoices and Customer entities. Continue identifying model components (entities, attributes, relationships) until all of the requirements are covered and all relevant business information is modeled.

Diagramming the Model

Several tools allow you to create ER diagrams, and Microsoft Visio for Enterprise Architects will be used in this book. This version of Visio is included in Visual Studio 2005 Team System (Developer, Tester, Architect) or as part of Visual Studio Professional with MSDN Premium.

Creating a Conceptual ER Diagram Using Microsoft Visio

1. From the Start menu, select Programs | Microsoft Office | Microsoft Office Visio For Enterprise Architects.

2. In the Choose Drawing Type window, select the Database category.

3. In the Database category, choose the Database Model Diagram or ER Source Model.

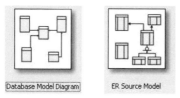

Creating Entities

To document an entity in an ER Visio diagram, complete the following steps.

Modeling Entities in Visio 2003

1. Drag and drop an entity shape from the Shapes toolbar to the diagram surface.

2. Select the recently added entity.

3. In the Database Properties window, choose the Definition category.

4. Name the entity using the Conceptual Name field.

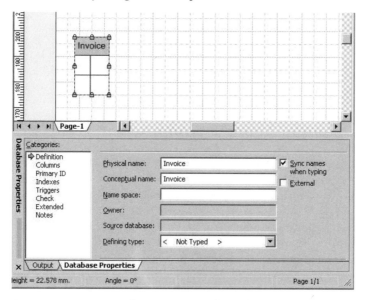

Try to maintain a simple naming standard when naming objects. The object names you choose should be easily identifiable by users.

Adding Attributes

To include attributes in the appropriate entity, complete the following steps.

Modeling Attributes in Visio 2003

1. Choose the Columns option in the Categories listbox, which is located to the left of the Database Properties window.

2. Add the attribute name in the Physical Name column.

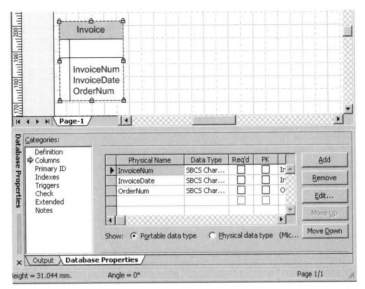

3. You may also choose the attribute datatype at this time, but datatypes will be discussed in greater detail in the sections dealing with logical modeling.

Adding Relationships

In an ER diagram, relationships are represented with arrows. The arrow representing a relationship always points to the referenced entity. This means that the model would verify that the referenced element exists, and the integrity of the data is preserved for every referencing element. For example, when creating a relationship between the Cities and States/Provinces entities, the model would not allow the inclusion of a city that references a State or Province that does not exist.

Many types of relationships can be modeled in ER diagrams. The most common and simple type of relationship is the *parent-child relationship*. In this relationship, for each entity A, there are many entities B. Entity A is called the parent entity, and Entity B is the child entity. Parent-child relationships are also referred to as *one-to-many relationships* because one entity in the parent entity may be referenced by many entities in the child entity.

Modeling a Parent-Child Relationship

1. Drag and drop a relationship shape from the Shapes toolbar to the diagram surface.

2. Select the head of the arrow, and drag and drop it over the parent entity.

In a relationship between entities, the parent entity is the one that is referenced. For example, in the Customer-Invoice relationship, Customer is the parent entity and Invoice is the child entity.

3.   Select the bottom of the arrow, and drag and drop it over the child entity.

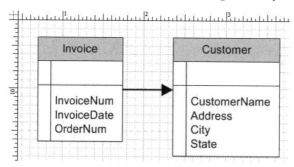

Other Types of Relationships

When creating a conceptual model, you may encounter some distinctive relationships that do not have a standard parent-child relationship between two entities. These relationships include intersection, multi-intersection, and self-referencing relationships.

Modeling intersection relationships   *Intersection relationships* possess a many-to-many association between entities, such as students and courses. Students may register for many courses, and courses may have numerous enrolled students. There is no parent-child relationship between students and courses. To model a many-to-many relationship, you will need an additional table that may or may not have additional attributes.

Modeling an Intersection Relationship

1.   Drag and drop three entity shapes from the Shapes toolbar to the diagram surface.

2.   Name the entities Students, Courses, and EnrolledStudents.

3.   Add the required attributes to the Students and Courses entities.

4.   Add two relationship shapes to the diagram surface.

5.   Drag and drop the heads of both arrows over the EnrolledStudents entity.

6.   Drag and drop the bottom of one relationship arrow over the Students entity and the bottom of the other relationship arrow over the Courses entity.

7.   Add attributes to the EnrolledStudents entity.

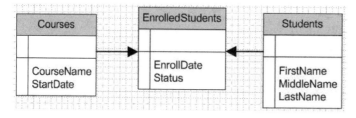

To model a many-to-many relationship, add an additional table and establish two one-to-many relationships between the intersection entity and the other entities.

Modeling multi-intersection relationships   The *multi-intersection relationship* uses the same guidelines as the intersection relationship, with the difference being that more than two tables participate in the relation. For example, assume that you want to enhance the previous model and capture information about scheduled courses in a university. You want to capture the relationship between courses, classrooms, professors, and schedules. The relationship can be modeled as shown in Figure 5-2.

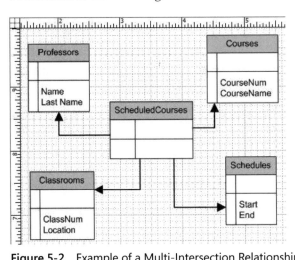

Figure 5-2   Example of a Multi-Intersection Relationship

Modeling self-referencing relationships   *Self-referencing relationships* involve entities that reference themselves. They do not have two different participating entities, but instead have only one entity participating in both ends of the relationship. An employee-boss relationship is one example of a self-referencing relationship. Every employee may have a boss or manager, who is also an employee. To model an employee-boss relationship, you will need to create a self-referencing relationship.

Modeling a Self-Referencing Relationship

1. Drag and drop one entity shape from the Shapes toolbar to the diagram surface.

2. Name the entity Employee.

3. Add the required attributes to the Employee entity.

4. Add one relationship shape to the diagram surface.

5. Drag and drop the head of the relationship arrow over the Employee entity.

6.   Drag and drop the bottom of the relationship arrow over the Employee entity.

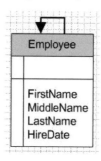

Approving the Model

After you have modeled all of the requirements and are satisfied with the model, it should be validated with users and customers. Take care to present the model to the domain experts. Domain experts are power users and business experts who intimately know how the business works, and they can be found at any level of the organization. Continue the process of model refinement until it satisfies all stakeholders.

> **Tip**   Validate the database model early in the development process, for this will prevent costly mistakes in the construction phase.

Designing a Database Logically to Leverage the Relational Engine

After the conceptual model is approved and obtains the consent of users and customers, database modelers create a logical design. A *logical design* is a database model that evolves from the conceptual model, for it takes the previously captured requirements and creates a vision of the software solution. A logical database diagram is created to answer questions such as the following: What datatypes should be used? How do you identify an entity? What rules should be enforced to validate the data?

Modeling terminology changes when it reaches the logical model. Table 5-1 may help you to distinguish the language used in each model.

Table 5-1   Modeling Terminology

Conceptual Model	Logical Model
Entity	Table
Attribute	Column
Relationship	Foreign Key

To create a logical model, complete the following steps:

1. Find the appropriate type for each column.

2. Find the primary key of each table.

3. Normalize the database.

4. Add additional validation rules.

> **More Info**   *Normalization* is the process in a relational database that both reduces redundancy and reduces the potential for anomalies, thus improving data integrity and consistency.

Creating Columns to Capture Object Attributes

Each time you define a column to capture an object attribute, you must define a datatype. The *datatype* is an attribute of each column that specifies what kind of data the column will store. For example, you may want the Name column to store string (alphanumeric) values, the Price column to store monetary data, and the OrderDate column to store only date and time data.

SQL Server 2005 supports twenty-eight system datatypes and also allows programmers to create their own. The datatypes provided by the system are shown in Table 5-2.

Table 5-2   SQL Server 2005 Datatypes

bigint	binary	bit	char	cursor
datetime	decimal	float	image	int
money	nchar	ntext	numeric	nvarchar
real	smalldatetime	smallint	smallmoney	sql_variant
table	text	timestamp	tinyint	varbinary
varchar	uniqueidentifier	xml		

Defining the appropriate datatype is critical in maintaining the integrity of the database. For example, if you use the char datatype to define the Price column, users may store names and addresses in this column, and no one will know the true value of the attribute. Good database designers invest a considerable amount of time analyzing what datatype should be applied to a column so as to create models that offer database integrity and good performance.

Declaring a Datatype Graphically

To define a datatype graphically, you may use your modeling tool or a T-SQL statement. To define a datatype using Microsoft Visio 2003, perform the following steps.

Defining a Datatype Using Microsoft Visio 2003

1. Select the table you want to model.

2.   If the Database Properties window is not displayed, right-click the table and choose Database Properties from the shortcut menu.

3.   Select Columns from the Categories list in the Database Properties window.

4.   Make sure that the Physical DataType (Microsoft SQL Server) option is selected.

5.   Select the column you want to model from the Column list.

6.   Enter the datatype in the Data Type column, or select the datatype from the Combo box.

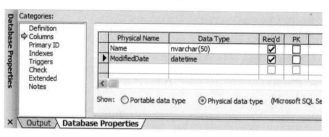

Using T-SQL Code to Define a Datatype

To define a datatype using T-SQL language, use the CREATE TABLE statement. This statement defines the table and its columns with the chosen datatypes. The simplified version of the CREATE TABLE statement is:

```
CREATE TABLE <NameofTable> (
    <ColumnName> <DataType>
  , <ColumnName> <DataType)
  , ...
)
```

For example, the following statement creates a department table.

```
CREATE TABLE Departments(
   DepartmentName NVARCHAR(50)
   , DivisionName NVARCHAR(50)
   , ModifiedDate DATETIME
)
```

Numeric Attributes

SQL Server 2005 offers wide support for numeric attributes, which include integer datatypes, precise decimal numbers, and approximate numbers. Each datatype category is useful in different situations.

Integers and quantities   *Integer columns* store whole numeric data containing no decimal components, meaning that integer attributes do not support fractions. *Integers* include natural positive numbers (1, 2, 3), natural negative numbers (−1,−2,−3), and 0. Integers are frequently used to model quantities. Examples of integer attributes include Age (in years), Quantity in

Stock, Shipped Quantity, Number of Employees, and Apartment Number. SQL Server 2005 provides five integer datatypes: bit, tinyint, smallint, int, and bigint. The difference between each datatype is the range of numbers they support and the storage space that each column of that datatype occupies. Table 5-3 provides specific information about integer datatype parameters that may help you make decisions about your choice of datatype.

Table 5-3 Integer Datatype Parameters

Datatype	Storage Space	Min Value to Max Value
bit	1/8 of byte	0 to 1
tinyint	1 byte	0 to 255
smallint	2 bytes	−32,768 to 32,767
int	4 bytes	−2,147,483,648 to 2,147,483,647
bigint	8 bytes	−9,223,372,036,854,775,808 to 9,223,372,036,854,775,807

Refer to the following guidelines to help you determine which integer datatype to use in different scenarios.

■ Use the bit datatype for True/False, Flag, or Status attributes. Examples include Sex (Male/Female), Reorder (True/False), Enable (True/False), and InProcess (0/1). Keep in mind that the bit datatype also permits the unknown value (NULL); therefore, it actually has three different statuses: 0, 1, and NULL.

■ Use the tinyint datatype for very small numbers. Examples include Number of Children, Line Number, Floor, and Age. The tinyint datatype stores only positive numbers (or zero) and does not allow negative numbers.

■ Use the smallint datatype for small numbers. Examples include Room Number, Years, and Seat Number.

■ Use the int datatype for almost every number you find in business applications. Examples include Quantity Ordered, Parts in Stock, Number of Shares, and Number of Passengers.

■ Use the bigint datatype only when very large numbers are required. These numbers are rarely required in business applications, but you may encounter them in scientific situations.

Precise numbers and accounting data   *Precise numbers* in T-SQL language allow the storage of numbers with decimal parts. This means that a number may contain fractions as long as it is expressed as a division of a power of ten. Financial and accounting information, including prices and amounts, are expressed with this datatype.

SQL Server 2005 provides four precise datatypes: decimal, money, numeric, and smallmoney. The difference between each datatype is the range of numbers they support and the storage space that each column of that datatype occupies. Other important factors include the datatype's precision and scale.

Precision is the maximum number of digits you want a datatype to store. For example, the number 12,345.12 contains seven digits. Precision includes all of the digits before and after the decimal point. The *scale* of the datatype is the number of decimal digits; therefore, the scale of 12,345.12 is two.

Table 5-4 provides specific information about precision datatypes that may help you make decisions when choosing these datatypes.

Table 5-4   Precision Datatype Parameters

Datatype	Space	Precision	Scale	Min Value to Max Value
decimal	5 bytes	9	0–5	–999,999,999 to 999,999,999
numeric	9 bytes	19	0–9	$-10^{19}+1$ to $10^{19}-1$
dec	13 bytes	28	0–13	$-10^{28}+1$ to $10^{28}-1$
	17 bytes	38	0–17	$-10^{38}+1$ to $10^{38}-1$
money	8 bytes	Approx. 18	4	–922,337,203,685,477.5808 to 922,337,203,685,477.5807
smallmoney	4 bytes	Approx. 9	4	–214,748.3648 to 214,748.3647

Note   The dec datatype is not included as a system datatype, but can be used to define columns in a table. The dec datatype is part of the SQL-92 ANSI standard.

The numeric and decimal datatypes are equivalent and can be used with different precisions and scales to accommodate most information. The smallmoney datatype can be used for prices, and the money datatype can be used for financial amounts.

Table 5-5 displays the minimum datatype required to store each number.

Table 5-5   Required Datatype Examples

Datatype	Example	Precision	Scale
decimal	54,143.9481	9	4
numeric	98,145,875,298.12	13	2
dec	0.12679	5	5
money	103,785,675.9573	Fixed	Fixed
smallmoney	45,985.4503	Fixed	Fixed

Scientific and engineering data   Scientific and engineering applications frequently use very large or very small numbers. For example, astronomy applications may store the mass and size of planets, stars, or galaxies. The mass of the sun is 1.9181×10^{30} Kg, which is a unit called solar mass. The mass of the Milky Way galaxy is about one trillion solar masses. To store the mass of a galaxy using a precise decimal number would not be appropriate.

For these purposes, SQL Server 2005 offers *approximate number* datatypes. These datatypes do not store an exact number, but instead use approximate floating-point data. SQL Server 2005 provides three approximate datatypes: float, real, and double. The real and double datatypes are float datatypes with predefined mantissa bits. Table 5-6 provides specific information about approximate datatypes that may help you make decisions about your choice of datatype.

Table 5-6   Approximate Datatype Parameters

Datatype	Storage Space	Mantissa Bits
float	4	1–24
	8	25–53
real	4	24
double	8	53

Important   Do not use approximate number datatypes (float, real, double) to store financial information because aggregations will result in round-off errors.

Because approximate number datatypes use natural logarithms to store values, the critical factor is the precision of the datatype. The real datatype uses twenty-four bits to store the mantissa, and the double datatype uses fifty-three bits, thereby controlling the precision and size of the datatype.

Note   A *mantissa* is the positive fractional part of the representation of a logarithm. For example, in reference to the number 12345.12, the log value is 9.42101612226667 and the mantissa is .42101612226667.

String Attributes

Users also need to store string attributes in the database. These attributes save information such as Name, Address, Title, and E-mail. These datatypes are composed of letters, numbers, and symbols. To store such attributes, SQL Server 2005 provides four different datatypes: char, nchar, varchar, and nvarchar. To better understand the terminology used in string types, refer to Table 5-7 below.

Table 5-7   String Datatype Terminology

String Types	Character	Unicode
Fixed	char	nchar
Variable	varchar	nvarchar

Variable datatypes use the *var* prefix, and unicode datatypes use the *n* prefix.

Unicode and character datatypes   Unicode and character datatypes use different methods to store (encode) strings. Unicode datatypes (nchar, nvarchar) use the unicode standard to convert characters into bit sequences (encode). Character datatypes use sets of rules called *collations* to perform the same task.

Unicode datatypes are an industry standard designed to allow text and symbols from all languages to be consistently represented and manipulated by computers. Therefore, information stored in unicode datatypes can be consistently communicated between computers, thereby always resulting in the decoding of the original character. In contrast, *character datatypes* use collations to control the physical storage of character strings by using a specific code page. If the code page differs between computers, the incorrect character may be decoded.

The main advantage of character datatypes is efficiency. In general, character datatypes are more efficient than unicode datatypes because most collations use one byte per character, while their unicode counterpart uses two bytes per character. For example, a char(20) column will require twenty bytes, whereas the same column defined as nchar(20) will use forty bytes. Some collations use two bytes per character.

Fixed and variable-length datatypes   Another option to consider when using string datatypes is whether to use fixed or variable-length datatypes. *Fixed datatypes* (char, nchar) use a permanent amount of space regardless of the value of the column or variable. For example, if you declare a column as type char(10) and it has the value of "Test," it will employ ten bytes, even though Test has only four letters. This occurs because SQL Server 2005 will add six spaces after the word *Test*, thus always filling in the ten characters. The same column defined as nchar(10) will employ twenty bytes. This behavior is known as *right padding*.

In contrast, *variable-length datatypes* adjust their storage to accommodate the value of the column, but require two additional bytes to control the length of the value. Therefore, if you declare a column as type varchar(10) and a row has the value of "Test," it will employ six bytes to store the value, two bytes for length control, and four bytes to store the actual value. The same column using nvarchar(10) will use ten bytes (two for length, eight for the actual value), and SQL Server 2005 will not add additional spaces.

String syntax   To define string attributes in T-SQL, use the following syntax.

```
CREATE TABLE <NameofTable> (
     <ColumnName> CHAR(<Size>)
   , <ColumnName> VARCHAR(<MaxSize>)
     <ColumnName> NCHAR(<Size>)
   , <ColumnName> NVARCHAR(<MaxSize>)
   , ...
)
```

For example, the following code will create a Department table to store the attributes Code, Name, and AlternateName.

```
CREATE TABLE Departments(
   DepartmentCode    CHAR(6)
   , DepartmentName VARCHAR(50)
   , AlternateName NVARCHAR(50)
)
```

Character datatypes (char, varchar) support up to 8,000 characters per column, and unicode datatypes (nchar, nvarchar) can hold up to 4,000 characters.

Long text datatypes   When the attribute you are capturing exceeds the maximum capacity of string datatypes, you may use the varchar(max) or nvarchar(max) datatype. Use these datatypes when the size of column values varies significantly and when the size might exceed 8,000 bytes. These datatypes support up to 2,147,483,647 characters (two gigabytes). The varchar(max) datatype uses collation to code characters, and nvarchar(max) uses unicode. Remember that unicode datatypes occupy two bytes per character; therefore, nvarchar(max) holds only 1,073,741,823 characters.

> **Note**   SQL Server 2005 also supports the text and ntext datatypes. Avoid using these datatypes because they are marked as obsolete, and future versions will remove them.

Choosing the appropriate datatype   Refer to the following guidelines to help you determine which datatype to use in each situation.

- Appropriately size the column to collect the values of the attribute, but do not add additional unnecessary space. Using an adequate length will aid in data validation and provide better performance.

- Use fixed-length datatypes (char, nchar) when the values of the attribute do not vary considerably in length. For example, to store a Social Security number, use a char datatype instead of varchar. This will result in better storage usage and performance.

- Use variable-length datatypes (varchar, nvarchar) when the values of the attribute vary considerably in length. For example, to store an address attribute, use a varchar datatype instead of char. This will result in better storage usage and performance.

- Use character datatypes when all users of the database utilize the same language or when you can set a general collation to represent all characters in their languages. Using character datatypes will result in more efficient databases.

- Use unicode datatypes when users will store strings from different writing systems (e.g., Latin, Kanji, Arabic, Greek) and you cannot set a general collation to represent all characters in their languages. Unicode will support a wider range of characters and avoid those errors produced when using different code pages.

Date and Time Attributes

In business applications, the need to store date and time attributes occurs frequently. For example, you may want to store the date and time that an order is received or shipped, the date an employee is hired, or the date of someone's birthday. SQL Server 2005 does not have separate datatypes for date and time attributes. It instead has two datatypes that combine date and time into a single attribute with different features (Size, Accuracy and Range). Table 5-8 provides specific information about datetime attributes that will help you better understand their characteristics.

Table 5-8   Datetime Attribute Parameters

Type	Size	Accuracy	Min to Max Value
datetime	8 bytes	3.33 milliseconds	January 1, 1753, to December 31, 9999
smalldatetime	4 bytes	1 minute	January 1, 1900, to June 6, 2079

Best Practices   Do not use string datatypes (char, nchar, varchar, nvarchar) to store dates. Storing dates as strings makes data validation more difficult, exposes the application to internalization errors, and is frequently detrimental to performance.

Binary Data

Some applications need to store images (such as JPG, GIF, and BMP files) or documents (such as Microsoft Excel workbooks or Microsoft Word documents). To support those needs, SQL Server 2005 supports binary datatypes. *Binary datatypes* are raw sequences of bytes that SQL Server 2005 does not try to encode or decode as it does with string datatypes. Binary information can be stored in three datatypes: binary(n), varbinary(n), and varbinary(max), as detailed below in Table 5-9.

Table 5-9   Binary Datatype Parameters

Datatype	Description	Max Width
binary(n)	Fixed-length binary data	8000 bytes
varbinary(n)	Variable-length binary data	8000 bytes
varbinary(max)	Long binary data	2,147,483,647 bytes

Best Practices   SQL Server 2005 also supports the image datatype. Avoid using the image datatype because it is marked as obsolete, and future versions will remove it.

The following is an example of how to declare binary datatypes in SQL server 2005.

```
CREATE TABLE Applicants(
  , ApplicantID INT
```

```
  , Name    VARCHAR(25)
  , LastName VARCHAR(25)
  , Curriculum VARBINARY(MAX)
  , PictureVARBINARY(300000)
)
```

Complex Attributes

SQL Server 2005 also offers additional datatypes, which are listed below.

- **Rowversion** A binary(8) datatype that is automatically updated when a row is inserted or updated. Because rowversion numbers are controlled per database, they are not sequential in the table; however, they are sequential per database. For example, if you define two tables, Orders and OrderDetails, and define a rowversion column in each table, the value 0 × 87D2 may be assigned to the Order table, and the value 0 × 87D3 may be assigned to the OrderDetail table. Rowversion columns are useful to control changes in rows.

- **Uniqueidentifier** A datatype used to stored globally unique identifiers (GUIDs). A GUID is a numbering mechanism that guarantees that the same number will not be generated in any table, database, or networked server in the world. A uniqueidentifier is a sixteen-byte number, like the following: 50295F55-4666-4358-B6C6-B9B709755BAC. Uniqueidentifiers are not automatically updated, as are rowversion numbers. You must use the *NEWID()* function to generate the GUID. Uniqueidentifiers are useful to identify, copy, and control rows in distributed databases.

- **XML** The xml datatype is one of the most interesting and complex datatypes offered by SQL Server 2005. This datatype is used to store XML documents and fragments as single values. For example, you may store documents that were generated by other applications or platforms, such as Purchase Orders or Shipment Confirmations. The xml datatype can also be used to store information that can be modeled in a relational manner, or it can be used when the schema of the information is unknown.

T-SQL user-defined datatypes If you want to create your own datatype to maintain consistency among tables that store the same attribute, you may use a T-SQL *user-defined type* (UDT). A UDT will help you create columns that contain the same datatype and length. For example, you may create a PhoneNumber attribute to ensure that all tables define phone numbers in the same manner. The following example creates a PhoneNumber attribute using T-SQL.

```
CREATE TYPE PhoneNumber
FROM VARCHAR(14);
```

Common language runtime-based UDTs If you want to create your own datatypes without being limited by system datatypes, you may create your own common language runtime (CLR) UDTs using .NET languages such as Visual Basic.NET, C#.NET, and C++.NET. To create a CLR UDT, you must create a structure and use the *Microsoft.SqlServer.Server.SqlUserDe-*

finedTypeAttribute. After the structure is created, it must be compiled as an assembly and deployed in the database. Finally, the server must be enabled to execute CLR code.

Validating the Data

Determining how your database will implement integrity is an important part of the database designing process. To do so, you must identify which values are valid for each column in your database. After the values have been identified, you then create constraints that help keep bad data from entering your database. SQL Server 2005 provides the following constraints: NOT NULL, DEFAULT, PRIMARY KEY, UNIQUE, CHECK, and FOREIGN KEY.

NOT NULL Constraints

The *NOT NULL constraint* is equivalent to declaring an attribute as being required instead of optional. As a result, it will not allow rows that do not have a value in that column. For example, in the following table, the Number, Name, Social Security Number, and Hire Date columns are required and the Termination Date is optional.

```
CREATE TABLE Employee (
        EmployeeNumber      INT             NOT NULL
      , EmployeeName        VARCHAR(50)     NOT NULL
      , EmployeeSSN         VARCHAR(15)     NOT NULL
      , HireDate            SMALLDATETIME   NOT NULL
      , TerminationDate     SMALLDATETIME   NULL
)
```

Try to design all columns with the NOT NULL constraint, and allow NULL values only in rare cases.

DEFAULT Constraints

Another useful constraint is *DEFAULT*, which allows you to declare a column value if one is not specified when the row is inserted. For example, if you have an E-mail column in the Employee table, recently hired employees may not have an e-mail account. If you do not want the column to support NULL values, you may create a DEFAULT constraint. The following code creates the table.

```
CREATE TABLE Employee (
 EmployeeNumberINTNOT NULL
, EmployeeNameVARCHAR(50)NOT NULL
, EmployeeSSNVARCHAR(15)NOT NULL
, EmailAccountVARCHAR(50)NOT NULL
DEFAULT('unknown@mycompany.com')
, HireDateSMALLDATETIMENOT NULL
, TerminationDateSMALLDATETIMENULL
)
```

PRIMARY KEY Constraints

Because a table is a set of rows, a row cannot be identified unless you define a primary key. The *primary key* is a column or combination of columns that identifies each row in the table. For example, the EmployeeNumber column identifies each row in the Employee table because it is a value that is both required (NOT NULL) and distinct in each row (employees do not share employee numbers). The following code creates the PRIMARY KEY constraint of the employee table.

```
CREATE TABLE Employee (
        EmployeeNumber          INT             NOT NULL
            PRIMARY KEY
        , EmployeeName           VARCHAR(50)     NOT NULL
        , EmployeeSSN            VARCHAR(15)     NOT NULL
        , EmailAccount           VARCHAR(50)     NOT NULL
            DEFAULT('unknown@mycompany.com')
        , HireDate               SMALLDATETIME   NOT NULL
        , TerminationDate        SMALLDATETIME   NULL
)
```

When the primary key involves multiple columns, the PRIMARY KEY constraint is defined at the table level with the following syntax.

```
CREATE TABLE StateProvince (
        CountryCode             CHAR(3)         NOT NULL
        , StateCode             CHAR(3)         NOT NULL
        , StateProvinceName     VARCHAR(50)     NOT NULL
        PRIMARY KEY (CountryCode, StateCode)
)
```

UNIQUE Constraints

When you want to enforce the stipulation that a value cannot be repeated in a table, you may define a *UNIQUE constraint.* For example, if you want the database to control that no employees use the same Social Security number, use a UNIQUE constraint. The following code will check that a Social Security number is used in only one row and that two rows do not have the same value.

```
CREATE TABLE Employee (
        EmployeeNumber          INT             NOT NULL
            PRIMARY KEY
        , EmployeeName           VARCHAR(50)     NOT NULL
        , EmployeeSSN            VARCHAR(15)     NOT NULL
            UNIQUE
)
```

UNIQUE constraints may also limit a combination of multiple columns. For example, if you want to limit repeated products in a purchase order, the following UNIQUE constraint may help you.

```
CREATE TABLE OrderDetails (
        OrderId                CHAR(6)            NOT NULL
      , OrderLine              INT                NOT NULL
      , ProductNumber          CHAR(10)           NOT NULL
      , Quantity               DECIMAL(10,2)      NOT NULL
      , Price                  DECIMAL(10,2)      NOT NULL
      , PRIMARY KEY(OrderId, OrderLine)
      , UNIQUE(OrderId, ProductNumber)
)
```

CHECK Constraints

Certain columns should be limited to a range of values, a pattern, or a certain condition. For example, the Sex column should be limited to Male or Female, the Amount column to positive values, and Social Security Numbers to a string pattern such as ###-##-####. To define such constraints, use CHECK expressions, such as those shown in the code below.

```
CREATE TABLE Employee (
    EmployeeNumberINT             NOT NULL
       CHECK(EmployeeNumber>0)
    , EmployeeSSN       VARCHAR(15)      NOT NULL
       CHECK(EmployeeSSN LIKE '[0-9][0-9][0-9][0-9]-[0-9][0-9]-
[0-9][0-9]-[0-9][0-9][0-9][0-9]')
    , HireDate          SMALLDATETIME    NOT NULL
       CHECK(HireDate>'19950101')
    , TerminationDateSMALLDATETIMENULL
       CHECK(TerminationDate IS NULL OR TerminationDate>HireDate)
)
```

FOREIGN KEY Constraints

The *FOREIGN KEY constraint* limits the values of a column to those that can be found in another table. For example, if you create a DepartmentCode column in the Employee table, you want the database to guarantee that this department exists in the Department table. The FOREIGN KEY constraint links the values of the column with the PRIMARY KEY or UNIQUE constraint in the referenced table, as shown in the following example.

```
CREATE TABLE StatesProvinces (
    CountryCode         CHAR(3)          NOT NULL
         FOREIGN KEY REFERENCES Countries(CountryCode)
    , StateCode         CHAR(3)          NOT NULL
    , StateProvinceName VARCHAR(50)      NOT NULL
    , PRIMARY KEY (CountryCode, StateCode)
    , UNIQUE (CountryCode, StateProvinceName)
)
```

Physically Creating a Database

The final step of the database design process is the physical design. This is the phase in which you finally create the database, tables, and remaining database objects.

Selecting an Appropriate Storage Design for a Database

When creating a database, it is important to understand what constitutes a database, how SQL Server 2005 stores information in the database, and, most importantly, what options exist when designing the database.

What Is a Database?

A *database* in a relational world is a repository of structured data or, in simpler terms, an organized collection of data. A database is where you create tables, constraints, datatypes, and other data-related objects. Because SQL Server 2005 is a client-server relational database management system (RDBMS), you will rarely access the database files from your application. You will use T-SQL statements to specify the actions that the server must take. Client applications will then open a connection to the server and database and operate within its boundaries.

How Is Information Stored?

A SQL Server database contains the following files, as illustrated in Table 5-10.

Table 5-10   Database Files

Database File	Optional/Required	File Extension	Objective
Primary	Required	.mdf	Stores database system information, plus the table and index structures where data resides
Secondary	Optional	.ndf	Stores table and index structures where data resides
Log	Required	.ldf	Provides transactional support to the database and temporarily stores changes in the database

The following list is a simplified version of the transactional process.

- Your application sends a group of T-SQL statements in a transaction. To learn more about transactions, see Chapter 10, Using Transactions to Provide Safe Database Concurrency in Microsoft® SQL Server™ 2005: Applied Techniques Step by Step.

- The server reads the information needed to perform changes to the database. This information is read from primary and/or secondary files. If the information was previously in RAM memory, this step is skipped.

- The server modifies the information in RAM memory and marks the information as "dirty." *Dirty* means that the information has been modified in RAM, but changes have not been saved to disk.

- The server saves all modifications in the transaction log. The *transaction log* keeps a record of all database modifications and will be used in case of server failure.

- The server informs the application that the transaction is committed. *Committed* means that the server has saved the modification and the application may continue.

- Eventually, an event called CHECKPOINT occurs in the server, and all dirty information of committed transactions is saved to disk in primary and secondary files.

Designing Database Storage

When designing database storage, consider the following guidelines.

- Use formatted disks from the New Technology File System (NTFS) to store database files. NTFS offers better security and recoverability than a file allocation table (FAT) file system.

- Do not use compressed volumes or files. Compressed volumes dramatically decrease the performance of a database.

- Use a separate disk or disk subsystem for log files because log files access information in a sequential manner, while data files are accessed randomly using separate disks to increase performance. Separating the log file also increases recoverability. Use different physical disks instead of partitions of the same disk.

- Use redundant array of inexpensive disks (RAID) technology to store database and log files. Primary and secondary database files are best stored in RAID 5 or RAID 10 disk subsystems. Log files are best stored in RAID 1 or RAID 10 disk subsystems.

- Spreading the database in multiple disk subsystems increases performance. Use as many disks as possible to distribute the database load. Performance is increased when using primary and secondary files, but not when using multiple log files.

Creating a Database

The following process describes how to create a database using Microsoft SQL Server Management Studio.

Using SQL Server Management Studio to Create a Database

1. From the Start menu, select Programs | Microsoft SQL Server 2005 | Sql Server Management Studio.

2. Connect to the database engine that will host the database.

3. In Object Explorer, right-click the Databases folder and choose New Database from the context menu.

4. When the New Database dialog box is displayed, name the database.

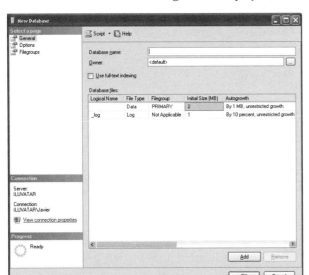

5. In the Database Files grid, scroll to the right to review the path of the file and, if necessary, change the path to support your storage design decisions.

6. If you want to use multiple data files, select the Add button to create secondary files.

7. If necessary, choose options in the Select A Page task pane on the left.

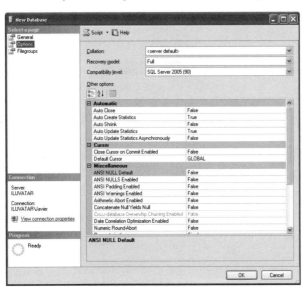

8. Configure the database options.

9. Click OK to create the database.

Using T-SQL to Create a Database

To create a database using T-SQL statements, use the following syntax.

```
CREATE DATABASE Tests
ON ( NAME = Tests_dat
, FILENAME = 'C:\Data\TestDat.mdf'
, SIZE = 20 MB )
LOG
ON ( NAME = Sales_log
, FILENAME = 'E:\Logs\TestLog.ldf'
, SIZE = 5MB );
```

Designing Database Schemas to Logically Group Database Objects

Schemas are namespaces that simplify database object management. By using schemas, you can organize tables and other database objects as well as make it easier to grant permissions. Use schemas to create categories of tables, help users and developers navigate your database, or create groups of tables that can be managed from a single point.

Using SQL Server Management Studio to Create Database Schemas

1. Open SQL Server Management Studio.

2. Connect to the database engine that hosts the database.

3. Expand the Databases folder, expand the database you will be working with, and then expand the Security folder.

4. Under the Security folder, right-click the Schemas folder and choose New Schema.

5. When the New Schema dialog box is displayed, name the schema.

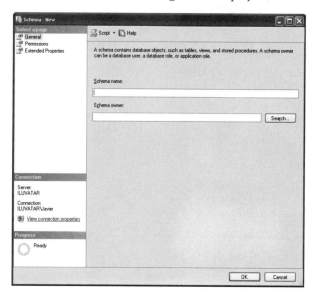

6. Press OK to create the schema.

Using T-SQL to Create Database Schemas

To create a schema using T-SQL statements, use the following syntax:

```
CREATE SCHEMA Inventory
```

Creating Tables to Implement a Design

After you have designed your solution, you will begin the implementation of your solution by creating tables to store the data.

Using SQL Server Management Studio to Create Tables

1. Open SQL Server Management Studio.

2. Connect to the database engine that will host the database.

3. Expand the Databases folder, and expand the database you will be working with.

4. Right-click the Tables folder and choose New Table.

5. Add a column using the Columns grid, name the column, assign a datatype, and specify whether the column will allow NULL values.

6. Additional column configurations may be set in the Column Properties section.

7. Add all necessary columns.

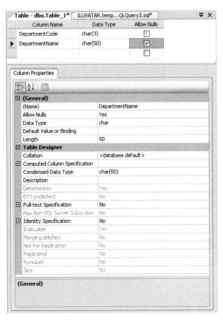

Defining the Primary Key in a Table Using SQL Server Management Studio

1. In the Table Definition window (shown in Step 7 above), select the columns you want to configure as the primary key. (You can re-open this window for an existing table by right-clicking the table in Object Explorer and choosing Modify from the context menu.)

2. Click the Set Primary Key button on the toolbar, or right-click the selected columns and choose Set Primary Key from the context menu.

Defining a CHECK Constraint Using SQL Server Management Studio

1. In the Table Definition window, click the Manage Check Constraints button in the toolbar.

2. Select the Add button.

3. In the Expression property, specify the validation expression.

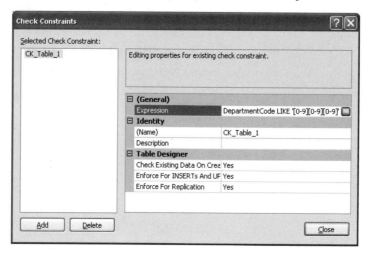

Using T-SQL to Create Tables

To create a table using T-SQL statements, use the following syntax.

```
CREATE TABLE Employee (
   EmployeeNumber        INT             NOT NULL
      PRIMARY KEY
      CHECK(EmployeeNumber>0)
   , EmployeeSSN          VARCHAR(15)     NOT NULL
      CHECK(EmployeeSSN
      LIKE
   '[0-9][0-9][0-9][0-9]-[0-9][0-9]-[0-9][0-9]-[0-9][0-9][0-9][0-9]')
      UNIQUE
   , HireDate             SMALLDATETIME   NOT NULL
      CHECK(HireDate>'19950101')
   , DepartmentCode  CHAR(3)         NOT NULL
      FOREIGN KEY REFERENCES Departments(DepartmentCode)
   , TerminationDateSMALLDATETIMENULL
   ,   CHECK(TerminationDate IS NULL OR TerminationDate>HireDate)
)
```

Conclusion

In this chapter, you reviewed the process that database developers undertake when designing a database. The first step involves the creation of a conceptual model that defines all user requirements. The model then evolves into a relational logical model and is finally implemented within a physical model.

Chapter 5 Quick Reference

To	Do This
Increase the quality of the database design	Create three database models: conceptual, logical, and physical.
Communicate the database design and validate the model	Create an ER diagram.
Increase the performance of the application	Use the appropriate datatype for each column.
Ensure the integrity of the data stored in the database	Use database constraints such as NOT NULL, DEFAULT, PRIMARY KEY, UNIQUE, CHECK, and FOREIGN KEY.

Part III
How to Query Data from Microsoft SQL Server 2005

Chapter 6

Reading Microsoft SQL Server 2005 Data from Client Applications

After completing this chapter, you will be able to:

- Know the different components and libraries you can use to connect to Microsoft SQL Server 2005

- Know when to use each of the available libraries

- Know how to access Microsoft SQL Server 2005 from your .NET applications

- Compare different choices for connecting to your databases

Microsoft SQL Server 2005 uses a client-server architecture that divides the workload of applications among server and client computers. In this chapter, you will learn about different programming interfaces that you can use when building client applications.

Introducing Microsoft Data Access Components

In 1996, Microsoft released Microsoft Data Access Components (MDAC 1.0). This was the first attempt at creating a unified database access framework to provide developers with a consistent way to develop database applications. Since that version, Microsoft has gradually enhanced their library with newer components, replacing and deprecating older ones. The latest version (MDAC 2.8 SP1) was released on May 10, 2005. Some of its components include ADO (ActiveX® Data Objects), ADO.NET, OLE DB (Object-Linking and Embedding Database), and ODBC (Open Database Connectivity).

Avoiding Deprecated MDAC Components

If you are developing new applications or upgrading existing ones, avoid using the following components because Microsoft will be removing them from future releases.

- **Microsoft JET (Joint Engine Technology)**   The first version of JET was developed in 1992. Many Microsoft products, including Microsoft Access, Microsoft Exchange, and Microsoft Visual Basic, used JET as their database engine.

- **MSDASQL (Microsoft OLE DB Provider for ODBC)**   Provides client ADO application access to ODBC connections through an OLE DB provider.

- **MSDADS**   An OLE DB provider that allows the construction of hierarchical relationships between rowsets.

- **Oracle ODBC**   An ODBC driver developed by Microsoft that provides access to Oracle database servers.

- **MSDAORA**   An OLE DB provider developed by Microsoft that provides access to Oracle database servers.

- **RDS**   A technology that allows retrieval of a set of data from a database server across the Internet or an intranet.

- **JET and Replication Objects (JRO)**   A component object model used to manage replication in Microsoft Access databases.

- **SQL XML**   Extends the SQL Server OLE DB provider, thereby allowing applications to retrieve XML streams. SQL XML is not deprecated, but is being removed from future MDAC releases.

Outlining the MDAC Architecture

From an architectural point of view, MDAC can be divided into three distinct layers, as shown in Figure 6-1.

1. Programming interface layer: Location of ADO and ADO.NET components

2. Database access layer: Location where different database vendors supply their database access providers (ODBC and OLE DB providers)

3. Database layer

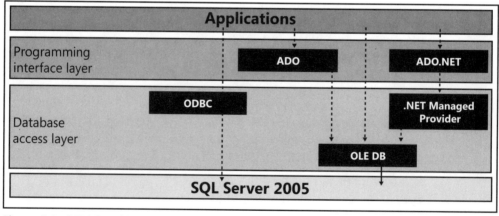

Figure 6-1   MDAC Architecture.

Understanding Open Database Connectivity (ODBC)

ODBC is a standard application programming interface (API) to utilize database management systems (DBMSs). The main objective of ODBC is to provide a generic standard supported by multiple programming languages, database systems, and operating systems. All major operating systems support the ODBC standard including Microsoft Windows, UNIX, Mac OS X, and Linux. There are also drivers for hundreds of DBMSs including Microsoft SQL Server, Microsoft Access, DB2, Oracle, and Sybase.

Creating a Data Source Name

The first step when using an ODBC data source is to create a data source name (DSN). A *DSN* stores information about how to connect to a data source. Microsoft Windows supports three types of DSNs:

- **User DSN**   Visible to the current user
- **System DSN**   Visible to all users on a single computer
- **File DSN**   Can be shared among multiple computers

Creating an ODBC Data Source

1. From the Start menu, choose Settings | Control Panel.
2. Double-click the Administrative Tools icon.
3. Double-click the Data Sources (ODBC) icon.
4. Select the tab for the type of data source you want to create (User DSN, System DSN, File DSN). For this example, select the User DSN tab.
5. Click the Add button to add a new data source.
6. In the Create New Data Source dialog box, select SQL Native Client and click the Finish button.

> **Note**   SQL Native Client allows applications to use the new features of SQL Server 2005. If your application also uses SQL Server 7.0 or 2000 and you do not want to install the new SQL Native Client, you may use the SQL Server driver.

7. In the Create A New Data Source To SQL Server dialog box, type the name of your choice for the data source in the Name textbox. You may also type a description in the Description textbox. Type the name of the server, or select a server from the Server drop-down listbox. Click Next to continue.

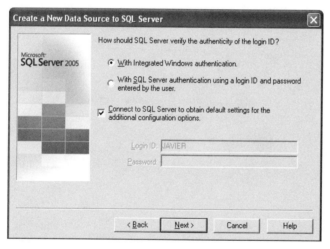

8. Select the preferred authentication method for the connection. Windows Authentication does not require a login and password because the user is already authenticated to the operating system; however, SQL Server 2005 authentication requires a login and password. Click Next to continue.

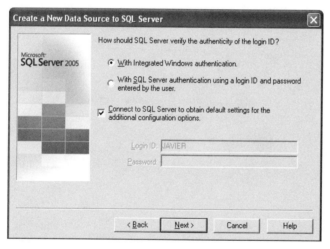

9. Select the Change The Default Database checkbox and select the appropriate database in the Database drop-down listbox. Click Next to continue.

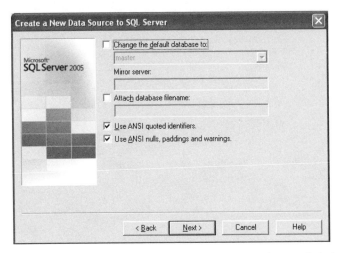

10. Review the additional options in the final window and click the Finish button.

11. In the ODBC Microsoft SQL Server Setup dialog box, review the configuration. Test the DSN by clicking the Test Data Source button and then click OK.

12. Click OK to finish the configuration.

Programming ODBC Applications

Although VB.NET and C# can be written to use ODBC directly, developers seldom take this approach because Microsoft provides simpler APIs with which to program ODBC applications, such as ADO and ADO.NET. For directly using the ODBC functions, Microsoft Visual C++ can be used. The following code tests a connection using the C language. This code can be accessed from \Ch06\Sample01.c in the sample files.

```
#include <stdio.h>
#include <sql.h>
#include <sqlext.h>

main()
{
  ExtractError
  SQLHENV env;
  SQLHDBC dbc;
  SQLHSTMT stmt;
  SQLRETURN ret;
  SQLCHAR outstr[1024];
  SQLSMALLINT outstrlen;

  /* Environment Handle */
  SQLAllocHandle(SQL_HANDLE_ENV, SQL_NULL_HANDLE, &env);
  /* ODBC 3 support */
  SQLSetEnvAttr(env, SQL_ATTR_ODBC_VERSION, (void *) SQL_OV_ODBC3, 0);
  /* Connection Handle */
  SQLAllocHandle(SQL_HANDLE_DBC, env, &dbc);
```

```
/* Open Connection to Adventureworks */
ret = SQLDriverConnect(dbc, (void *)1, "DSN=AdventureWorks;", SQL_NTS,
            outstr, sizeof(outstr), &outstrlen,
            SQL_DRIVER_COMPLETE);
if (SQL_SUCCEEDED(ret))
  {
  printf("Connected\n");
  SQLDisconnect(dbc);
  }
else
  {
  fprintf(stderr, "Failed to connect\n");
  }
/* Free handles */
SQLFreeHandle(SQL_HANDLE_DBC, dbc);
SQLFreeHandle(SQL_HANDLE_ENV, env);
}
```

> **Note**   This example uses C language because demonstrating how to create an ODBC con-
> nection is clearer in C. This connection can be created with other languages, but the complex-
> ity of the code would hide what needs to be demonstrated here, which is the connection
> definition.

Understanding OLE DB and ADO

OLE DB is an API designed by Microsoft to access different data stores in a uniform manner.
Instead of using a single interface, such as ODBC, OLE DB is a set of interfaces implemented
using the Component Object Model (COM). OLE DB is a successor of ODBC and extends
ODBC functionality to provide access to nonrelational databases, such as spreadsheets and
text files.

ADO is a set of COM components that provides a high-level interface to OLE DB. Its main
objects are the *Connection*, *Command*, and *Recordset* objects. The following code (which you
can access from \Ch06\Sample02.bas in the sample files) uses the ADO object model to read
a list of departments and is written using Visual Basic for Applications.

```
Public Function ReadData() As ADODB.Recordset
    Dim cn As ADODB.Connection
    Dim cmd As ADODB.Command
    Dim rs As ADODB.Recordset
    ' Setup Connection
    Set cn = New ADODB.Connection
    cn.Provider = "SQLOLEDB"
    cn.ConnectionString = _
        "Server=ILUVATAR;Database=AdventureWorks;Trusted_Connection=yes"
    ' Setup Command
    Set cmd = New ADODB.Command
    cmd.CommandText = "SELECT Name FROM HumanResources.Department"
    cmd.CommandType = adCmdText
    ' Read Data
```

```
        cn.Open
        cmd.ActiveConnection = cn
        Set rs = cmd.Execute()
        cn.Close
        Set ReadData = rs
End Function
```

The architecture of ADO can be summarized as shown in Figure 6-2.

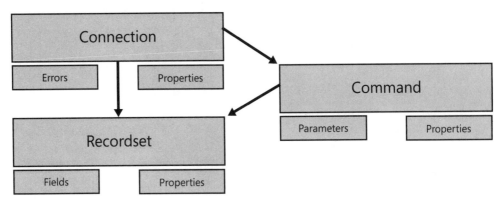

Figure 6-2 ADO Architecture.

ADO offers a simpler model than its predecessors RDO (Remote Data Objects) and DAO (Data Access Objects). For example, when using ADO, you may create a recordset without a connection. Internally, when the recordset is opened, the connection will be created and opened. When the recordset is closed, the connection will also be closed.

Using an ADO Connection Object

The *Connection object* is used to represent the link to the database and the database provider. Through the ADO *Connection* object, you can set the connection string, connect to the database, open the connection, and close the connection. The ADO connection also is used to manage transactions. You will learn more about transactions in Chapter 10, Using Transactions to Provide Safe Database Concurrency in Microsoft® SQL Server™ 2005: Applied Techniques Step by Step.

The trickiest part of the ADO connection is to set the correct connection string. An easy way to accomplish this is to create a Microsoft Data Link (.udl) file and then copy and paste the string.

Creating an Appropriate Connection String

1. In Windows Explorer, navigate to My Documents.

2. From the File menu, choose New | Text Document.

3. Name the file **Database.txt**.

4. Rename the file **Database.udl**. The icon of the file should change.

> **Tip**   By default, Windows Explorer hides extensions of known file types. To display file extensions in Windows Explorer, choose Folder Options from the Tools menu. Select the View tab. In the Advanced Settings section, uncheck the Hide Extension For Known File Types option.

5. Double-click the Database.udl file to display the Data Link Properties window. Select the Provider tab.

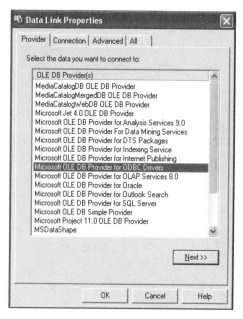

6. Select the SQL Native Client provider and click Next.

7. In the Datasource textbox, type the server name.

8. In the Enter Information To Log On To The Server section, choose Use Windows NT Integrated Security if you want to use Windows Authentication or type a username and password.

9. In the Enter The Initial Catalog To Use drop-down listbox, select the appropriate database. Click the Test Connection button to test the connection, then click OK.

10. Click OK to confirm the configuration.

11. Right-click the Database.udl file in Windows Explorer and select Open With from the context menu.

12. Select Notepad from the list of programs and click OK.

13. Copy the string connection and use it in your application.

Using an ADO Command Object

The ADO *Command object* is used to execute database queries that return records in an ADO *Recordset* object. The ADO *Command* object can also be used to modify records (update, insert, delete) in the database. The major feature of the ADO *Command* object is the ability to use parameters and reuse the same object for multiple queries.

Using an ADO Recordset Object

The ADO *Recordset object* is the most important object in ADO because it is used to hold a set of records that can be navigated and modified by the application. A *Recordset* object consists of records and fields (columns). The following code displays the list of departments stored in the AdventureWorks database using Visual Basic for Applications. You can access the code from \Ch06\OLEDBSample.bas in the sample files.

```
Public Sub DisplayDepartments()
   Dim rs As New ADODB.Recordset
   rs.Open "SELECT Name FROM HumanResources.Department", _
      "Provider=SQLNCLI.1;Integrated Security=SSPI;" + _
      "Initial Catalog=AdventureWorks;Data Source=(local)"
   While Not rs.EOF
      MsgBox rs.Fields(0)
      rs.MoveNext
   Wend
End Sub
```

Understanding ADO.NET

ADO.NET is the evolution of ADO. Its main advantages are listed below.

- **Interoperability**   ADO.NET is more interoperable because it uses *XML*—a simple and very flexible format through which to exchange data.

- **Maintainability**   In ADO.NET, it is simpler to write and maintain multi-tiered applications because it is designed to exchange disconnected data.

- **Programmability**   Strongly typed programming is possible in ADO.NET. The use of strong types makes it easier to write and read code.

- **Performance**   ADO requires COM and COM marshalling. This is not necessary in ADO.NET because data is exchanged in XML format.

- **Scalability**   Since ADO.NET uses a disconnected dataset, database connections and locks are minimized, thereby increasing the scalability of the application.

The following code (accessed as \Ch06\Sample03.vb in the sample files) uses the ADO.NET object model to read names of departments from the AdventureWorks database.

```
Public Function ReadData() As DataSet
   Dim da As New SqlClient.SqlDataAdapter( _
```

```
        "SELECT Name FROM HumanResources.Department", _
        "Server=(local);Database=AdventureWorks;Trusted_Connection=yes")
    Dim ds As New DataSet
    da.Fill(ds)
    Return ds
End Function
```

Outlining the ADO.NET Architecture

ADO.NET is a set of classes designed to work with data. ADO.NET uses two main components to provide data access. The first component is the dataset. A *dataset* is a disconnected, in-memory copy of data. From the developer's perspective, a dataset is an in-memory database—independent from the source—that can be updated and manipulated. After the application has finished working with the dataset, changes can then be sent forward to the database.

The second component of the ADO.NET architecture is the *data provider*, which is responsible for interacting with the database. The data provider is composed of a set of classes designed to work together, including the *Connection*, *Command*, *DataReader*, and *DataAdapter* classes, as shown in Figure 6-3.

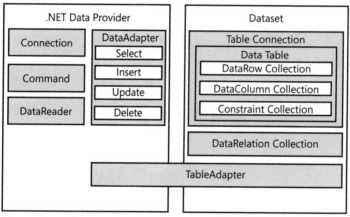

Figure 6-3   Classes in the data provider component of ADO.NET.

Using ADO.NET Namespaces

The .NET Framework uses logical namespaces to divide functionality. ADO.NET is primarily implemented in the *System.Data* namespace. Other namespaces are listed in Table 6-1.

Table 6-1   ADO.NET Namespaces

Namespace	Description	Main Classes
System.Data	Core classes that represent the ADO.NET architecture	*Dataset, DataTable*
System.Data.Common	Base classes shared by .NET data providers	*DbConnection, DbCommand, DbDataReader, DataAdapter*

Table 6-1   ADO.NET Namespaces

Namespace	Description	Main Classes
System.Data.SqlClient	SQL Server .NET data provider	*SqlConnection, SqlCommand, SqlDataReader, SqlDataAdapter*
System.Data.OleDb	Generic .NET data provider for OLE DB data sources	*OleDbConnection, OleDbCommand, OleDbDataReader, OleDbDataAdapter*
System.Data.OracleClient	Microsoft .NET data provider for Oracle	*OracleConnection, OracleCommand, OracleDataReader, OracleDataAdapter*

Introducing the .NET SQL Server Data Provider

The .NET Framework data provider for SQL Server 2005 includes all of the classes required to access SQL Server datatabases from applications written in .NET languages, such as VB.NET and C#. The namespace includes the following classes: *SqlConnection*, *SqlCommand*, *SqlDataReader*, and *SqlDataAdapter*.

Using the SqlConnection Class

The *SqlConnection class* represents the link to the database. Its main property is the connection string, which sets the parameters to establish a connection with a SQL Server database. Two important methods of the *SqlConnection* class are *Open* and *Close*, which are responsible for starting and ending the connection with the server.

The following code (accessed as \Ch06\Sample04.vb in the sample files) uses Windows security to test a connection with the local server.

```
Sub ConnectIntegrated()
    Dim con As New SqlClient.SqlConnection("Data Source=(local);Initial Catalog=Adven
tureWorks;Integrated Security=True")
    Try
        con.Open()
        MsgBox("Connection Successful")
        con.Close()
    Catch ex As Exception
        MsgBox("Connection Failed")
    End Try
End Sub
```

The following code (also accessed from \Ch06\Sample04.vb in the sample files) uses SQL Server security to test the connection.

```
Sub ConnectSQLSecurity()
    Dim con As New SqlClient.SqlConnection("Data Source=(local);" + _
        "Initial Catalog=AdventureWorks;User ID=sa;Password=P@assword")
    Try
        con.Open()
```

```
            MsgBox("Connection Successful")
            con.Close()
        Catch ex As Exception
            MsgBox("Connection Failed")
        End Try
    End Sub
```

Connection strings in ADO.NET are similar to ADO connections. However, in a *SqlConnection*, it is not necessary to set the database driver because the object model already knows that it is going to access a SQL Server database.

Using the SqlCommand Class

The *SqlCommand class* is used to represent Transact-SQL (T-SQL) statements to execute in the database. A *SqlCommand* can be used to execute stored procedures or T-SQL statements, or it can be used to access a table directly. Use the *CommandType* property to specify which type of statement the object represents.

The *SqlCommand* class provides three main methods:

- *ExecuteNonQuery*   Executes the command and returns the number of rows affected by the statement.

- *ExecuteScalar*   Executes the command and returns a single value.

- *ExecuteReader*   Builds a *SqlDataReader* that can be used to read a set of records. (This method is discussed in the next section.)

> **Note**   *SqlCommand* also provides the *ExecuteXmlReader* method (which returns an *XmlReader* object) that should be used when including the FOR XML clause in the SELECT statement.

The following code (accessed as \Ch06\Sample05.VB in the sample files) reads the name of the department with ID=3 in the database by using the *ExecuteScalar* method.

```
Sub DoExecuteScalar()
    Dim con As New SqlClient.SqlConnection( _
        "Server=(local);Database=AdventureWorks;Trusted_Connection=yes")
    Dim Com As New SqlClient.SqlCommand( _
        "SELECT Name FROM HumanResources.Department WHERE DepartmentID=3", con)
    Dim Name As String = ""
    Try
        con.Open()
        Name = Com.ExecuteScalar.ToString
        MsgBox(String.Format("The name is {0}", Name))
        con.Close()
    Catch ex As Exception
        MsgBox("Connection Failed")
    End Try
End Sub
```

Using the SqlDataReader Class

The *SqlDataReader class* provides reading access to a forward-only set of streamed rows. This class is used to read rows from a command into the application. The *SqlDataReader* object is created through the *SqlCommand.ExecuteReader* method. The *SqlDataReader* class contains the *Read* method to obtain the next record, as well as many *Get* methods to read different types of columns in the row. The *Read* method can be run multiple times and will return false after the last row has been read. All of the *Get* methods support an integer parameter to specify the column number in the record.

> **More Info** *SqlDataReader* also supports multiple *GetSql* methods, which can be used to read the different datatypes of columns by using sql datatypes instead of standard .NET datatypes.

The following code (accessed as \Ch06\Sample06.vb in the sample files) reads departments from the AdventureWorks database by using a *SqlDataReader*.

```vb
Sub DoExecuteReader()
    Dim con As New SqlClient.SqlConnection( _
        "Server=(local);Database=AdventureWorks;Trusted_Connection=yes")
    Dim Com As New SqlClient.SqlCommand( _
        "SELECT DepartmentID, Name FROM HumanResources.Department", con)
    Dim Name As String = ""
    Dim DepartmentId As Integer = 0
    Dim dr As SqlClient.SqlDataReader
    Try
        con.Open()
        dr = Com.ExecuteReader
        Do While dr.Read
            DepartmentId = CInt(dr(0))
            Name = dr(1).ToString
            MsgBox(String.Format("{0}:{1}", DepartmentId, Name))
        Loop
        dr.Close()
        con.Close()
    Catch ex As Exception
        MsgBox("Connection Failed")
    End Try
End Sub
```

Using the SqlDataAdapter Class

The *SqlDataAdapter class* is used to fill a dataset and includes a set of data commands with which to select and update the database. *SqlDataAdapter* has four commands responsible for each of the operations in the database: SELECT, INSERT, DELETE, and UPDATE. The *SqlDataAdapter* class hides the complexity of *SqlDataReaders* and offers a simpler object model with which to create data-centric applications.

To create a *SqlDataAdapter* graphically by using the SqlDataAdapter control in Visual Studio 2005, complete the following steps.

Creating a SqlDataAdapter Graphically

1. From the Start menu, choose All Programs | Microsoft Visual Studio 2005 | Microsoft Visual Studio 2005 to open Visual Studio 2005.

2. From the File menu, choose New | Project.

3. In the Project Types section, select Visual Basic and then choose the Windows Application template.

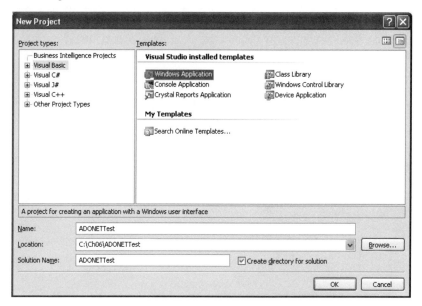

4. Name the project **ADONETTest** and click OK to create the project.

5. If the Toolbox is not visible, select Toolbox from the View menu.

6. Right-click the Toolbox and select Choose Items from the context menu.

7. On the .NET Framework Components tab of the Choose Toolbox Items window, select the following components: *SqlCommand*, *SqlConnection*, and *SqlDataAdapter*. The *SqlDataReader* class does not have a graphical designer. Click OK to add the components.

8. From the Toolbox, drag a DataGridView control onto the form. Right-click it and select Properties from the context menu.

9. In the Properties window, locate the (Name) property and change it to **dgDepartments**. Locate the Dock property and select Left (by clicking the left bar in the selector window when you expand the property value).

10. From the Toolbox, drag a button onto the form, and then drag a second button onto the form.

11. As you did previously with the grid, locate the (Name) property for one of the buttons. Change the name to **btnRead** and then change the other button's name to **btnUpdate**.

12. Change the Text property of each button to Read and Update to match their names.

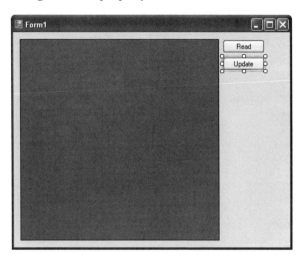

13. Add a SqlDataAdapter control (from the DataSet group of the Toolbox) to the window. The Data Adapter Configuration Wizard is displayed.

14. Select the connection to use. If this is the first time that you have accessed SQL Server 2005 from Visual Studio, click the New Connection button. Configure the server name, authentication method, and database in the Add Connection window.

15. Click Next to continue.

16. In the Choose A Command Type screen of the Data Adapter Configuration Wizard, make sure that the Use SQL Statements option is selected. In Chapter 9, Retrieving Data Using Programmable Objects, you will learn about stored procedures.

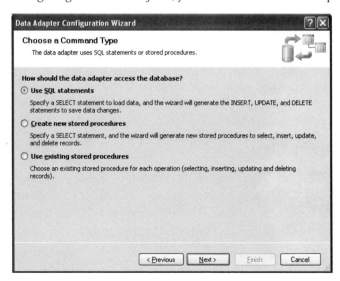

17. In the Generate The SQL Statements screen of the wizard, type the following command. You can access this code from \Ch06\Sample07.sql in the sample files.

```
SELECT      DepartmentID, Name, GroupName
FROM        HumanResources.Department
```

18. Click Next to continue. Review how the *SqlDataAdapter* will be configured, including the four commands: SELECT, INSERT, UPDATE, and DELETE. Click Finish to configure the *SqlDataAdapter*.

19. Double-click the Read button and write the following code (included in the sample files as \Ch06\Sample08.vb).

```
.   Private Sub btnRead_Click(ByVal sender As System.Object, _
        ByVal e As System.EventArgs) Handles btnRead.Click
        Dim ds As New DataSet
        SqlDataAdapter1.Fill(ds)
        With dgDepartments
            .DataSource = ds
            .DataMember = "Department"
        End With
    End Sub
```

20. Select the Form1.cs [Design] tab or click the Form1.cs node in Solution Explorer to return to the Form1 design window. Double-click the btnUpdate button.

21. Write the following code (included in the sample files as \Ch06\Sample09.vb).

```
    Private Sub btnUpdate_Click(ByVal sender As System.Object, _
        ByVal e As System.EventArgs) Handles btnUpdate.Click
        Dim ds As DataSet = CType(dgDepartments.DataSource, DataSet)
        SqlDataAdapter1.Update(ds)
    End Sub
```

22. Press F5 to save and run the application. Click the Read button to fill the DataGridView. Make modifications, and then click the Update button to save the information in the database.

Important   Do not delete the first rows from the Departments table (DepartmentID 1 to 16) because they are referenced by the Employee table. If you want to test how the DELETE command works, add a row, update the database, and then delete the row later.

Using the TableAdapter Class

ADO.NET 2.0 introduces a new class called *TableAdapter*. *TableAdapter* substitutes the functionality of *SqlDataAdapter* by providing built-in communications between the application and the database. *TableAdapters* may contain any number of T-SQL statements or stored procedures that return filled data tables or update data from the data table back to the database.

Creating a TableAdapter

1. From the Start menu, choose All Programs | Microsoft Visual Studio 2005 | Microsoft Visual Studio 2005.

2. From the File menu, select New | Project.

3. In the Project Types section, select Visual Basic and choose the Windows Application template.

4. Name the project **ADONETTest2** and click OK to create the project.

5. If the Toolbox is not visible, choose Toolbox from the View menu.

6. Add a DataGridView and one button to the form. Name the DataGridView **dgDepartments**, and name the button **btnUpdate**. Change the text of btnUpdate to Update.

7. Select the dgDepartments data grid view, and click the DataGridView Tasks button (small right-arrow button in the upper-right corner of the data grid view).

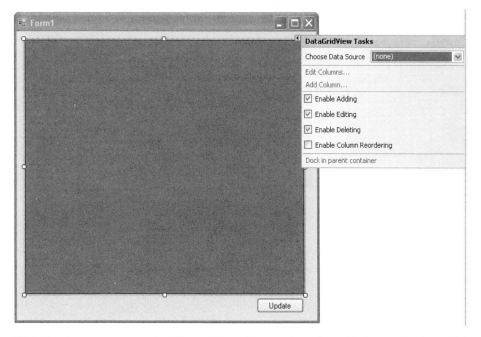

8. Click the down arrow on the Choose Data Source drop-down listbox and select Add Project Data Source at the bottom.

9. In the Datasource Configuration Wizard, select the Database icon and click Next to continue.

10. Select the AdventureWorks connection that you created in the previous procedure and click Next to continue.

11. In the Save The Connection String To The Application Configuration File screen of the wizard, click Next to continue.

12. In the Choose Your Database Objects screen of the wizard, expand the Tables node. Expand the Department table, and select the DepartmentID, Name, and GroupName columns by putting a check in the checkboxes.

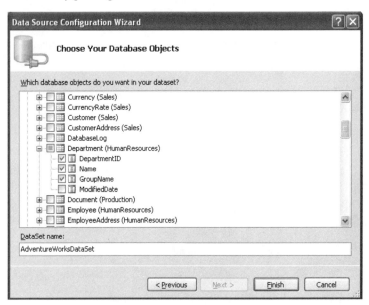

13. Click Finish to configure the data source.

14. Notice that the wizard created a dataset in the project (visible in Solution Explorer) and three database objects in the tray below the form: AdventureWorksDataset, department-BindingSource, and departmentTableAdapter.

15. Double-click the Update button and write the following code:

```
private void btnUpdate_Click(object sender, EventArgs e)
{
    this.departmentTableAdapter.Update(this.adventureWorksDataSet.Department);
}
```

16. Save and run the application. The data grid is automatically filled with data when the window is displayed. Make modifications, and then click the Update button to save the information back to the database.

Introducing SQL Native Client

The new SQL Native Client is a single dynamic link library (DLL) that can be used in OLE DB and ODBC interfaces because it includes both data providers. By using SQL Native Client, applications can use the new SQL Server 2005 features. Some new SQL Server 2005 features that require SQL Native Client are XML Datatype Support, Multiple Active Result Sets, and Query Notification.

Using the XML Datatype

As you learned in Chapter 5, Designing a Database to Solve Business Needs, SQL Server 2005 includes a new datatype designed to store XML documents and XML fragments in the database. Because this datatype was not included in previous versions of SQL Server, the standard SQL Server client does not provide support for this datatype. SQL Native Client adds the DBTYPE_XML datatype in the OLE DB provider and the SQL_SS_XML datatype in the ODBC provider. From the ADO.NET programming perspective, applications do not need to be changed to access the xml datatype because it is always converted to a string type.

Using Multiple Active Result Sets (MARS)

A new feature of SQL Server 2005 supports multiple active result sets (MARS). In previous versions of SQL Server, the application would fail if it tried to use multiple active statements. For example, the following code (included as \Ch06\Sample10.vb in the sample files) fails in the *cmdUpd.ExecuteNonQuery()* statement because it tries to open a result set in the same connection as that which the *cmdSel* object is using.

```
Dim conn As New SqlClient.SqlConnection( _
    "Data Source=(local);Initial Catalog=AdventureWorks;Integrated Security=True")
Dim cmdsel As New SqlClient.SqlCommand( _
    "SELECT DepartmentID FROM HumanResources.Department", conn)
Dim cmdUpd As New SqlClient.SqlCommand( _
    "UPDATE HumanResources.Department SET ModifiedDate=GETDATE() " + _
    "WHERE DepartmentID=@DepartmentId", conn)
Dim par As SqlClient.SqlParameter = _
    cmdUpd.Parameters.Add("@DepartmentId", SqlDbType.Int)
conn.Open()
Dim dr As SqlClient.SqlDataReader = cmdsel.ExecuteReader
While dr.Read
    par.Value = CInt(dr(0))
    'Other operations
    cmdUpd.ExecuteNonQuery()
End While
dr.Close()
conn.Close()
```

 The previous code returns an *InvalidOperationException* with the following message:

```
There is already an open DataReader associated with this Command
which must be closed first.
```

When using MARS, the same code above will succeed. To enable MARS, add the following text to the connection string:

```
MultipleActiveResultSets=True
```

Using Query Notification

Because many applications use the ADO.NET disconnected model, they cache tables in memory. Therefore, data in the server may change without the application's knowledge. To avoid this situation, SQL Native Client provides the Query Notification feature.

Creating an Application that Uses Query Notification

1. From the Start menu, choose All Programs | Microsoft Visual Studio 2005 | Microsoft Visual Studio 2005.

2. From the File menu, choose New | Project.

3. In the Project Types section, select Visual Basic and choose the Windows Application template.

4. Name the project **NotificationTest** and click OK to create the project.

5. If the Toolbox is not visible, select Toolbox from the View menu.

6. Add a DataGridView and name it **dgDepartments**.

7. Double-click the Windows Form (not the DataGridView) to add the *Load* event.

8. Scroll to the top of the code and, just below the first lines, add the following *Imports* statement (included in the sample files as \Ch06\Sample11.vb) to reference the SQL Client namespace.

```
Imports System.Data.SqlClient
```

9. Within the *Form1* class declaration, declare the *depend* variable of *SqlDependency* type, enabled to manage events, as follows (also located in \Ch06\Sample11.vb):

```
Dim WithEvents depend As SqlDependency
```

10.   In the form's *Load* event, write the following code (also located in
      \Ch06\Sample11.vb):

```
Dim AdventureWorks As String = _
    "Data Source=(local);Initial Catalog=AdventureWorks;" + _
    "Integrated Security=True"
Dim Conn As New SqlConnection(AdventureWorks)
Dim CmdSel As New SqlCommand( _
    "SELECT DepartmentID, Name FROM HumanResources.Department", Conn)
depend = New SqlDependency(CmdSel)
Dim da As New SqlDataAdapter(CmdSel)
Dim ds As New DataSet
SqlDependency.Start(AdventureWorks)
da.Fill(ds)
dgDepartments.DataSource = ds
dgDepartments.DataMember = "Table"
```

11.   Add the *depend_OnChange* event as follows (included in the sample files as
      \Ch06\Sample12.vb):

```
Private Sub depend_OnChange(ByVal sender As Object, _
    ByVal e As System.Data.SqlClient.SqlNotificationEventArgs) _
    Handles depend.OnChange
    MsgBox("Data has changed in the server, reload the dataset")
End Sub
```

> **Note**   Make sure that the Service Broker is enabled in the SQL Server instance. To do
> this, open SQL Server Surface Area Configuration, as explained in Chapter 3, Reviewing
> Microsoft SQL Server 2005 Management Tools. Click the Surface Area Configuration For
> Features link at the bottom of the window.

12.   Save and run the application by pressing F5. The department data will be displayed.

13.   Without closing the application, open SQL Server Management Studio by choosing
       Start | All Programs | Microsoft SQL Server 2005 | SQL Server Management Studio.

14.   Connect to the database engine using Windows Authentication.

15.   In Object Explorer, expand the server node. Expand the Databases folder, the Adven-
       tureWorks database node, and the Tables folder.

16.   Right-click the HumanResources.Department table and select Open Table from the con-
       text menu.

17.   Modify any of the department names, and the *depend_OnChange* event will fire, display-
       ing the message box you coded in Step 10 above.

Conclusion

This chapter reviewed some of the client-side options that are available to you when creating SQL Server 2005 applications. You learned about ODBC programming, ADO and ADO.NET object models, and some features of SQL Native Client programming.

Chapter 6 Quick Reference

To	Do This
Access information quickly	Use ODBC (but write your code in C).
Access information from COM-compliant languages, such as VBA (Visual Basic for Applications)	Use OLE DB.
Create .NET applications that are data ready	Use ADO.NET components from your preferred .NET language.
Use all of the SQL Server 2005 capabilities	Use SQL Native Client.
Perform multiple operations against the same connection	Use MARS options.

Chapter 7

Selecting the Data You Need

After completing this chapter, you will be able to:

- Select data from single and multiple tables
- Design and use scalar user-defined functions
- Use system functions
- Design and use stored procedures that return scalar values
- Use the XML datatype

Databases store information. This chapter will show you how to build sentences to retrieve data from databases. The chapter starts by presenting simple Transact-SQL (T-SQL) SELECT statements. Next will follow information about using inner and outer joins for retrieving data from multiple tables. The chapter ends by examining XPATH and XQUERY statements for handling data in XML format. Since it is important to know how to obtain the right data in the most efficient manner, the chapter will also discuss performance issues along the way.

Selecting Data from a Single Table

The simplest way to obtain data from a single table is by executing the SELECT statement. This statement is used to retrieve data stored in relational databases. The following example uses the SELECT statement to obtain the content of a table that stores the headers of purchase orders.

Running a SELECT Statement in SQL Server Management Studio

1. From the Start menu, select Programs | Microsoft SQL Server 2005 | SQL Server Management Studio.

2. Connect to your Microsoft SQL Server 2005 instance.

3. In Object Explorer, expand the Databases node, and then select the AdventureWorks database.

4. Click the New Query toolbar button to display a query window.

5. In query window, enter the following T-SQL sentence. This sentence can be accessed from \Ch07\Samples01.sql in the sample files.

```
SELECT *
FROM Sales.SalesOrderHeader
```

6. Click the Execute toolbar button.

Part of the result is shown below (the results are shown scrolled to the right).

	AccountNumber	CustomerID	ContactID	SalesPersonID	TerritoryID	BillToAddressID	ShipToAddressID	ShipMethodID	Credit
1	10-4020-000676	676	378	279	5	985	985	5	1628
2	10-4020-000117	117	216	279	5	921	921	5	5618
3	10-4020-000442	442	281	282	6	517	517	5	1346
4	10-4020-000227	227	564	282	6	482	482	5	1045
5	10-4020-000510	510	97	276	4	1073	1073	5	4322
6	10-4020-000397	397	458	280	1	876	876	5	806
7	10-4020-000146	146	114	283	1	849	849	5	1523
8	10-4020-000511	511	828	276	4	1074	1074	5	1334
9	10-4020-000646	646	542	277	3	629	629	5	1037
10	10-4020-000514	514	151	282	6	529	529	5	1566
11	10-4020-000578	578	295	283	1	895	895	5	1553

Query executed successfully.   (56)   AdventureWorks   00:00:08   31465 rows

The statement above returns all of the fields of the SalesOrderHeader table because the asterisk (*) requests all columns. It is typically not necessary to request all columns in a table, and doing so when not needed may cause several problems.

- An application may not work properly when new columns are added to a database. The application will continue to retrieve all of the columns, and the new, unexpected columns will not be handled correctly.

- The Query Optimizer will not use some indexes when you select all of the columns in a table. Selecting only the columns that you are going to use allows the Optimizer use the appropriate indexes. However, if you select all of the columns, the indexes cannot be used.

For these reasons, it is best not to use the asterisk (*) in your queries. As an example, suppose that you need data from the OrderDate, SalesOrderNumber, CustomerId, Subtotal, TaxAmt, and TotalDue columns. The following query will obtain only the columns you need.

```
SELECT OrderDate,SalesOrderNumber,CustomerID,Subtotal,TaxAmt,TotalDue
FROM Sales.SalesOrderHeader
```

The statement above returns all of the rows in the SalesOrderHeader table from the database, comprising 31,465 rows; it can take a few seconds to return the data. When a table contains a small number of rows, the time it takes to return the data is acceptable. But if a table contains millions of OrderHeaders, returning all of this data is not an option. Therefore, you must retrieve only the rows you are going to use. When selecting your data, answer the following two questions: What columns do you need? What rows do you need? By correctly answering these questions, you can create server-friendly queries and efficiently obtain the most useful information.

Returning to the example above, suppose that the answers to these two questions are that you need the OrderDate, SalesOrderNumber, CustomerId, Subtotal, TaxAmt, and TotalDue columns, but you only need the data from those shipped on July 8, 2001. The query you must write to obtain this particular information should look like the following:

```
SELECT OrderDate,SalesOrderNumber,CustomerID,Subtotal,TaxAmt,TotalDue
FROM Sales.SalesOrderHeader
WHERE ShipDate='20010708'
```

Below are the results of executing this query (note that the OrderDate is displayed, not the ShipDate).

	OrderDate	SalesOrderNumber	Customerid	Subtotal	TaxAmt	TotalDue
1	2001-07-01 00:00:00.000	SO43659	676	24643,9362	1971,5149	27231,5495
2	2001-07-01 00:00:00.000	SO43660	117	1553,1035	124,2483	1716,1794
3	2001-07-01 00:00:00.000	SO43661	442	39422,1198	3153,7696	43561,4424
4	2001-07-01 00:00:00.000	SO43662	227	34689,5578	2775,1646	38331,9613
5	2001-07-01 00:00:00.000	SO43663	510	503,3507	40,2681	556,2026
6	2001-07-01 00:00:00.000	SO43664	397	29312,401	2344,9921	32390,2031
7	2001-07-01 00:00:00.000	SO43665	146	17199,2839	1375,9427	19005,2087
8	2001-07-01 00:00:00.000	SO43666	511	6079,6842	486,3747	6718,051
9	2001-07-01 00:00:00.000	SO43667	646	7326,5034	586,1203	8095,7863
10	2001-07-01 00:00:00.000	SO43668	514	43272,067	3461,7654	47815,6341
11	2001-07-01 00:00:00.000	SO43669	578	881,4687	70,5175	974,0229
12	2001-07-01 00:00:00.000	SO43670	504	7344,5034	587,5603	8115,6763

Query executed successfully.   (56)   AdventureWorks   00:00:00   43 rows

You obtained only forty-three of the 31,465 rows contained in the SalesOrderHeader table, and these rows contain only the columns you specifically need. With this new knowledge about writing queries, you can optimize your queries to obtain benefits on the server layer.

> **Note**   The previous figure displays the standard way to represent dates by using four digits for the year (yyyy), two more for the month (mm), and two more for the day (dd). This format helps to avoid internationalization issues when using dates. If necessary, you can also add hours, minutes, and seconds when using this format (yyyymmdd hh:mm:ss.ddd).

Using AND and OR Operators

You may occasionally need to combine more than one condition to obtain the data you need. To combine conditions, you can use the AND and OR operators.

The *AND operator* is used when you want multiple conditions to be true. Suppose that you want to access the orders shipped on July 8, 2001, but only those orders from the customer with Customer Id number 676. You can obtain this information by combining conditions on the WHERE clause using the AND operator. The statement to obtain this data will look like the following:

```
SELECT OrderDate,SalesOrderNumber,CustomerID,Subtotal,TaxAmt,TotalDue
FROM Sales.SalesOrderHeader
WHERE ShipDate='20010708' and CustomerID=676
```

The *OR operator* is used when you want at least one of the conditions to be true. Suppose that you need to obtain the orders shipped on July 8, 2001, as well as those shipped on July 9, 2001. You can again obtain this information by combining restrictions on the WHERE clause using the OR operator. The statement to obtain this data will look like the following:

```
SELECT OrderDate,SalesOrderNumber,CustomerID,Subtotal,TaxAmt,TotalDue
FROM Sales.SalesOrderHeader
WHERE ShipDate='20010708' or ShipDate='20010709'
```

In other situations, you might need to combine both AND and OR operators to obtain the desired data. To combine both operators, you must pay attention to *operator precedence.* Operator precedence can be demonstrated with the following example. Suppose that you need to obtain the orders shipped on July 8, 2001, in which the Total Due is greater than $10K or less than $2K. The statement to obtain this data will be:

```
SELECT OrderDate,SalesOrderNumber,CustomerID,Subtotal,TaxAmt,TotalDue
FROM Sales.SalesOrderHeader
WHERE ShipDate='20010708' and (TotalDue<=2000 or TotalDue>=10000)
```

The parentheses in the example above are important because they set the operator precedence. The result becomes quite different if parentheses are not used. When parentheses are included in the statement, you obtain all of the orders shipped with a Total Due amount of less than $2,000 or greater than $10,000 from only those orders shipped on July 8, 2001. When parentheses are not included, the AND operator is evaluated first, returning all orders shipped on July 8, 2001, with a Total Due amount of less than $2,000. The OR operator is then evaluated, and you obtain all orders shipped with a Total Due amount greater than $10,000 regardless of the date the order was shipped. You can see how important it is to use parentheses to specify the operator precedence when combining AND and OR operators.

Comparing NULL Values

Databases allow you to store NULL values in some fields. A *NULL* value means that a field contains no value or that the value is unavailable. The IS NULL clause is used to find NULL values.

Suppose that you need to access all of the Order Headers that have a NULL value for the CurrencyRate field. In this situation, you can use the IS NULL sentence as shown below.

```
SELECT OrderDate,SalesOrderNumber,CustomerID,Subtotal,TaxAmt,TotalDue
FROM Sales.SalesOrderHeader WHERE CurrencyRateID is null
```

You can also use a more familiar syntax, such as the following:

```
SELECT OrderDate,SalesOrderNumber,CustomerID,Subtotal,TaxAmt,TotalDue
FROM Sales.SalesOrderHeader WHERE CurrencyRateID=null
```

When using the above syntax, you do not receive any rows by default because the server uses ANSI (American National Standards Institute) rules. ANSI rules specify that, when comparing two NULL values, the result is neither true nor false; therefore, there are no rows to be returned. You can change the behavior of the server to have the same behavior as the IS NULL clause by using SET ANSI_NULLS OFF. The following example demonstrates how to change the behavior of the server.

```
SET ANSI_NULLS OFF
SELECT OrderDate,SalesOrderNumber,CustomerID,Subtotal,TaxAmt,TotalDue
FROM Sales.SalesOrderHeader WHERE CurrencyRateID=NULL
```

This query will return the same rows that you receive when using the IS NULL clause. Yet, the best way to query NULL values is to use the IS NULL clause, as ANSI recommends.

You may need to obtain only the rows in a table that have values. By combining the NOT clause with IS NULL, you can retrieve the rows that have a value for the specified columns. In the following example, you retrieve the rows that have an actual value in the CurrencyRate column from the SalesOrderHeader table.

```
SELECT OrderDate,SalesOrderNumber,CustomerID,Subtotal,TaxAmt,TotalDue
FROM Sales.SalesOrderHeader WHERE NOT CurrencyRateID IS NULL
```

Using the CASE Statement

Because data stored in a database may not be in the right representation for a particular situation, you can transform it to make it useful. In the following example, the CASE clause is used to specify a new field that is related to another field stored in a database. A new type called FreightType has been created, and this type can have three values—Soft, Normal, and Hard—depending on the value of Freight stored in the database. The FreightType will be Soft if freight is less than 25, Normal if between 25 and 700, and Hard if greater than 700.

```
SELECT ShipDate,SalesOrderNumber,CustomerID,Subtotal,TaxAmt,TotalDue,
    CASE WHEN Freight<25 THEN 'Soft'
        WHEN Freight between 25 and 700 THEN 'Normal'
        ELSE 'Hard'
    END FreightType
FROM Sales.SalesOrderHeader
WHERE ShipDate='20010708'
```

The following figure illustrates the result of executing this query.

	Shipdate	SalesOrderNumber	Customerid	Subtotal	TaxAmt	TotalDue	FreightType
1	2001-07-08 00:00:00.000	SO43659	676	24643.9362	1971.5149	27231.5495	Normal
2	2001-07-08 00:00:00.000	SO43660	117	1553.1035	124.2483	1716.1794	Normal
3	2001-07-08 00:00:00.000	SO43661	442	39422.1198	3153.7696	43561.4424	Hard
4	2001-07-08 00:00:00.000	SO43662	227	34689.5578	2775.1646	38331.9613	Hard
5	2001-07-08 00:00:00.000	SO43663	510	503.3507	40.2681	556.2026	Soft
6	2001-07-08 00:00:00.000	SO43664	397	29312.401	2344.9921	32390.2031	Hard
7	2001-07-08 00:00:00.000	SO43665	146	17199.2839	1375.9427	19005.2087	Normal
8	2001-07-08 00:00:00.000	SO43666	511	6079.6842	486.3747	6718.051	Normal
9	2001-07-08 00:00:00.000	SO43667	646	7326.5034	586.1203	8095.7863	Normal
10	2001-07-08 00:00:00.000	SO43668	514	43272.067	3461.7654	47815.6341	Hard
11	2001-07-08 00:00:00.000	SO43669	578	881.4687	70.5175	974.0229	Soft

> **Tip**   The CASE clause is a powerful tool to use in queries. You can also create a CASE statement for calculated fields. Because you can index the calculated columns in a database, these indexes can then be used to improve performance on some queries using these calculated values.

Using Search Arguments

Suppose that you need to obtain the Subtotal, TaxAmt, and Total for all orders in the SalesOrderHeader table from July 2001. This can be accomplished in two different ways. The first is as follows:

```
SELECT Subtotal,TaxAmt,TotalDue
FROM Sales.SalesOrderHeader
WHERE YEAR(ShipDate)=2001 AND MONTH(ShipDate)=7
```

> **More Info**   System functions, such as *year* and *month*, will be introduced later in this chapter.

The other method is found below.

```
SELECT Subtotal,TaxAmt,TotalDue
FROM Sales.SalesOrderHeader
WHERE ShipDate BETWEEN '20010701' AND '20010731'
```

There are no differences between the results of these two queries, for both obtain the orders shipped during July 2001. However, there are differences in the execution of these queries. The first query retrieves the date and month; after obtaining all rows, the calculation and comparison are completed. The second query makes only the comparison, not the calculation. If an index exists for these columns, it will be used in the second query but not in the first one. Therefore, the second query will be faster.

> **Note**   You can create an index using the following command:
>
> ```
> CREATE INDEX ix_SalesOrderHeader_shipdate
> ON Sales.SalesOrderHeader (Shipdate)
> ```

As shown on the following page, the first sentence needs to scan the entire index to obtain the month and year and then compare them with the constants. The second sentence performs an *index seek* operation, whereby only the needed records of the index will be read, thus achieving better performance and consuming less server resources.

Query 1: Query cost (relative to the batch): 50%
SELECT Subtotal,TaxAmt,TotalDue FROM Sales.SalesOrderHeader WHERE YEAR(ShipDate)=2001 AND MONTH(ShipDate)=7

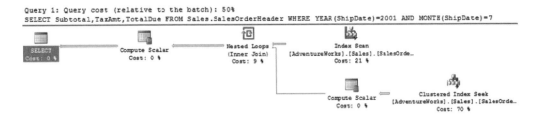

Query 2: Query cost (relative to the batch): 50%
SELECT [Subtotal],[TaxAmt],[TotalDue] FROM [Sales].[SalesOrderHeader] WHERE [ShipDate]>=@1 AND [ShipDate]<=@2

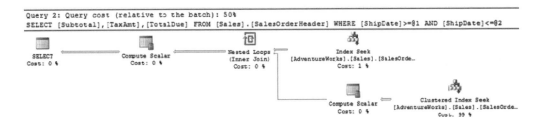

> **Note**   You can compare the execution of the two sentences by selecting both sentences
> on SQL Server Management Studio and displaying the estimated execution plan by pressing
> Crtl + L or by choosing Display Estimated Execution Plan from the Query menu.

Various strategies exist to optimize T-SQL queries by using indexes. Avoiding the use of functions, operations, and transformations on fields makes these strategies more efficient. After designing your queries, you can use the database Tuning Advisor to find indexes, find partitioning strategies, and find other recommendations to improve execution performance.

Selecting Data from Multiple Tables

Because well designed databases are normalized following certain designing rules, not all of the data you need may be located in the same table. You may therefore need to use more than one table in your query to obtain the desired data. Suppose you need to obtain the Product Name from an order, but the order information is stored in two different tables: the OrderDetails table that contains the Product Id and the Product table that contains the name. The statement below demonstrates one way to retrieve information from multiple tables. The SQL Server statements in this section can be accessed from \Ch07\Samples02.sql in the sample files.

```
SELECT Sales.SalesOrderDetail.SalesOrderId,
       Sales.SalesOrderDetail.SalesOrderDetailId,
       Production.Product.ProductId,
```

```
         Production.Product.Name,
         Sales.SalesOrderDetail.UnitPrice,
         Sales.SalesOrderDetail.UnitPriceDiscount,
         Sales.SalesOrderDetail.LineTotal
FROM     Sales.SalesOrderDetail,
         Production.Product
WHERE    Sales.SalesOrderDetail.ProductID=Production.Product.ProductId
  AND    Sales.SalesOrderDetail.SalesOrderId=43659
```

Using Aliases

When using multiple tables on the FROM clause, you should specify the schema, table name, and field name in the SELECT clause to avoid using ambiguous names that may be found in several tables. The schema, table name, and column name were specified in the statement above to obtain the Product Id (Production.Product.ProductId). By using this notation, you avoid the problem that could arise because the ProductId field is also the name of a field in the Sales.SalesOrderDetails table. If you do not specify the entire name, you should at least specify enough information to avoid ambiguity, that is: Product.ProductId and SalesOrderDetails.ProductId.

Avoiding ambiguity often makes names very long. While this is not a problem involving network traffic or server processing, it is a problem for those who code the statements. The length of a statement makes it easier to commit syntax errors, and long statements are more complicated to understand. You can use aliases to avoid this problem in both the FROM and SELECT clauses. *Aliases* allow you to replace long table names by shorter expressions. Below is the same example using aliases in the FROM clause.

```
SELECT SAL_SOD.SalesOrderId,
       SAL_SOD.SalesOrderDetailId,
       PRO_P.ProductId,
       PRO_P.Name,
       SAL_SOD.UnitPrice,
       SAL_SOD.UnitPriceDiscount,
       SAL_SOD.LineTotal
FROM   Sales.SalesOrderDetail SAL_SOD,
       Production.Product PRO_P
WHERE  SAL_SOD.ProductID=PRO_P.ProductId
  AND  SAL_SOD.SalesOrderId=43659
```

Caution   Be careful when selecting aliases so that they are not confusing. Avoid the use of acronyms with confusing letters or any letters with similar appearance. You should also avoid confusing combinations, such as the use of two consecutive letters in different order on the same query (SD and DS). It would be easy to switch these two consecutive letters, and the switch could produce unexpected results.

Using the INNER JOIN Syntax

The syntax in the previous example is still confusing because you are combining different options on the WHERE clause. SAL_SOD.ProductId=PRO_P.ProductID is used for joining the two tables, and SAL_SOD.SalesOrderID=43659 applies a filter to the result set. ANSI introduced the INNER JOIN operator to the SQL Server standard in the SQL-92 specification. The *INNER JOIN* operator allows you to specify in the FROM clause how two tables are to be joined, as shown in the following example.

```
SELECT SAL_SOD.SalesOrderId,
       SAL_SOD.SalesOrderDetailId,
       PRO_P.ProductId,
       PRO_P.name,
       SAL_SOD.UnitPrice,
       SAL_SOD.UnitPriceDiscount,
       SAL_SOD.LineTotal
FROM   Sales.SalesOrderDetail SAL_SOD
       INNER JOIN Production.Product PRO_P
       ON SAL_SOD.ProductID=PRO_P.ProductId
WHERE  SAL_SOD.SalesOrderId=43659
```

This example demonstrates that the WHERE clause contains only the filter condition and that the JOIN condition is written by using the ON clause instead of the WHERE clause.

Of course, you can use more than one condition to join tables. Suppose that another table is used to store the primary photo of your product for the entire catalog. With the next sentence, you can obtain the Product Id, Product Name, and Modified Date for the primary photo.

```
SELECT PR_P.ProductID,PR_P.Name,PR_PPP.[Primary],PR_PPP.ModifiedDate
FROM Production.Product PR_P
     INNER JOIN Production.ProductProductPhoto PR_PPP
     ON PR_P.ProductID=PR_PPP.ProductId and PR_PPP.[Primary]=1
WHERE PR_P.ProductID<100
```

> **Note** Note that the word *Primary* is found inside brackets [] because Primary is a reserved word. It could also be used as the name of a field, although this is not recommended. When a reserved word is used as a field or table name, it is placed inside brackets [].

In the statement above, the AND operator is used to find only the primary photo. You could also use the OR operator and different comparison operators, such as >, >=,<, or <=, on JOIN clauses if necessary.

Using More than Two Tables

It is sometimes necessary to use more than two tables. Although you can use as many tables as needed to obtain information, it is best to use the minimum number of tables on your joins to achieve better performance. Queries are more efficient when there are fewer tables on the join, so try not to use more than four to six tables on FROM clauses. The following example uses three tables on the join because the relationship between Production.Product and Production.ProductPhoto is a many-to-many relationship, as shown in the figure below.

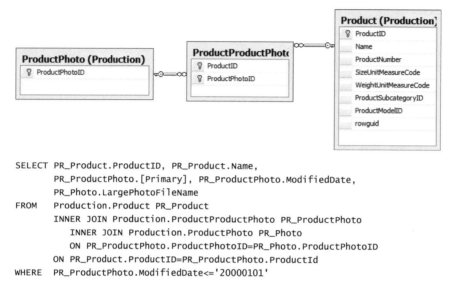

```
SELECT  PR_Product.ProductID, PR_Product.Name,
        PR_ProductPhoto.[Primary], PR_ProductPhoto.ModifiedDate,
        PR_Photo.LargePhotoFileName
FROM    Production.Product PR_Product
        INNER JOIN Production.ProductProductPhoto PR_ProductPhoto
            INNER JOIN Production.ProductPhoto PR_Photo
            ON PR_ProductPhoto.ProductPhotoID=PR_Photo.ProductPhotoID
        ON PR_Product.ProductID=PR_ProductPhoto.ProductId
WHERE   PR_ProductPhoto.ModifiedDate<='20000101'
```

Using LEFT JOIN

Sometimes the relationship between tables is optional, not mandatory. Vendors are typically (but not always) associated with specific products. Assume that you have acquired a new vendor who is not yet associated with any product. If you use the INNER JOIN syntax to join vendor and product information, only vendors with associated products will appear in the results. If you need to obtain information about all of your vendors, even those who are not associated with any product, then you must use the LEFT JOIN syntax as shown in the following example. When using *LEFT JOINS*, all records from the left table are shown plus only the needed rows from the right table. If a relationship does not exist for a particular row, then all columns on the right table return a NULL value.

```
SELECT  V.VendorID,V.AccountNumber,V.[Name],
        P.ProductID,P.[Name]
FROM    Purchasing.Vendor V
        LEFT JOIN Purchasing.ProductVendor PV
            INNER JOIN Production.Product P
            ON PV.ProductID=P.ProductID
        ON V.VendorID=PV.VendorID
```

As shown on the following page, some vendors contain the NULL value as their Product ID because they do not have any associated products.

If you need to obtain only those vendors without associated products, you could add a WHERE clause to specify that the ProductID value must be NULL, as shown in the following example.

```
SELECT V.VendorID,V.AccountNumber,V.[Name],
       P.ProductID,P.[Name]
FROM   Purchasing.Vendor V
       LEFT JOIN Purchasing.ProductVendor PV
           INNER JOIN Production.Product P
           ON PV.ProductID=P.ProductID
       ON V.VendorID=PV.VendorID
WHERE  P.ProductID is null
```

The figure below displays a database diagram representing the relationship between the Vendor and Product tables.

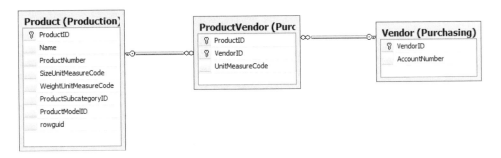

Note   Note that a LEFT JOIN was used for the relationship between Purchasing.Vendor and Purchasing.ProductVendor. An INNER JOIN was used for the relationship between Purchasing.ProductVendor and Production.Product because all vendors with or without an associated product were needed. The LEFT JOIN guaranties that all vendors will be included in the results. The INNER JOIN clause will return rows only when a record exists on Purchasing.ProductVendor.

In the result window below, you see that only vendors without associated products are shown.

	VendorID	AccountNumber	Name	ProductID	Name
1	89	SPORTSH0001	Sports House	NULL	NULL
2	6	GREENLA0001	Green Lake Bike Company	NULL	NULL
3	49	MAGICCY0001	Magic Cycles	NULL	NULL
4	29	INTEGRAT0001	Integrated Sport Products	NULL	NULL
5	9	ADATUM0001	A. Datum Corporation	NULL	NULL
6	95	TEAMATH0001	Team Athletic Co.	NULL	NULL
7	63	MERITBI0001	Merit Bikes	NULL	NULL
8	18	G&KBI0001	G & K Bicycle Corp.	NULL	NULL
9	67	KNOPFLER0001	Knopfler Cycles	NULL	NULL

Using RIGHT JOIN

Not all products are associated with all vendors. Therefore, if you use a sentence like the one below to try to obtain all products, you will miss some rows.

```
SELECT P.ProductID,P.[Name],PV.VendorID
FROM Purchasing.ProductVendor PV
    INNER JOIN Production.Product P
    ON PV.ProductID=P.ProductID
```

For instance, Product ID 3 (BB Ball Bearing) is not associated with any vendor, and therefore this product does not appear in the results, as shown in the following figure.

	ProductID	Name	VendorID
1	1	Adjustable Race	83
2	2	Bearing Ball	57
3	4	Headset Ball Bearings	85
4	317	LL Crankarm	50
5	317	LL Crankarm	84

To obtain all products, you must use a *RIGHT JOIN* as shown in the following sentence.

```
SELECT p.ProductID,P.[Name],PV.VendorID
FROM Purchasing.ProductVendor PV
    RIGHT JOIN Production.Product P
    ON PV.ProductID=P.ProductID
```

The result includes all products, even those that do not have any associated vendor.

In the figure below, you can see that Product ID 3 and Product ID 316 have a NULL value on the VendorID column.

	ProductID	Name	VendorID
1	1	Adjustable Race	83
2	2	Bearing Ball	57
3	3	BB Ball Bearing	NULL
4	4	Headset Ball Bearings	85
5	316	Blade	NULL
6	317	LL Crankarm	50

The main difference between a LEFT JOIN and a RIGHT JOIN is the position in your sentence of the table that should return all rows. By using these statements, you can avoid missing data due to an absent relation.

> **More Info**   A RIGHT JOIN and LEFT JOIN can also be written as RIGHT OUTER JOIN and LEFT OUTER JOIN. Writing OUTER JOINS in this way is the clearest—but also wordiest—method to use, which is why a shorter syntax was used in the example.

Using FULL JOIN

You can use a LEFT JOIN or RIGHT JOIN to obtain all of the records from either the left or right table, but you may need to obtain all of the records in both tables. In this situation, you can use the FULL JOIN syntax to obtain all records. Suppose that you need to obtain all vendors and all products with or without relations. To do so, you can use the following statement.

```
SELECT V.VendorID,V.AccountNumber,V.[Name],
       P.ProductID,P.[Name]
FROM   Purchasing.Vendor V
       FULL JOIN Purchasing.ProductVendor PV
           FULL JOIN Production.Product P
           ON PV.ProductID=P.ProductID
       ON V.VendorID=PV.VendorID
```

> **Note**   Note that two FULL JOIN clauses are used because the relationship between Vendors and Products is made between the Purchasing.ProductVendor table. It is therefore necessary to use three tables on your join.

The following figure demonstrates how all records of both tables (Purchasing.Vendor and Production.Product) are contained in the results of the query, with NULL values displayed when necessary.

	VendorID	AccountNumber	Name	ProductID	Name
696	NULL	NULL	NULL	867	Women's Mountain ...
697	NULL	NULL	NULL	854	Women's Tights, L
698	NULL	NULL	NULL	853	Women's Tights, M
699	NULL	NULL	NULL	852	Women's Tights, S
700	89	SPORTSH0001	Sports House	NULL	NULL
701	6	GREENLA0001	Green Lake Bike Company	NULL	NULL
702	49	MAGICCY0001	Magic Cycles	NULL	NULL
703	29	INTEGRAT0001	Integrated Sport Products	NULL	NULL

Reading Single Values

There are multiple ways to obtain single values in SQL Server 2005. Each method is evaluated to help you make better choices between the different options.

Using System-Supplied Scalar Functions

SQL Server 2005 provides several functions that return single values. These functions can help you obtain part of a value, a value in a different format, random values, environment data, and so forth. There are several function categories, and an example of each category follows.

Aggregate Functions

Aggregate functions help you to obtain summarized values, and they include the *COUNT, SUM, AVG, MAX,* and *MIN* functions. These functions are used on grouped expressions to obtain aggregated values.

Suppose that you need to obtain the number of orders from a sales table. You can obtain the value by using the following sentence. The sentences in this section can be accessed from \Ch07\Samples03.sql in the sample files.

```
SELECT COUNT(*) NumOfElements
FROM Sales.SalesOrderHeader
```

You can use more than one aggregate function on a single statement, as shown in the following sentence.

```
SELECT COUNT(*) NumOfElements,max(OrderDate) LastSaleDate
FROM Sales.SalesOrderHeader
```

Suppose that you need to obtain the number of elements and the date of the last sale for every territory. To obtain this information, you can combine aggregate functions with the GROUP BY clause, as shown below.

```
SELECT ST.TerritoryId,ST.Name,
       COUNT(*) NumOfElements,max(OrderDate) LastSaleDate
FROM Sales.SalesOrderHeader  SOH
    INNER JOIN Sales.SalesTerritory  ST
       ON SOH.TerritoryId=ST.TerritoryID
GROUP BY ST.TerritoryId,ST.Name
```

The following figure presents the result.

	Territor...	Name	Eleme...	LastSaleOn
1	3	Central	385	2004-06-11 00:00:00.000
2	6	Canada	4067	2004-07-31 00:00:00.000
3	9	Australia	6843	2004-07-31 00:00:00.000
4	7	France	2672	2004-07-29 00:00:00.000
5	10	United Kingdom	3219	2004-07-31 00:00:00.000
6	1	Northwest	4594	2004-07-31 00:00:00.000
7	4	Southwest	6224	2004-07-31 00:00:00.000
8	2	Northeast	352	2004-06-19 00:00:00.000
9	5	Southeast	486	2004-07-31 00:00:00.000
10	8	Germany	2623	2004-07-31 00:00:00.000

Configuration Functions

Configuration functions help you to determine the execution environment. Multiple functions, shown in Table 7-1, can be used to obtain different information about the environment.

Table 7-1   Configuration Functions

Function	Description
@@Datefirst	Returns the number of the first day of the week. You can change this value by using the SET DATEFIRST statement.
@@DBTS	Returns the last timestamp value used on the current database. This value changes on every connection because each change on each table has a timestamp value that is guaranteed to be unique.
@@LANGID, @@LANGUAGE	Returns the default language for the actual connection. You can change these settings by using the SET LANGUAGE statement.
@LOCKTIMEOUT	Shows the actual lock timeout value. Special values are –1: waits until the lock has been released and 0: does not wait for any time period. Other values indicate waiting time in milliseconds.
@@NESTLEVEL	Specifies the nested level. If a stored procedure calls another stored procedure, the nested level is two inside the called stored procedure, and so on.
@@SPID	Represents the identifier of the actual connection.

> **More Info**   You can obtain a detailed explanation of each of these functions, plus others that are not explained in this book, by searching the SQL Server Books Online topic, "Configuration Functions."

Cursor Functions

Cursor functions are useful for managing cursors. The function @@cursor_rows, for example, returns the number of qualifying rows opened on a connection. When @@cursor_rows id = –1, this means that it is a dynamic cursor. On a dynamic cursor, the number of rows can change by time, and therefore this function always returns –1. @@cursor_rows will return 0 if there are no opened cursors. It will return a positive number with the number of qualifying rows if the cursor is already opened and populated. It will return a negative number if the cursors are still populating asynchronously. The *CURSOR_STATUS* function will help you determine the status of the cursor.

The most frequently used function when using cursors is @@FETCH_STATUS. This function will help you to determine when you are at the end of the cursor. A value of 0 means that the last FETCH statement was successful. A value of –1 means that the last FETCH statement failed, most likely because the row was beyond the result set. A value of –2 means that the row to be fetched is missing.

Date and Time Functions

Most code needs to perform date and time transformations. You can easily perform these transformations by using the *date and time system functions*. The *YEAR*, *MONTH*, and *DAY* functions receive a date and return the year, month, or day of the provided date. Observe the following code:

```
SELECT YEAR('2006/02/03')
```

This code will return the year 2006. The *MONTH* function applied to this date will return 2, and the *DAY* function applied to the same date will return 3.

The *GETDATE* and *GETUTCDATE* functions help you to determine the current date (including the time). The *GETDATE* function obtains the date and time for the current server time zone (configured in the regional settings), and the *GETUTCDATE* function obtains the UTC time (Coordinated Universal Time of Greenwich).

The *DATEPART* and *DATENAME* functions help you to obtain sections of the time (such as hours or minutes), as well as the names of the day or month.

The *DATEADD* and *DATEDIFF* functions are helpful when you need to perform operations with dates. For example, you can use these functions to calculate the age of your customers based on the date of birth stored in your database.

Mathematical Functions

Several *mathematical functions* exist to help you perform complex mathematical operations. The *ABS* function returns the absolute value of a number. The *SQUARE* function returns the square root of a number. Other functions include *POWER*, *EXP*, *FLOOR*, and *COS*.

Metadata Functions

Metadata functions are used to discover information about databases and database objects. There are twenty-nine different metadata functions. The *DATABASEPROPERTY* and *DATA-BASEPROPERTYEX* functions help you to obtain metadata about databases such as the recovery model, collation, or ANSI defaults. The following example demonstrates some of the uses of these functions.

```
SELECT DATABASEPROPERTY('master','IsAnsiNullDefault')
SELECT DATABASEPROPERTYEX('master','collation')
```

Other functions are related to columns, such as the *COL_LENGTH*, *COL_NAME*, and *INDEX_COL* functions. These are used to discover configuration information related to columns. There are also metadata functions related to files, file groups, objects, types, and full text services.

> **More Info** You can find detailed information about these and other functions by using SQL Server Books Online.

Security Functions

Security functions return information about logins, users, and permissions. There are multiple security function improvements to be found in SQL Server 2005. Some functions, such as *CURRENT_USER, IS_MEMBER*, and *IS_SRVROLEMEMBER*, help you to determine the members of a group or role, as shown below.

```
SELECT IS_SRVROLEMEMBER('sysadmin')
SELECT IS_SRVROLEMEMBER('sysadmin',current_user)
```

Other SQL Server 2005 functions help you to discover permissions on different principals. The *HAS_PERMS_BY_NAME* function receives information about principals, classes, and permissions. With these values, it returns an integer with a NULL value if the query fails, it returns 0 when the user does not have permission, and it returns 1 when the user has permission. The following statement uses the *HAS_PERMS_BY_NAME* function.

```
SELECT HAS_PERMS_BY_NAME(NULL,NULL,'CREATE ANY DATABASE')
```

The first parameter represents the securable—in this case, the default value of the server itself is indicated by NULL—so you can use NULL. The second parameter represents the securable class, and it is NULL for the same reason.

Other security functions are *SCHEMA_NAME, SESSION_USER, USER_NAME*, and *USER_ID*, as well as others.

String Functions

String functions help you to manipule strings (char, varchar, nchar, or nvarchar types). The *LEFT, RIGHT*, and *SUBSTRING* functions help you to manipulate strings to obtain certain parts of them.

Review the following statement:

```
SELECT LEFT('My Word',2),RIGHT('My Word',4),SUBSTRING('My Word',4,4)
```

This statement returns the words *My, Word*, and *Word*. The first clause returns the two first characters beginning at the left of the word. The second clause returns the four last characters beginning at the right of the word. The last clause returns four characters beginning at the fourth character (W, in this case).

Other functions, such as *LOWER, REVERSE, UPPER, STUFF*, and *REPLICATE*, are used to obtain additional information about strings. More information about these functions can be found on SQL Server Books Online.

System Functions

Several *system functions* exist to obtain information about objects, server-wide values, and settings of a particular SQL Server instance. Some of these functions can help you to catch errors or identify values, collations, and transformations.

The *CAST* and *CONVERT* functions can help you with explicit conversions between datatypes, as shown below.

```
SELECT CAST('1234' AS int), CONVERT(datetime,'20060101',112)
```

This sentence returns the number 1234 as well as the date January 1, 2006, 00:00:00.000 hours. The value 112 represents the style of the string value; in this case, 112 indicates a format that includes four digits for years. You can obtain more information about the *CAST* and *CONVERT* functions on SQL Server Books Online.

The *ERROR_LINE*, *ERROR_MESSAGE*, *ERROR_NUMBER*, *ERROR_PROCEDURE*, *ERROR_SEVERITY*, and *ERROR_STATE* functions return information about the last error. In SQL Server 2005, you can use a TRY CATCH statement to catch errors. You can use these functions inside the CATCH statement to determine what error occurred in the system, the error number, procedure, severity, and so on.

```
DECLARE @i INT
SET @i=0
BEGIN TRY
    SELECT 10/@i
END TRY
BEGIN CATCH
SELECT Line=ERROR_LINE(),
       Message=ERROR_MESSAGE(),
       ErrNumber=ERROR_NUMBER(),
       [Procedure]=ERROR_PROCEDURE(),
       Severity=ERROR_SEVERITY(),
       State=ERROR_STATE()
end catch
```

> **Note**   Another way to specify aliases is to use the syntax above (*Alias=ColumnName*). This syntax is only valid for use in the SELECT clause; you cannot use this syntax on the FROM clause.

The *NEWID()* function returns a new unique identifier. This identifier can be used as a default value for columns on your database.

```
CREATE TABLE Messages (idMessage uniqueidentifier NOT NULL default NEWID(),
                       Messagebody varchar(max),
                       CONSTRAINT idMessages PRIMARY KEY NONCLUSTERED (idMessage) )
```

The *@@IDENTITY, SCOPE_IDENTITY, IDENT_CURRENT, IDENT_INCR,* and *IDENT_SEED* functions are helpful for identifying metadata identities and the recent values of these identities. Consider the following example:

```
CREATE TABLE Table1 (id int identity(1,1),
                     othercolumns int DEFAULT 0)
GO
CREATE TABLE Table2 (id int identity(1,1),
                     othercolumns int DEFAULT 0)
GO
INSERT INTRO Table1 DEFAULT VALUES
GO
CREATE TRIGGER tr_table1_insert ON Table1
FOR INSERT
 AS
  BEGIN
    INSERT INTO table2 DEFAULT VALUES
  END
GO
INSERT INTO table1 DEFAULT VALUES
SELECT @@IDENTITY,IDENT_CURRENT('Table1'),SCOPE_IDENTITY()
```

The last query returns the values 1, 2, and 2. The @@IDENTITY value represents the last identity value inserted on the current connection (the value is 1 because the last identity value inserted on table2 was 1). The *IDENT_CURRENT* function represents the actual last identity value on Table1, but if another connection changes the value, *IDENT_CURRENT* returns the value as changed by this other connection. The *SCOPE_IDENTITY()* function returns the last identity value inserted in the current scope (the trigger is out of this scope). All three are useful functions, but understanding the exact meaning of each one will help you to use them properly.

Other system functions include *@@ROWCOUNT, ISNULL, ISDATE,* and *SESSION_USER.*

System Statistical Functions

System statistical functions return statistical information about the system. For example, *@@CPU_BUSY* returns the time that SQL Server 2005 has spent working since it was last started.

> **Caution** Be careful when using the *@@CPU_BUSY* and *@@IO_BUSY* functions. If your server is running for a long time, these functions can receive an arithmetic overflow warning. In this situation, these variables will have no meaning.

The following statement returns the use of the central processing unit (CPU) in milliseconds.

```
SELECT @@CPU_BUSY * CAST(@@TIMETICKS AS float)/1000 [Milliseconds CPU]
```

The @@TOTAL_READ and @@TOTAL_WRITE functions return the number of disk (not cache) reads and writes since SQL Server 2005 was last started. Other statistical functions include @@CONNECTIONS, @PACK_SENT, @@PACK_RECEIVED, and @@IDLE.

Ranking Functions

SQL Server 2005 provides four ranking functions: RANK, DENSE_RANK, NTILE, and ROW_NUMBER. The ROW_NUMBER functions return the row number in a particular order or inside a particular partition. The next statement provides an example.

```
SELECT AddressLine1,City,PostalCode,
       ROW_NUMBER() OVER(ORDER BY Postalcode,AddressLine1),
       ROW_NUMBER() OVER(PARTITION BY PostalCode ORDER BY Postalcode,AddressLine1)
FROM Person.Address
ORDER BY PostalCode,AddressLine1
```

The first ROW_NUMBER() function will return values from 1 to the total number of rows affected by the query. The second ROW_NUMBER() function will return values from 1 up to the number of rows having the same postal code.

The RANK and DENSE_RANK functions return the rank of every row within the partition specified. RANK will return the same ranking value for all elements that have the same value within the ORDER BY clause. Review the following statement:

```
SELECT AddressLine1,City,PostalCode,
       RANK() OVER(ORDER BY PostalCode),
       DENSE_RANK() OVER(ORDER BY PostalCode)
FROM Person.Address
ORDER BY PostalCode,AddressLine1
```

Ranking functions (RANK, DENSE_RANK) return the position of the row within the partition. In the previous example, it will return a different value for each postal code (the postal code is the field specified in the ORDER BY clause). The difference between RANK and DENSE_RANK is that DENSE_RANK returns consecutive values for each group. However, RANK returns 1 for all records in the first group of postal codes, then the ordinal position of the first record of the second group for all the records in the second group, then the ordinal position of the first record of the third group for all the records in the third group, and so on.

The NTILE function divides the information into a specified number of groups.

```
SELECT AddressLine1,City,PostalCode,
       NTILE(10) OVER(ORDER BY PostalCode,AddressLine1)
FROM Person.Address
ORDER BY PostalCode,AddressLine1
```

In the statement above, NTILE divides all the records into ten groups.

Designing and Using Scalar UDFs

User-defined functions (UDFs) in SQL Server 2005 are similar to functions in programming languages—they accept parameters and return values. These values can be both scalar and table values. Only scalar functions will be discussed in this chapter; in-line and table functions will be covered in Chapter 9: Retrieving Data Using Programmable Objects.

UDFs help you to hide development complexity. These functions have access to every table (depending on permissions) and view, but they cannot call stored procedures or perform UPDATE or INSERT statements.

Designing UDFs that Do Not Access Tables or Views

Scalar UDFs are helpful when organizing data. Suppose that you need descriptions for merchandise status and that these descriptions will rarely if ever be updated. You can use a UDF instead of a table to provide the descriptions, as shown in the following example. The code in this section can be accessed from \Ch07\Samples04.sql in the sample files.

```
CREATE FUNCTION States(@idState tinyint)
RETURNS nvarchar(15)
AS
 BEGIN
   RETURN (CASE @idState WHEN 0 THEN N'Stock Pending'
                 WHEN 1 THEN N'Prepared'
                 WHEN 2 THEN N'On truck'
                 WHEN 3 THEN N'In warehouse'
                 WHEN 4 THEN N'Finished'
               ELSE N'UNKNOWN'
          END)
 END
GO
SELECT dbo.states(0),dbo.States(1),dbo.States(100)
```

You can use this function to return the description of the state. The SELECT statement in the above example will return Stock Pending, Prepared, and Unknown. UDFs that do not access tables do not use many resources, and they can help you to envelope complexity and avoid hard-coding information throughout your application.

Designing UDFs that Access Tables or Views

You can also use UDFs to access tables. By doing so, you can isolate certain types of complex business rules that are related to data. Review the following sample:

```
CREATE FUNCTION MostRecentSaleByCustomer(@CustomerID int)
RETURNS INT
AS
BEGIN
    DECLARE @SalesOrderId int
    SELECT TOP 1 @SalesOrderId=SalesOrderId
    FROM Sales.SalesOrderHeader
```

```
      WHERE CustomerID=@CustomerID
      ORDER BY OrderDate Desc
RETURN @SalesOrderId
END
GO
SELECT * FROM Sales.SalesOrderHeader WHERE
      SalesOrderId=dbo.MostRecentSaleByCustomer(676)
```

This function returns the most recent sale for a particular customer. Using *GROUP BY* functions is an alternative but cumbersome way to obtain this information for a set of customers; the complexity is reduced dramatically by using a UDF.

> **Caution**   In the previous example, a UDF was used for only one row, so there were no performance issues involved with the use of this function. However, be careful when using UDFs. If the UDF performs a simple search on a table, the Query Optimizer will not be able to optimize the call because the search is hidden within the UDF; consequently, every row will execute the scalar function. When using UDFs inside queries returning multiples rows, it is recommended that you avoid using scalar UDFs to access other tables. If you do use scalar UDFs, be sure that the queries will not affect too many records.

Designing and Using Stored Procedures to Retrieve Scalar Values

The use of stored procedures is a good strategy when you need to encapsulate data-related business logic. Stored procedures can be used not only to retrieve scalar values, but also to return result sets with multiple rows. This chapter focuses only on how to use stored procedures to retrieve scalar values.

Using Output Parameters

The most natural way to return scalar values from a stored procedure is to use output parameters. Most datatypes can be returned as output parameters including the new xml type, varchar(max) types, and text types. Review the following stored procedure. The code in this section can be accessed from \Ch07\Samples05.sql in the sample files.

```
CREATE PROC ReturnAVowel (@WhatVowel tinyint,@Vowel char(1) output)
AS
BEGIN
   SELECT @Vowel= CASE @WhatVowel WHEN 1 THEN 'A'
                                  WHEN 2 THEN 'E'
                                  WHEN 3 THEN 'I'
                                  WHEN 4 THEN 'O'
                                  WHEN 5 THEN 'U'
                                  ELSE NULL
               END
END
```

Suppose that you execute this stored procedure as shown in the following statement.

```
DECLARE @Vowel char(1)
EXEC ReturnAVowel 1,@Vowel
SELECT 'Vowel'=@Vowel
```

The result is not the letter *A*. The result is the NULL value because you need to use the OUT-PUT keyword when executing the stored procedure, as shown in the following statement.

```
DECLARE @Vowel char(1)
EXEC ReturnAVowel 1,@Vowel OUT
SELECT 'Vowel'=@Vowel
```

In this example, the result is *A*, as expected. Note that the example uses the OUT clause. Both OUT and OUTPUT are valid clauses.

A stored procedure is able to return more that one value. Review the following statement:

```
CREATE PROC ReturnAVowelAndItsAsciiCode
    (@WhatVowel tinyint,@Vowel char(1) OUTPUT,@Asciicode tinyint OUTPUT)
AS
BEGIN
  SELECT @Vowel= CASE @WhatVowel  WHEN 1 THEN 'A'
                                  WHEN 2 THEN 'E'
                                  WHEN 3 THEN 'I'     .
                                  WHEN 4 THEN 'O'
                                  WHEN 5 THEN 'U'
                             ELSE NULL
              END
  SET @AsciiCode=ASCII(@Vowel)
END
```

Now, this statement is used to execute the stored procedure:

```
DECLARE @Vowel char(1),
        @AsciiCode tinyint
EXEC ReturnAVowelAndItsAsciiCode 1,@Vowel OUTPUT,@AsciiCode OUTPUT
SELECT 'Vowel'=@Vowel,'Ascii code '=@AsciiCode
```

Note   All stored procedures can return integer values by using the RETURN clause. However, do not use the RETURN clause to return values between applications or as mechanisms for returning scalar values. If you decide to use the RETURN statement, its purpose should be to return flow-related data, such as logical failures or status. It should never be used to return other kinds of data.

Reading Relational and XML Data

Chapter 5, Designing a Database to Solve Business Needs, introduced the new xml datatype to store XML data natively in SQL Server 2005. Yet SQL Server 2005 offers several other technologies to manipulate relational data as XML data (or, conversely, to manipulate XML data as relational data) without having to store it. You might want to manipulate XML data as relational data because:

1. XML data is self describing. Applications can consume XML data without prior knowledge of its schema or structure.

2. XML is order dependent.

3. XML data is searchable by using special query languages, such as XQUERY and XPATH.

Relational formatting does not conform to these characteristics.

Viewing XML Results in SQL Server Management Studio

The easiest way to view XML results when using SQL Server Management Studio is to set the Results Pane view to Grid view instead of Text view.

Setting the Results Pane View

1. From the Query menu in SQL Server Management Studio, choose Results To | Results To Grid.

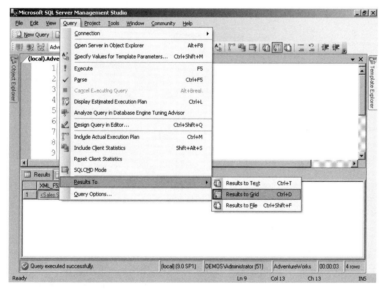

2. After executing the query, the Results Pane will show a link instead of the result.

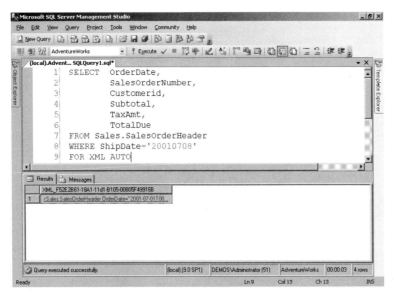

3. When you click the link, a new window will open in SQL Server Management Studio and show you the XML result. This new window is an XML Editor window.

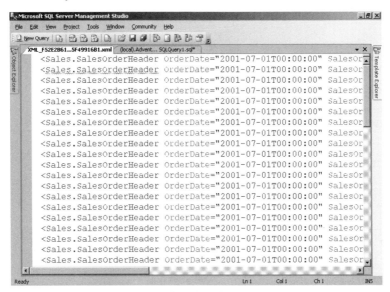

Converting Relational Data to XML Format

The SELECT statement supports the FOR XML clause. This clause is used to transform the result of a query into XML format. You can start learning about XML in a simple way by using the first query that you learned in this chapter. The code in this section can be accessed from the sample files as \Ch07\Samples06.sql.

```
SELECT OrderDate,SalesOrderNumber,CustomerID,Subtotal,TaxAmt,TotalDue
FROM Sales.SalesOrderHeader
WHERE ShipDate='20010708'
FOR XML AUTO
```

The partial result of executing this query should look like the following:

```
<Sales.SalesOrderHeader OrderDate="2001-07-01T00:00:00" SalesOrderNumber="SO43659"
CustomerID="676" Subtotal="24643.9362" TaxAmt="1971.5149" TotalDue="27231.5495" />
<Sales.SalesOrderHeader OrderDate="2001-07-01T00:00:00" SalesOrderNumber="SO43660"
CustomerID="117" Subtotal="1553.1035" TaxAmt="124.2483" TotalDue="1716.1794" />
...
<Sales.SalesOrderHeader OrderDate="2001-07-01T00:00:00" SalesOrderNumber="SO43701"
CustomerID="11003" Subtotal="3399.9900" TaxAmt="271.9992" TotalDue="3756.9890" />
```

The resulting XML is not considered to be well formed because it does not contain a single root node. You can modify the query to create a well formed XML statement, as shown below.

```
SELECT OrderDate,SalesOrderNumber,CustomerID,Subtotal,TaxAmt,TotalDue
FROM Sales.SalesOrderHeader
WHERE ShipDate='20010708'
FOR XML AUTO, ROOT ('TotalSales')
```

The partial result of executing this query should look like the following:

```
<TotalSales>
<Sales.SalesOrderHeader OrderDate="2001-07-01T00:00:00" SalesOrderNumber="SO43659"
 CustomerID="676" Subtotal="24643.9362" TaxAmt="1971.5149" TotalDue="27231.5495" />
<Sales.SalesOrderHeader OrderDate="2001-07-01T00:00:00" SalesOrderNumber="SO43660"
 CustomerID="117" Subtotal="1553.1035" TaxAmt="124.2483" TotalDue="1716.1794" />
...
<Sales.SalesOrderHeader OrderDate="2001-07-01T00:00:00" SalesOrderNumber="SO43701"
 CustomerID="11003" Subtotal="3399.9900" TaxAmt="271.9992" TotalDue="3756.9890" />
</TotalSales>
```

Notice that the table name (Sales.SalesOrderHeader) is used as the XML node name. By declaring a table alias, you can change the element name. Below, the query is modified again to use your own name for each XML node.

```
SELECT OrderDate,SalesOrderNumber,CustomerID,Subtotal,TaxAmt,TotalDue
FROM Sales.SalesOrderHeader MySales
WHERE ShipDate='20010708'
FOR XML AUTO, ROOT ('TotalSales')
```

The partial result of executing this query should look like the following:

```
<TotalSales>
<MySales OrderDate="2001-07-01T00:00:00" SalesOrderNumber="SO43659"
 CustomerID="676" Subtotal="24643.9362" TaxAmt="1971.5149" TotalDue="27231.5495" />
<MySales OrderDate="2001-07-01T00:00:00" SalesOrderNumber="SO43660"
 CustomerID="117" Subtotal="1553.1035" TaxAmt="124.2483" TotalDue="1716.1794" />
...
<MySales OrderDate="2001-07-01T00:00:00" SalesOrderNumber="SO43701"
```

```
      CustomerID="11003" Subtotal="3399.9900" TaxAmt="271.9992" TotalDue="3756.9890" />
</TotalSales>
```

The same process is applied when you want to use a different name for each *XML* attribute instead of using the column name. Notice the variations in the following query and investigate the result by executing it.

```
SELECT  OrderDate 'Date',
        SalesOrderNumber 'OrderNumber',
        CustomerID 'ID',
        Subtotal,
        TaxAmt 'Taxes',
        TotalDue
FROM Sales.SalesOrderHeader MySales
WHERE ShipDate='20010708'
FOR XML AUTO, ROOT('TotalSales')
```

In the previous examples, the resulting XML is built as attribute-based XML. In the following example, you will modify the query to receive element-based XML.

```
SELECT OrderDate,SalesOrderNumber,CustomerID,Subtotal,TaxAmt,TotalDue
FROM Sales.SalesOrderHeader MySales
WHERE ShipDate='20010708'
FOR XML AUTO, ROOT ('TotalSales'), ELEMENTS
```

The partial result of executing this query should look like the following:

```
<TotalSales>
  <MySales>
    <OrderDate>2001-07-01T00:00:00</OrderDate>
    <SalesOrderNumber>SO43659</SalesOrderNumber>
    <CustomerID>676</CustomerID>
    <Subtotal>24643.9362</Subtotal>
    <TaxAmt>1971.5149</TaxAmt>
    <TotalDue>27231.5495</TotalDue>
  </MySales>
  <MySales>
    <OrderDate>2001-07-01T00:00:00</OrderDate>
    <SalesOrderNumber>SO43660</SalesOrderNumber>
    <CustomerID>117</CustomerID>
    <Subtotal>1553.1035</Subtotal>
    <TaxAmt>124.2483</TaxAmt>
    <TotalDue>1716.1794</TotalDue>
  </MySales>
...
</TotalSales>
```

When using the FOR XML clause, queries can include any of the other clauses that have already been discussed.

You can look at a more complex example by retrieving results from multiple tables.

```
SELECT  Vendor.VendorID,
        Vendor.AccountNumber,
        Vendor.[Name],
        Product.ProductID,
        Product.[Name]
FROM Purchasing.Vendor Vendor
    LEFT JOIN Purchasing.ProductVendor PV
        INNER JOIN Production.Product Product
        ON PV.ProductID=Product.ProductID
    ON Vendor.VendorID=PV.VendorID
ORDER BY Vendor.VendorID
FOR XML AUTO, ROOT('Vendors')
```

The partial result of executing this query should look like the following:

```
<Vendors>
  <Vendor VendorID="1" AccountNumber="INTERNAT0001" Name="International">
    <Product ProductID="462" Name="Lower Head Race" />
  </Vendor>
  <Vendor VendorID="2" AccountNumber="ELECTRON0002"
   Name="Electronic Bike Repair &amp; Supplies">
    <Product ProductID="511" Name="ML Road Rim" />
    <Product ProductID="510" Name="LL Road Rim" />
    <Product ProductID="512" Name="HL Road Rim" />
  </Vendor>
  <Vendor VendorID="3" AccountNumber="PREMIER0001" Name="Premier Sport, Inc.">
    <Product ProductID="513" Name="Touring Rim" />
  </Vendor>
  <Vendor VendorID="4" AccountNumber="COMFORT0001" Name="Comfort Road Bicycles">
    <Product ProductID="507" Name="LL Mountain Rim" />
    <Product ProductID="508" Name="ML Mountain Rim" />
  </Vendor>
<Vendors>
```

When using the FOR XML AUTO clause, be aware that:

- XML AUTO generates a new hierarchy level for each table in the SELECT query.

- Table and column aliases can be used to rename the elements in the resulting XML.

- All columns are formatted in the same way as either attributes or elements, but it is impossible to mix the different formatting modes.

If formatting modes cannot be mixed, how do you provide a different format (either attribute based or element based) for each column in the result? To solve this problem, SQL Server 2005 introduces the FOR XML PATH clause, which allows you to declare independent formatting options for each of the columns in a query.

Copy the following query to SQL Server Management Studio and compare the results with those from the previous query. The syntax is explained in Table 7-2.

```
SELECT  Vendor.VendorID 'Vendor/@ID',
        Vendor.AccountNumber 'Vendor/Account',
        Vendor.[Name] 'Vendor/Name',
```

```
        Product.ProductID 'Vendor/Product/@ID',
        Product.[Name] 'Vendor/Product/Name'
FROM Purchasing.Vendor Vendor
    LEFT JOIN Purchasing.ProductVendor PV
        INNER JOIN Production.Product Product
        ON PV.ProductID=Product.ProductID
    ON Vendor.VendorID=PV.VendorID
ORDER BY Vendor.VendorID
FOR XML PATH(''), ROOT('Vendors')
```

The partial result of executing this query should look like the following:

```
<Vendors>
  <Vendor ID="1">
    <Account>INTERNAT0001</Account>
    <Name>International</Name>
    <Product ID="462">
      <Name>Lower Head Race</Name>
    </Product>
  </Vendor>
  <Vendor ID="2">
    <Account>ELECTRON0002</Account>
    <Name>Electronic Bike Repair &amp; Supplies</Name>
    <Product ID="511">
      <Name>ML Road Rim</Name>
    </Product>
  </Vendor>
...
<Vendors>
```

By using the FOR XML PATH clause, the column aliases provide further formatting informa-tion to SQL Server 2005.

Table 7-2   Column Alias Syntax

Column Alias	Instructions to SQL Server 2005
element_name	Copy the value of this column into an element called *element_name* under the context element (the last processed node).
	Example: 'Vendor'
element_name1/ element_name2	Copy the value of this column into an element called *element_name2* under an element called *element_name1*.
	Example: 'Vendor/Account'
@attribute_name	Copy the value of this column into an attribute called *attribute_name* under the context element (the last processed node).
	Example: '@ID'
element_name/ @attribute_name	Copy the value of this column into an attribute called *attribute_name* under an element called *element_name*.
	Example: 'Vendor/@ID'

It is also important to be aware of the following information concerning the use of the FOR XML AUTO clause.

- Developers have full control over the number of levels that the XML structure will contain.

- XML attribute declarations must be declared before XML element declarations; therefore, column order does matter. Column order also indicates the context node with which to locate column values for which you do not specify the position in the XML structure.

- Table aliases are ignored by the formatting mechanism in the XML PATH clause.

> **Note**   The FOR XML clause supports four formatting modes: RAW, AUTO, EXPLICIT, and PATH. Only basic usage of the FOR XML AUTO and FOR XML PATH clauses have been covered in this chapter. For more information on how to use the other formatting modes, see the SQL Server Books Online topic, "Constructing XML Using FOR XML."

Converting XML Data to Relational Format

You must now focus on the opposite scenario. Assume that you want to transform your XML data into a tabular (relational) format. SQL Server 2005 provides different technologies to accomplish this, but you are going to focus on the *nodes()* method of the new xml datatype.

Converting XML Data into a Relational Format Using the nodes() Method

1. Load the XML data into an xml datatype variable using the following T-SQL statements. The code in this section can be accessed from \Ch07\Samples07.sql in the sample files.

```
DECLARE @MYDATA XML
SET @MYDATA = '<Vendors>
  <Vendor VendorID="1" AccountNumber="INTERNAT0001" Name="International">
    <Product ProductID="462" Name="Lower Head Race" />
  </Vendor>
  <Vendor VendorID="2" AccountNumber="ELECTRON0002"
   Name="Electronic Bike Repair Supplies">
    <Product ProductID="511" Name="ML Road Rim" />
    <Product ProductID="510" Name="LL Road Rim" />
    <Product ProductID="512" Name="HL Road Rim" />
  </Vendor>
  <Vendor VendorID="3" AccountNumber="PREMIER0001" Name="Premier Sport, Inc.">
    <Product ProductID="513" Name="Touring Rim" />
  </Vendor>
  <Vendor VendorID="4" AccountNumber="COMFORT0001" Name="Comfort Road Bicycles">
    <Product ProductID="507" Name="LL Mountain Rim" />
    <Product ProductID="508" Name="ML Mountain Rim" />
  </Vendor>
  <Vendor VendorID="5" AccountNumber="METROSP0001" Name="Metro Sport Equipment">
    <Product ProductID="528" Name="Seat Lug" />
  </Vendor>
```

```
<Vendor VendorID="6" AccountNumber="GREENLA0001" Name="Green Lake Bike Company">
  <Product />
</Vendor>
</Vendors>'
```

2. Construct a query using the *value()* method to extract specific values as well as the *nodes()* method to transform the XML into tabular format.

```
SELECT XMLColumn.value('@VendorID','int') 'VendorID',
       XMLColumn.value('@AccountNumber','nvarchar(100)') 'Account_Number',
       XMLColumn.value('@Name','nvarchar(100)') 'Account_Name',
       XMLColumn.value('(Product/@ProductID)[1]','int') 'FirstProduct'
FROM @MYDATA.nodes('Vendors/Vendor') ResultTable(XMLColumn)
```

3. You can use this result set as you would any other relational table. When you execute this code, the result should look like the following figure.

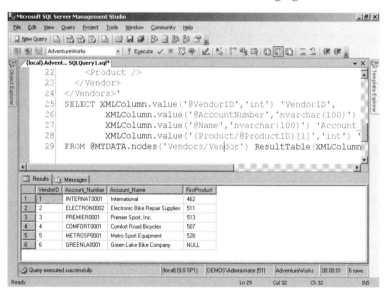

The *nodes()* method returns a table with a single column (of type xml). The values inside this XML column are the result of the XPATH query sent as an input parameter to the *nodes()* method call. In the previous example, the XPATH query Vendors/Vendor indicates that you would like to select all of the nodes called Vendor that exist under a node called Vendors.

The *value()* method extracts a single value from the XML, transforms it into a SQL Server datatype, and returns a scalar value. The syntax in the above example is explained in Table 7-3.

Table 7-3   Input Parameter Syntax

Input Parameter	Instructions to SQL Server 2005
@attribute_name, int	Extract the value from the *attribute_name* attribute as an int datatype.

Table 7-3   Input Parameter Syntax

Input Parameter	Instructions to SQL Server 2005
element_name, nvarchar(100)	Extract the value from the *element_name* element as an nvarchar(100) datatype.
element_name/@attribute_name, nvarchar(100)	Extract the value from the *attribute_name* attribute located under the *element_name* element as an nvarchar(100) datatype.
(element_name/@attribute_name)[1], int	Extract the first value found from the *attribute_name* attribute under the *element_name* element as an int datatype.

Note   This chapter has barely scratched the surface of this topic. To learn more about using the XML data *nodes()* method, read the SQL Server Books Online topic, "nodes() Method (xml Data Type)."

Note   If you want to extract relational data from XML data without using the xml datatype, SQL Server 2005 offers another technique called OpenXML. For more information about how to use this other technology, read the SQL Server Books Online topic, "Querying XML Using OPENXML."

Querying XML and Relational Data Using XQuery

XQUERY is a language designed to query XML data. It is a full programming language that is used to execute complex extractions, joins, and filters around your XML data. SQL Server 2005 is aligned with the July 2004 working draft of XQUERY and supports a subset of this query language. The *query()* method of the xml datatype provides the ability to execute an XPATH or XQUERY expression, and it returns the resulting XML fragment.

Using XQUERY in Queries

1. Load the XML data into an xml datatype variable, as in the previous procedure. The code in this section can be be accessed from \Ch07\Samples08.sql in the sample files.

```
DECLARE @MYDATA XML
SET @MYDATA = '<Vendors>
  <Vendor VendorID="1" AccountNumber="INTERNAT0001" Name="International">
    <Product ProductID="462" Name="Lower Head Race" />
  </Vendor>
  <Vendor VendorID="2" AccountNumber="ELECTRON0002"
   Name="Electronic Bike Repair Supplies">
    <Product ProductID="511" Name="ML Road Rim" />
    <Product ProductID="510" Name="LL Road Rim" />
    <Product ProductID="512" Name="HL Road Rim" />
  </Vendor>
  <Vendor VendorID="3" AccountNumber="PREMIER0001" Name="Premier Sport, Inc.">
    <Product ProductID="513" Name="Touring Rim" />
```

```
    </Vendor>
    <Vendor VendorID="4" AccountNumber="COMFORT0001" Name="Comfort Road Bicycles">
      <Product ProductID="507" Name="LL Mountain Rim" />
      <Product ProductID="508" Name="ML Mountain Rim" />
    </Vendor>
    <Vendor VendorID="5" AccountNumber="METROSP0001" Name="Metro Sport Equipment">
      <Product ProductID="528" Name="Seat Lug" />
    </Vendor>
    <Vendor VendorID="6" AccountNumber="GREENLA0001" Name="Green Lake Bike Company">
      <Product />
    </Vendor>
  </Vendors>'
```

2. Construct a query using the *query()* method to extract specific sections of the XML data.

```
SELECT @MYDATA.query('//Product[@ProductID>510]')
```

This simple *XQUERY* expression indicates that you would like to traverse the complete XML tree ("//") and extract the Product elements that contain a ProductID attribute with a value larger than 510.

3. When executing this code, the result should look like the following:

```
<Product ProductID="511" Name="ML Road Rim" />
<Product ProductID="512" Name="HL Road Rim" />
<Product ProductID="513" Name="Touring Rim" />
<Product ProductID="528" Name="Seat Lug" />
```

Another way of writing this same query would be:

```
SELECT @MYDATA.query('
    for $product in //Product
    where data($product/@ProductID) > 510
    return
        <result>
            {$product}
        </result>
    ')
```

This is also an *XQUERY* expression, which is called a *FLWOR* (for, let, where, order by, return) expression. The result of executing this type of query should resemble the following:

```
<result>
  <Product ProductID="511" Name="ML Road Rim" />
</result>
<result>
  <Product ProductID="512" Name="HL Road Rim" />
</result>
<result>
  <Product ProductID="513" Name="Touring Rim" />
</result>
<result>
  <Product ProductID="528" Name="Seat Lug" />
</result>
```

The XQUERY language supports encapsulating programming logic as functions. The *data()* function (used in the previous example) is part of the XQUERY language and extracts the values out of XML elements.

> **Note** XQUERY is a complete programming language for which a thorough explanation is beyond the scope of this book. A recommended starting point for more information about XQUERY is to read the subtopics under the section, "XQuery Against the xml Data Type," in SQL Server Books Online.

Sorting Data

You can sort data in your queries by using the ORDER BY clause. The most common construction is to use the name of a column to specify the desired order. Refer to the following example. The code in this section can be accessed from \Ch07\Samples09.sql in the sample files.

```
SELECT SalesOrderId,OrderDate,SalesOrderNumber,CustomerID,Subtotal,TaxAmt,TotalDue
FROM Sales.SalesOrderHeader
WHERE CustomerID=676
ORDER BY OrderDate
```

The query above will return a list of orders from customer 676, arranged by the date of the order in an ascending fashion, with the oldest order listed first. If you want the orders with the most recent dates listed first, you can use the DESC clause, as shown below.

```
SELECT SalesOrderId,OrderDate,SalesOrderNumber,CustomerID, Subtotal,TaxAmt,TotalDue
FROM Sales.SalesOrderHeader
WHERE CustomerID=676
ORDER BY OrderDate DESC
```

The query above will return the SalesOrderNumber SO67260 in the first row because that is the most recent order.

The previous examples are ordered by date. You can also order your query by different datatypes, such as numbers and strings, but you cannot order your query by XML. Refer to the following example:

```
SELECT *
FROM Sales.Individual
WHERE ModifiedDate BETWEEN '20041018' AND '20041020'
ORDER BY Demographics
```

If you execute the query above on the AdventureWorks database, you will receive the following message:

```
Msg 305, Level 16, State 1, Line 1
The xml data type cannot be compared or sorted, except when using
the IS NULL operator.
```

The xml, text, ntext, or image datatypes cannot be used in the ORDER BY clause.

You may need to order your query by data that must be calculated first. Queries can use aliases to specify the name of calculated columns. You can also use this name when specifying the order, as shown below.

```
SELECT SalesOrderId,OrderDate,SalesOrderNumber,CustomerID,
       Subtotal+TaxAmt+Freight as Total
FROM Sales.SalesOrderHeader
WHERE CustomerID=676
ORDER BY Total DESC
```

In some cases, ordering by only one column is not enough to specify the desired order. Suppose that you need to obtain the sales of customers 676 and 677. You need the sales ordered by Total, but you do not want to merge the sales of different customers. The following statement solves the problem.

```
SELECT SalesOrderId,OrderDate,SalesOrderNumber,CustomerID,
       Subtotal+TaxAmt+Freight as Total
FROM sales.SalesOrderHeader
WHERE CustomerID in (676 ,677)
ORDER BY CustomerID,Total DESC
```

In other situations, the desired order depends on a parameter. The following example demonstrates how to solve this issue.

```
DECLARE @orderby varchar(10)
SET @orderby='date'
SELECT SalesOrderId,OrderDate,SalesOrderNumber,CustomerID,
       Subtotal+TaxAmt+Freight as Total
FROM sales.SalesOrderHeader
WHERE CustomerID in (676 ,677)
ORDER BY case @orderby WHEN 'date' THEN SalesOrderHeader.OrderDate
                       WHEN 'total' THEN 5
                       ELSE SalesOrderHeader.SalesorderId
         END
```

Note that the name "total" has been replaced by the number 5. This occurred because the use of aliases is not permitted when they are inside of CASE statements. You can therefore replace the alias with the order number of the column (5, in this case).

> **Caution**   When using CASE statements to specify varying orders, be sure that performance is not compromised. A discussion of performance is not within the scope of this chapter, but by viewing the estimated execution plan in SQL Server Management Studio, you can discover whether using a CASE statement will negatively impact performance.

Conclusion

Microsoft SQL Server 2005 is a very powerful tool with which to query databases. SQL Server 2005 helps you to obtain data from one or several tables, thereby allowing you to filter, join, and order different sets of data within the same language. By using scalar functions, you can write more comprehensive queries. Output parameters allow you to return scalar data. The new xml datatype presents a new way to not only query relational data, but also to store and return irregular information.

Chapter 7 Quick Reference

To	Do This
Query databases	Use the SELECT, CASE, JOIN, AND, and OR operators.
Select data from multiple tables	Use INNER JOIN, LEFT JOIN, RIGHT JOIN, or FULL JOIN.
Obtain summarized values	Use aggregate functions: *COUNT*, *SUM*, *AVG*, and *MIN*.
Perform complex operations Set information about the system or security	Use system-supplied scalar functions: configuration, cursor, date time, mathematical, security, and other functions.
Define your own functions	Use UDFs to accept and return values in new functions.
Store, retrieve, or manipulate XML documents	Use the new xml datatype in SQL Server 2005.

Chapter 8
Creating Views to Encapsulate Queries

After completing this chapter, you will be able to:

- Create and query views
- Select data from a single view
- Mix data from views and tables
- Work with views from within client applications

A Microsoft SQL Server 2005 database can host a wide range of database objects that provide you with more options and flexibility when designing data-centric applications. A view is one of these database objects. In this chapter, you will learn how to create and manage a view. You will also learn how to query data from a view and combine data from a view and base tables. Lastly, you will learn how to use views from client applications.

Selecting Data from a Single View

You can think of a *view* as a stored query that encapsulates the complexity of a query and presents the desired data to users or applications. When you create a view, SQL Server 2005 only stores the definition for the view. No data is stored unless the view will be indexed. Therefore, a view is basically a SELECT statement stored in a database for later use. Once a view is created, you can obtain results from the SELECT statement by querying the view instead of running the complex SELECT statement against the base tables.

Creating a View

You can create a view graphically in SQL Server Management Studio or by using the CREATE VIEW statement.

Creating a View in SQL Server Management Studio

1. Start SQL Server Management Studio by selecting Programs | Microsoft SQL Server 2005 | SQL Server Management Studio from the Start menu. Connect to the appropriate SQL Server instance.

2. From Object Explorer, expand the AdventureWorks database.

3. Right-click the Views folder and select New View from the context menu.

4. The Add Table dialog box appears. Choose the Department, Employee, and EmployeeDepartmentHistory tables. Click Add, and then click Close.

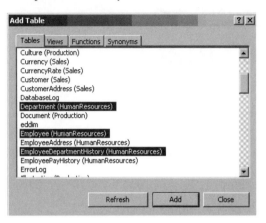

5. Select the Name column on the Department table. Select the NationalIDNumber and Title columns from the Employee table.

6. Click outside of the tables you added and select Properties Window from the View menu. In the Properties window, choose HumanResources in the Schema property.

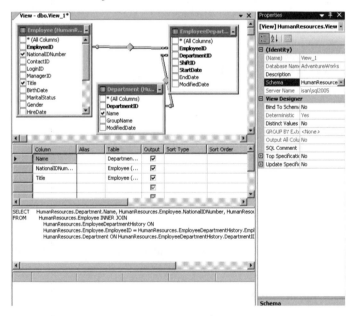

7. Click the Save View toolbar button and enter **vTest** as the view name.

Creating a View Using T-SQL

The following sample code creates a view called ProductSales in the Sales schema that provides information about the units sold for each product. You can access this sample code from \Ch08\SampleCh0801.sql.

```
USE AdventureWorks
GO
CREATE VIEW Sales.ProductSales
AS
SELECT     Production.Product.Name AS Product,
           SUM(Sales.SalesOrderDetail.OrderQty) AS ProductSales
FROM       Production.Product INNER JOIN
               Sales.SalesOrderDetail ON Production.Product.ProductID =
                   Sales.SalesOrderDetail.ProductID INNER JOIN
                       Sales.SalesOrderHeader ON
                           Sales.SalesOrderDetail.SalesOrderID =
                               Sales.SalesOrderHeader.SalesOrderID
GROUP BY Production.Product.Name
```

In SQL Server 2005, a view can contain a maximum of 1,024 columns. You can create views only in the local database.

> **Tip**   Using the ORDER BY clause inside a view does not guarantee that the results will be ordered when you query the view.

Obtaining Information about Views

Once a view is created in a database, you can obtain information about the view from the sys.views catalog view. The following is a sample query of the sys.views catalog view. You can access this sample code from \Ch08\SampleCh0802.sql.

```
USE AdventureWorks
GO
SELECT * FROM sys.views
```

You can also view the original code by querying the sys.sql_modules catalog view. The following example provides information about the definition for the AdventureWorks views. You can access this sample code from \Ch08\SampleCh0803.sql.

```
USE AdventureWorks
GO
SELECT name, definition
FROM sys.sql_modules INNER JOIN sys.views
    ON sys.sql_modules.object_id=sys.views.object_id
```

Before you modify, rename, or delete a view, it is important to know what objects depend on the view. For example, changing the name or definition of a view can cause dependent objects to fail if the dependent objects are not updated to reflect the changes that have been made to the view. The stored procedure sp_depends allows you to determine the identity of the base objects on which the view depends. The following code describes how to obtain information about the objects used in the Sales.ProductSales view. You can access this sample code from \Ch08\SampleCh0804.sql.

```
USE AdventureWorks
GO
EXECUTE sp_depends 'Sales.ProductSales'
```

If you execute the code above, you should receive output resembling that found in Table 8-1.

Table 8-1   Sample Output for sp_depends

Name	Type	Updated	Selected	Column
Sales.SalesOrderDetail	user table	no	yes	SalesOrderID
Sales.SalesOrderDetail	user table	no	yes	OrderQty
Sales.SalesOrderDetail	user table	no	yes	ProductID
Sales.SalesOrderHeader	user table	no	yes	SalesOrderID
Production.Product	user table	no	yes	ProductID
Production.Product	user table	no	yes	Name

You can also obtain dependency information graphically within SQL Server Management Studio.

Accessing Dependency Information

1. Right-click the desired view and choose View Dependencies from the context menu.

2. Select the Objects On Which [*view*] Depends option.

   You can now navigate through the dependencies tree, obtaining information about tables, columns, indexes, and user-defined types.

You can query a view using a SELECT statement in the same way that you query a table. The following sample code demonstrates how to query the Sales.ProductSales view. You can access this sample code from \Ch08\SampleCh0805.sql.

```
USE AdventureWorks
GO
SELECT * FROM Sales.ProductSales
```

Creating View Options

SQL Server 2005 allows you to configure views using attributes in the CREATE VIEW statement. The following list provides a description of various view attributes.

- **Encryption**   The encryption attribute encrypts the entries within sys.sql_modules that contain the text of the view definition. Once a view has been encrypted, it is no longer possible to see the original view definition. Therefore, you should document all view statements and be careful when encrypting them. The following example creates an encrypted view. You can access this sample code from \Ch08\SampleCh0806.sql.

```
USE AdventureWorks
GO
CREATE VIEW dbo.TestEncryption
WITH ENCRYPTION
AS
SELECT * FROM Production.Product
```

  Once you have created the encrypted view, try to obtain the view description from the sys.sql_modules catalog view using the following SELECT statement. You can access this sample code from \Ch08\SampleCh0807.sql.

```
SELECT name, definition
FROM sys.sql_modules INNER JOIN sys.views
    ON sys.sql_modules.object_id=sys.views.object_id
WHERE Name = 'TestEncryption'
```

  You will receive a NULL description due to the view encryption, even though you are the view owner.

- **Schemabinding**   The schemabinding attribute allows you to bind the view definition with the schema of the base tables queried in the view. When you specify the schema-binding attribute, base tables cannot be modified if the change affects the view defini-tion. To use the schemabinding attribute, you must query the base objects with the two-part name (schema.table) for referenced objects. Schemabinding can be used if the view queries local database objects only. If you do not specify the schemabinding option, you must execute the sp_refreshview stored procedure when a base table is modified.

- **View_Metadata**   Client-side application program interfaces (APIs) have the option of requesting a browse-mode query to enable client-side APIs to implement updatable cli-ent-side cursors. This browse-mode metadata includes information about the base tables. You must specify the view_metadata option to support the delivery of browse-mode metadata.

- **Check**   By specifying the check option in the CREATE VIEW statement, the database engine forces all modification statements executed against the view to follow the criteria within the SELECT statement. When you modify a row through a view, the check option ensures that the data is visible after the modification is committed.

Modifying a View Definition

As with other database objects, you can modify a view definition through the SQL Server Man-agement Studio graphical interface or you can use the ALTER VIEW statement. If you want to modify a view, you should write the entire statement again even though you only want to modify one view attribute. This step is important because, when you have encrypted a view, you cannot see the original view definition once it has been encrypted. The following example demonstrates how to add the view_metadata attribute to the dbo.TestEncryption view. You can access this sample code from \Ch08\SampleCh0808.sql.

```
USE AdventureWorks
GO
ALTER VIEW dbo.TestEncryption
WITH ENCRYPTION,VIEW_METADATA
AS
SELECT * FROM Production.Product
```

You can also remove a view with the DROP VIEW statement as shown in the following example. You can access this sample code from \Ch08\SampleCh0809.sql.

```
USE AdventureWorks
GO
DROP VIEW dbo.TestEncryption
```

> **Important**   Before you modify or drop a view, you should check for view dependencies. Dependencies could raise errors in the alter and drop operations.

Updating Data through a View

Although the primary reason for creating a view is to obtain information for queries and reports, you can execute INSERT, UPDATE, and DELETE sentences over the base tables through a view. To perform these actions, the view must meet the following conditions.

- Modifications can only reference columns from one base table.
- Columns cannot be derived.
- Modified columns cannot be affected by GROUP BY, HAVING, or DISTINCT clauses.
- The TOP clause cannot be specified in the view definition.

The following example demonstrates how to update the Person.Address.City column through the vEmployeeAddress view. You can access this sample code from \Ch08\SampleCh0810.sql.

```
USE AdventureWorks
GO
CREATE VIEW HumanResources.vEmployeeAddress
AS
SELECT NationalIDNumber,LoginID,Title,AddressLine1,City,PostalCode
FROM HumanResources.Employee INNER JOIN HumanResources.EmployeeAddress
    ON HumanResources.Employee.EmployeeID =
    HumanResources.EmployeeAddress.EmployeeID
```

```
    INNER JOIN Person.Address
    ON Person.Address.AddressID = HumanResources.EmployeeAddress.AddressID
GO
UPDATE HumanResources.vEmployeeAddress
   SET City = 'Everett' WHERE NationalIDNumber= 14417807
```

Partitioned Views

SQL Server 2005 allows you to create views that reference tables from different databases and servers. You can partition your data among several servers and then create views to consolidate the information. Suppose that you are working with a client table containing millions of rows. You can partition the table horizontally and filter clients by location. You could create a USA_Customers table, an EMEA_Customers table, and so on, and each table could be stored in a different SQL Server instance. You could then create a view that combined all of these tables and manage modifications to the data through INSTEAD OF triggers. INSTEAD OF triggers will be discussed in Chapter 12, Updating Data from Microsoft SQL Server 2005. This process is known as *partitioned views* and is a way to scale out your SQL Server environment.

Note   To query data from a remote instance, you should create a linked server before accessing the remote instance.

The following example works with a linked server named ISAN that connects to another SQL Server instance with a TestPartitionedViews database. This database also contains an EMEA_Customers table. The following Transact-SQL (T-SQL) sentences demonstrate how to create the local resources and partitioned views. You can access this sample code from \Ch08\SampleCh0811.sql.

```
CREATE DATABASE TestPartitionedViews
GO
USE TestPartitionedViews
GO
CREATE TABLE USA_Customers (CustomerID int, CustomerName varchar(200), Region varchar(20))
GO
CREATE VIEW Customers
AS
SELECT * FROM USA_Customers
UNION
SELECT * FROM ISAN.TestPartitionedViews.dbo.EMEA_Customers
GO
```

You could then create an INSTEAD OF trigger to support modifications to the base tables through the Customers view.

Note   Partitioned views that access data in tables from the local server are supported in SQL Server 2005 for backward compatibility only. In SQL Server 2005, you should use partitioned tables as the preferred partitioning approach.

Mixing Data from Views and Tables

It is a common practice to write queries that involve data from views and tables. You can mix data from both views and tables in several ways, such as joining tables with views. The following example demonstrates how to mix data from the HumanResources.vEmployeeDepartment view and the HumanResources.EmployeeAddress and Person.Address table. You can access this sample code from \Ch08\SampleCh0812.sql.

```
SELECT HumanResources.vEmployeeDepartment.*, AddressLine1, City, PostalCode
FROM HumanResources.EmployeeAddress INNER JOIN Person.Address
    ON HumanResources.EmployeeAddress.AddressID = Person.Address.AddressID
    INNER JOIN HumanResources.vEmployeeDepartment
    ON HumanResources.EmployeeAddress.EmployeeID = HumanResources.vEmployeeDepartment.EmployeeID
```

Working with Views within Client Applications

By accessing views from client applications instead of accessing base tables directly, you can hide the database design complexity of client applications. When you work with a view from within a client application, there is no difference between the view and a table. You can query the view by using a *SQLCommand* object and navigate through the result set with a *SQLReader* object. The following example demonstrates how to query a view using Visual Basic.NET. You can access this sample code from \Ch08\SampleCh0813.vb.

```
' Create an instance of a SQLConnection object
Dim oConn as New SQLClient.SQLConnection
' Create an instance of a SQLCommand object
Dim oCmd as New SQLClient.SQLCommand
' Create an SQLReader object
Dim oReader as SQLClient.SQLReader
' Define the connection string
oConn.ConnectionString= _
    "server=localhost;database=AdventureWorks;Integrated Security=SSPI"
' Define command properties
oCmd.Connection=oConn
oCmd.CommandText="SELECT * FROM Sales.vSalesPerson"
' Open the connection
oConn.Open()
' Execute the command
oReader=oCmd.ExecuteReader
While oReader.Read
    ... <Process record by record>
End While
' Close the connection
oConn.Close()
```

You can also create a data source within Visual Studio that receives data from a view.

Creating a Data Source with Visual Studio 2005

1. Start Visual Studio 2005. From the Start Menu, choose All Programs | Microsoft Visual Studio 2005 | Microsoft Visual Studio 2005.

2. From the File menu, choose New | Project.

3. In the New Project dialog box, select the Windows Application template in the Visual Basic project types and click OK.

4. From the Data menu, choose Show Data Sources.

5. Click the Add New Data Source toolbar button in the Data Sources window. The Data Source Configuration Wizard appears.

6. Select Database and click Next.

7. In the Choose Your Data Connection step, click the New Connection button.

8. In the Add Connection dialog box, specify your SQL Server instance in the Data Source and Server Name boxes. Select the AdventureWorks database under the Select Or Enter A Database Name option of the Connect To A Database frame. Click OK.

9. In the Choose Your Data Connection step, click Next.

10. In the Save The Connection String To The Application Configuration File step, uncheck the Yes checkbox and click Next.

11. In the Choose Your Database Objects step, expand the Views node, select the vEmployee view, and then click Finish.

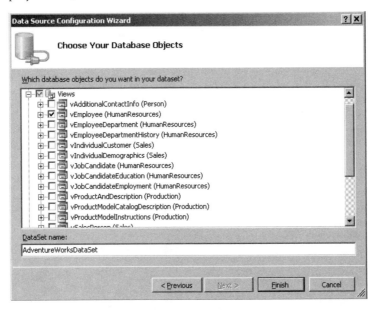

12. In the Data Sources window, select the vEmployee node, which will change to a combo box. Click the down arrow and select Details.

13. Drag and drop vEmployee from the Data Sources window to Form1.

14. Run the application. You can see data from the view and can navigate through the data, as shown below.

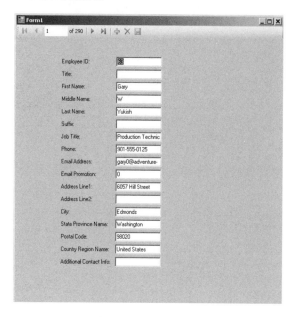

Conclusion

In this chapter, you learned how to create, modify, and manage views. Views allow you to encapsulate the complexity of a query so that you can provide more flexible and legible metadata to client applications.

Chapter 8 Quick Reference

To	Do This
Create a view in SQL Server Management Studio	Right-click the Views folder in the desired database.
	Choose New View.
	Add base tables used in the view.
	Select the columns to show.
Obtain information about views	Use the sys.views and sys.sql_modules system catalog views.
Access information about view dependencies in SQL Server Management Studio	Right-click the desired view.
	Choose View Dependencies.
Modify the view definition	Use the ALTER VIEW statement.
Update rows from a view	Make sure you update rows from only one table.

To	Do This
Bind the view to based tables	Use the schemabinding option.
Create a partitioned view	Create linked servers to access remote SQL Server instances.
	Create a view with a UNION operator to combine data from all of the instances.
	Create INSTEAD OF triggers to redirect operations.
Encrypt the view definition	Use the WITH ENCRYPTION option.

Chapter 9
Retrieving Data Using Programmable Objects

After completing this chapter, you will be able to:

- Create functions that work like built-in Microsoft SQL Server 2005 functions

- Develop stored procedures, which are small programs stored inside Micrososft SQL Server 2005 that query and update databases

- Develop programs using T-SQL, Visual Basic.NET, or other .NET Framework languages

- Know when programmable objects are best used

In this chapter, you will learn that Microsoft SQL Server 2005 can be more than simply a data repository. It is possible to write programs to run inside SQL Server 2005.

Introduction

Any relational database server, such as SQL Server 2005, is essentially a data repository. As you discovered in previous chapters, you design a database under the rules of relational database theory—that is, using tables, primary keys, foreign keys, and so on. The SQL Server language is then used to query and update data in the server. There is nothing wrong with this process, for several major applications do just that and nothing more.

However, when you start creating real applications, it becomes apparent that going back and forth to the database takes considerable work. For instance, to simply verify whether a table is empty, you must open a connection, submit a query such as SELECT COUNT(*) FROM MyTable, close the connection, and then compare the first column of the first line of the result set with zero. You must also check for errors.

This seems like too much work for such a simple operation. Not only is there a great deal of programming involved, but performance is not optimum. To perform any operation in a database server, you must go through the network, and the network may be slow. Even a fast network involves some latency to transmit packages. You and others may call the database several times, and each call competes with other calls. As these costs accumulate, performance suffers.

You can easily code this logic and run it in the database server itself by using stored procedures and user-defined functions (UDFs). Both stored procedures and UDFs are defined, at least traditionally, by using the Transact-SQL (T-SQL) language. This language includes all of the SQL Server commands that you already know, plus some "procedural language" constructs for things such as:

- Defining and using variables (DECLARE, SET)
- Controlling flow (IF, ELSE, RETURN)
- Using loops (WHILE, BREAK, CONTINUE)
- Defining a block (BEGIN, END)

Starting with SQL Server 2005, you can also write UDFs and stored procedures by using a Microsoft .NET language, such as Visual Basic.NET. Using Visual Basic.NET in this way will be discussed later in this chapter.

Working through a Simple Problem

Take a look at the PurchaseOrderHeader table from the AdventureWorks sample database. This table stores the "header" of sales orders, such as Date, Total, Buyer, and so on. It does not contain the individual items, which are stored in a separate table.

PurchaseOrderHeader (Purchasing)		
Column Name	Data Type	Allow Nulls
🔑 PurchaseOrderID	PurchaseOrderHeader (Purchasing)	
RevisionNumber	tinyint	☐
Status	tinyint	☐
EmployeeID	int	☐
VendorID	int	☐
ShipMethodID	int	☐
OrderDate	datetime	☐
ShipDate	datetime	☑
SubTotal	money	☐
TaxAmt	money	☐
Freight	money	☐
TotalDue		☐
ModifiedDate	datetime	☐
		☐

Suppose that you need to calculate the average value of every purchase order made by a given customer. The query might look something like the following code. You can access this sample code from the sample files as \Ch09\Samples01.sql.

```
SELECT    ISNULL(AVG(TotalDue), 0) as Amount
FROM      Sales.SalesOrderHeader
WHERE     (CustomerID = 23)
```

This is the result:

	Amount
1	15553.0575

The number 23 in the code above is the CustomerID. For other customers, you would supply their CustomerID instead of 23.

> **Note**   The *ISNULL* function is used to return an alternate value (in this case, 0) if the specified CustomerID does not exist.

You might want to discover the average purchase of a customer when given the customer name. The Sales.Store table contains a Name column and a CustomerID column. You can obtain the CustomerID for a given name by using the following query.

```
SELECT CustomerID FROM Sales.Store
WHERE Name = 'Bike World'
```

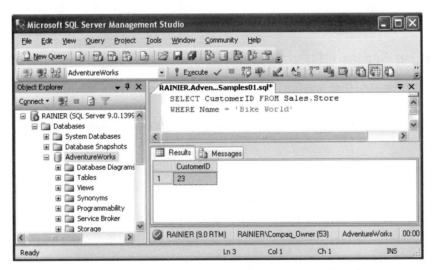

Given the CustomerID, you can use the previous query to find the average purchase amount. The two queries can be combined in the following statement.

```
SELECT ISNULL(AVG(Sales.SalesOrderHeader.TotalDue), 0) AS Amount
FROM Sales.SalesOrderHeader
WHERE CustomerID = (
    SELECT CustomerID FROM Sales.Store
    WHERE Name = 'Bike World')
```

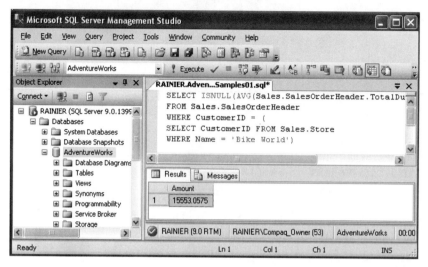

Note that Bike World is a customer name. Notice that the first three lines of this query are similar to those found in the first block of code above. What if you could put the common functionality in a single location? By doing this, you could not only reuse this piece of code, but you could easily change it everywhere it is reused by altering only one location.

Understanding Scalar UDFs

A *scalar UDF* is similar to what most programming languages call a function. It can accept parameters, execute logic, and return data. The returned data must be a scalar type, that is, a string, number, or date value. It cannot be a table or a cursor. A scalar UDF can be used anywhere that a built-in SQL Server function is allowed, and it must also be deterministic.

A *deterministic* function cannot call functions that return different values each time one is called, such as some *Date/Time* functions. Also, it cannot alter the database. On the other hand, a deterministic function may be used with more freedom in a T-SQL query. All T-SQL UDFs must be deterministic or an error will be generated.

The general syntax for defining a scalar UDF is:

```
CREATE FUNCTION [owner_name.] function_name
    ( [{ @parameter_name  scalar_parameter_type [ = default]} [,...n]])
RETURNS scalar_return_type
[WITH <function_option>]
[AS]
BEGIN
    function_body
    RETURN scalar_expression
END
```

In this case, you will define the function as follows on the next page. You can access this sample code from the sample files as \Ch09\Samples02.sql.

```
CREATE FUNCTION GetAvgCust(@CustomerID int)
   RETURNS money
AS
BEGIN
   DECLARE @Amount MONEY
   SET @Amount = 0
   SELECT    @Amount = AVG(TotalDue)
   FROM        Sales.SalesOrderHeader
   WHERE    (CustomerID = @CustomerID)
   RETURN ISNULL(@Amount, 0)
END
```

This function will accept a CustomerID and return the average purchase amount for that customer. You can easily call that function from SQL Server Management Studio, as shown below.

```
PRINT dbo.GetAvgCust(23)
```

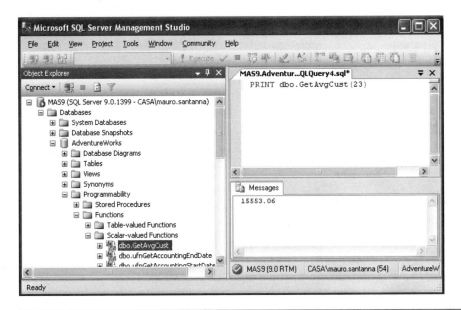

Note   You can use a UDF as if it were a built-in T-SQL function in places such as queries or expressions.

You can also use the function in more complicated scenarios. To retrieve the average purchase amount when given the customer name, you can use the following query.

```
SELECT CustomerID, Name, dbo.GetAvgCust(CustomerID) AS Amount
FROM Sales.Store
WHERE Name = 'Bike World'
```

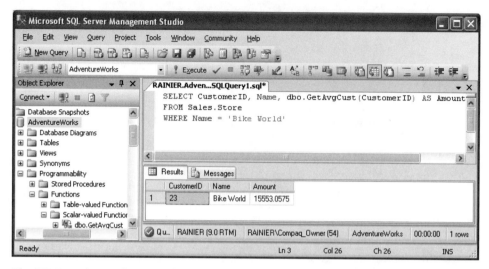

The UDF can be used repeatedly. For instance, suppose that you want the customer names of those whose purchase orders average more than $100,000. You can write a simple query, such as the following:

```
SELECT Name, dbo.GetAvgCust(CustomerID) as Amount FROM Sales.Store
WHERE dbo.GetAvgCust(CustomerID) > 120000
```

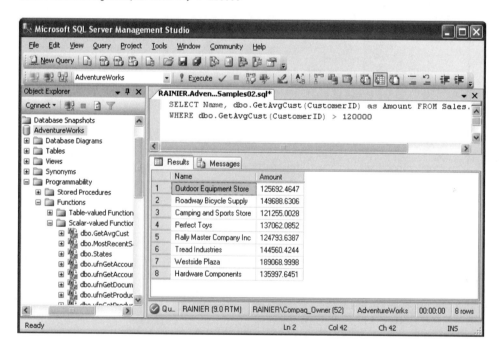

Retrieving Result Sets

In the example presented in the previous section, you reused a query that accepted a parameter and returned a scalar value (a money type, in our example). You may need similar solutions when you want to define something resembling a *parameterized* view, that is, a view that varies depending on a parameter. Suppose that you want to separate the orders that are larger than a certain value. You can write a query against the Sales.SalesOrderHeader table as shown below. You can access this sample code from the sample files as \Ch09\Samples03.sql.

```
SELECT SalesOrderID, CustomerID, TotalDue
FROM Sales.SalesOrderHeader
WHERE (TotalDue > 170000)
```

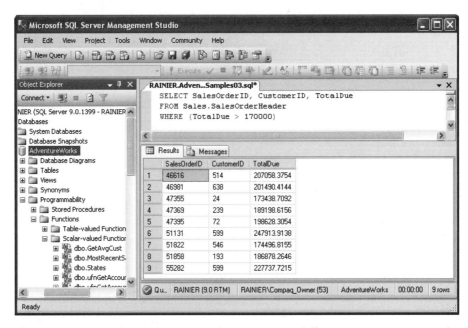

If you want to use that query over and over again in different scenarios, you might choose to create another type of UDF: an in-line UDF.

Using In-Line UDFs

Think of the *in-line UDF* as a parameterized SELECT query or a parameterized view. This type of UDF carries some restrictions: because it can only contain a single SELECT statement within it, it therefore cannot be very complicated. It can accept parameters, but cannot change the state of the database. The general format of an in-line UDF is:

```
CREATE FUNCTION [owner_name.] function_name
    ( [{ @parameter_name  scalar_parameter_type [ = default]} [,..n]])
RETURNS TABLE
[WITH <function_option>]
[AS]
    RETURN select_statement
```

Referring back to the example used in the previous section, you can wrap the query inside an in-line UDF with the following code.

```
CREATE FUNCTION GetSales(@Amount money)
RETURNS TABLE
AS
    RETURN
    SELECT     SalesOrderID, CustomerID, TotalDue
    FROM         Sales.SalesOrderHeader
    WHERE     (TotalDue > @Amount)
```

Once defined, you can use the in-line UDF with parameters as if it were a table, as presented in the following code.

```
SELECT * FROM dbo.GetSales(170000)
```

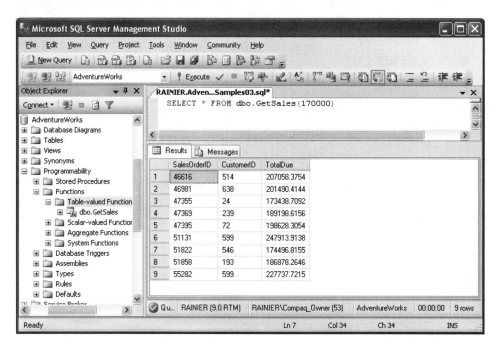

The in-line UDF can also be combined with other tables, such as in a JOIN clause.

```
SELECT GetSales.SalesOrderID, GetSales.CustomerID,
       GetSales.TotalDue, Sales.Store.Name
FROM dbo.GetSales(170000) AS GetSales INNER JOIN
Sales.Store ON GetSales.CustomerID = Sales.Store.CustomerID
```

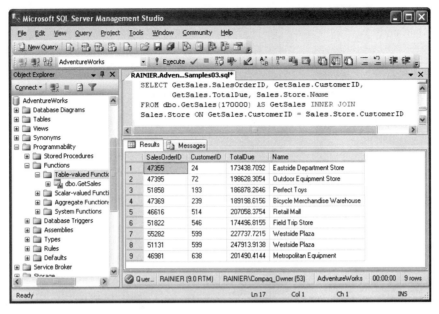

Using Phantom Tables

In-line UDFs work well if all of the code you wish to write is contained in a single SELECT statement. However, you cannot write complex code inside an in-line UDF, and the return type is limited by the schema of the SELECT query that you use.

Assume that you need a table with the compound interest accrued over a period of time. The number of periods is variable, as are the interest rates. For instance, for twelve periods at 1 percent per period, the table would look like the following figure.

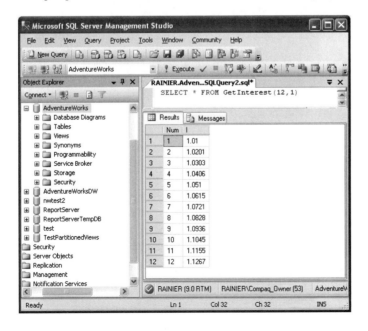

You can generate such a table in many ways. It could be created as an array inside the application. You might instead prefer to create a database table because it is easy to create reports based on database tables or because you need to join the table with other database tables. Using a database table, however, poses some of the following problems.

- You would need to repopulate the table before each use.

- A conflict would be created if your application has several simultaneous users who want to examine different time periods or rates because the table would have to be the same for every user.

You may mitigate the problem by utilizing temporary tables (each user would have her own copy), but you would still need to know when to populate the table and call the specific code.

Using Table-Valued UDFs

A *table-valued UDF* is a UDF that can return a table. Since you define the table's schema inside the function itself, the table does not need to be based on other database tables.

The interest rate table provides a good example. Just like a scalar UDF, it can contain multiple statements. The following is the general format of a table-valued UDF.

```
CREATE FUNCTION [owner_name.] function_name
    ( [{ @parameter_name  scalar_parameter_type [ = default]} [,..n]])
RETURNS @table_variable_name TABLE (table_definition)
[WITH function_option]
AS BEGIN
Function_body
RETURN
END
```

The code below returns the interest table for our example. You can access this sample code from the sample files as \Ch09\Samples04.sql.

```
CREATE FUNCTION dbo.GetInterest( @NumPeriods int, @PercentInterest money  )
RETURNS @InterestTable TABLE
    (
        Num int,
        I money
    )
AS
BEGIN
    DECLARE @N int
    SET @N = 0
    DECLARE @ITot money
    SET @ITot = 1
    WHILE @N < @NumPeriods
    BEGIN
        SET @N = @N + 1
        SET @ITot = @ITot * (1 + (@PercentInterest / 100))
        INSERT INTO @InterestTable VALUES(@N, @ITot)
```

```
        END
        RETURN
END
```

> **Tip** You define the schema of a table-valued UDF inside the function itself after the RETURN clause.

A table-valued UDF is an excellent alternative to a view because it accepts parameters and may contain several complex statements, while a view can only contain a single SQL Server statement.

The table-valued UDF can be used as a table. For instance, to generate a dataset with ten time periods at 6 percent interest per period, you would use:

```
SELECT * FROM GetInterest(10, 6)
```

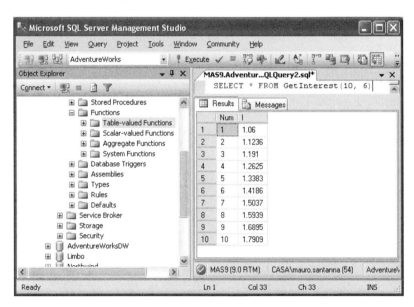

Now suppose that you want to determine the future value of your biggest sales (above $200,000) over the next three years using an interest rate of 8 percent per year. The query used to obtain your sales over $200,000 is:

```
SELECT * FROM dbo.GetSales(200000)
```

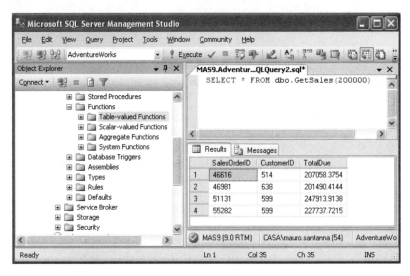

You can join this query with another that returns the interest rate.

```
SELECT GetSales.SalesOrderID, GetInterest.Num as Year,
    GetSales.TotalDue * GetInterest.I AS FutureValue
FROM dbo.GetSales(200000) AS GetSales CROSS JOIN
dbo.GetInterest(3, 8) AS GetInterest
ORDER BY GetSales.SalesOrderID
```

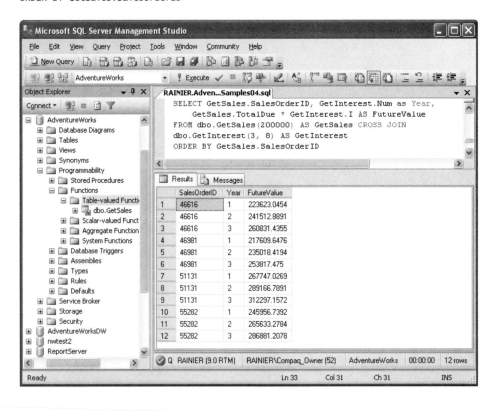

Updating Data

You cannot use a UDF to insert data into a table. Although a UDF can query the database since it is by definition deterministic, it cannot change the database. If you want to update the database, you must use a slightly different method: a stored procedure.

Simplifying Procedures

A *stored procedure* is a small program that runs inside the database server. One reason to write a stored procedure is because some programs are easier to write directly in the database server using T-SQL rather than going back and forth between the application and the server. Consider this simple situation: You have created a database table to store city names and states, as shown below.

	Column Name	Data Type	Allow Nulls
🔑	CITY_ID	int	☐
	STATE	char(2)	☐
	CITY_NAME	char(40)	☐

The following script is written to create the table. You can access the sample code from the sample files as \Ch09\Samples05.sql.

```
CREATE TABLE Cities(
    [CITY_ID] [int] IDENTITY(1,1) NOT NULL,
    [STATE] [char](2) NOT NULL,
    [CITY_NAME] [char](40) NOT NULL,
 CONSTRAINT [PK_Cities] PRIMARY KEY CLUSTERED
(
    [CITY_ID] ASC
) ON [PRIMARY]
) ON [PRIMARY]
```

You need to develop an insertion routine that performs the following logic: If the City/State pair does not exist, then insert it, obtain the new value of the Identity column (the primary key), and return it. If the City/State pair already exists, then return the primary key value of the existing column in the table.

The following VisualBasic.NET/ADO.NET code is written to accomplish this insertion routine. Do not be concerned if you are not familiar with Visual Basic. The point being illustrated here is that a great deal of work is necessary to accomplish such a simple task. This function is included in the sample files as \Ch09\InsertCityQ.vb.

```
Imports Microsoft.SqlServer.Server
Imports System.Data.SqlData

Function InsertCityQ(ByVal City As String, ByVal State As String) As Integer
    Dim RetVal = 0
    ' Create and open the connection
```

```
Dim Cnx As New SqlConnection( _
"Data Source=.;Initial Catalog=AdventureWorks;Integrated Security=True")
Cnx.Open()
Try
    ' Check if the city is already in the table
    Dim CmdCount As New SqlCommand( _
        "SELECT COUNT(*) FROM Cities WHERE " & _
        "(STATE = @STATE AND CITY_NAME = @CITY)", Cnx)
    CmdCount.Parameters.Add("@STATE", Data.SqlDbType.Char).Value = State
    CmdCount.Parameters.Add("@CITY", Data.SqlDbType.Char).Value = City
    Dim Count As Integer = CInt(CmdCount.ExecuteScalar())
    If Count <= 0 Then
        ' It is not, insert into table
        Dim CmdInsert As New SqlCommand( _
            "INSERT INTO Cities(STATE, CITY_NAME) VALUES (@STATE, @CITY)", Cnx)
        CmdInsert.Parameters.Add("@STATE", Data.SqlDbType.Char).Value = State
        CmdInsert.Parameters.Add("@CITY", Data.SqlDbType.Char).Value = City
        CmdInsert.ExecuteNonQuery()
        ' Retrieve the identity value (primary key)
        Dim CmdID As New SqlCommand("SELECT @@identity", Cnx)
        RetVal = CInt(CmdID.ExecuteScalar())
    Else
        ' Yes, it is in the table. Go retrieve the primary key
        Dim CmdPK As New SqlCommand("SELECT CITY_ID FROM Cities WHERE " & _
            "(STATE = @STATE AND CITY_NAME = @CITY)", Cnx)
        CmdPK.Parameters.Add("@STATE", Data.SqlDbType.Char).Value = State
        CmdPK.Parameters.Add("@CITY", Data.SqlDbType.Char).Value = City
        Dim DR As SqlDataReader = CmdPK.ExecuteReader()
        ' Check if the result set is invalid for some strange reason
        If DR Is Nothing Then
            RetVal = -1
        Else
            ' Ok, it is valid, now read one line
            If DR.Read() Then
                ' Retrieve the value of column CITY_ID
                Dim nCity_ID As Integer = DR.GetOrdinal("CITY_ID")
                RetVal = DR.GetInt32(nCity_ID)
            Else
                ' Return -1 if the resultset is empty for some strange reason
                RetVal = -1
            End If
        End If
    End If
Finally
    ' Close the connection
    Cnx.Close()
End Try
' Return the primary key value
Return RetVal
End Function
```

The following script creates a stored procedure that accomplishes the same result.

```
Create procedure InsertCity(@STATE char(2), @CITY char(40))
AS
```

```
BEGIN
  DECLARE @RetVal int
  SET @RetVal = 0
-- Check if the city is already in the table
  IF EXISTS (SELECT * FROM Cities WHERE (STATE = @STATE AND CITY_NAME = @CITY))
  BEGIN
-- Yes, it is in the table. Go retrieve the primary key
    set @RetVal = (SELECT CITY_ID FROM Cities
        WHERE (STATE = @STATE AND CITY_NAME = @CITY))
  END
  ELSE
  BEGIN
-- It is not, insert into table
    INSERT INTO Cities(STATE, CITY_NAME) VALUES (@STATE, @CITY)
-- Retrieve the identity value (primary key)
    SET @RetVal = @@identity
  END
  RETURN (@RetVal)
END
```

The T-SQL code is much simpler to write for several reasons.

■ Specific T-SQL functions can be used that are not directly available to Visual Basic programs, such as EXISTS in the example above.

■ Using parameters is a simpler process in T-SQL than in Visual Basic.

■ The identity value is easier to retrieve because no query is necessary. You simply use @@identity.

■ In this example, there is no need to manage a cursor (*SqlDataReader* in the Visual Basic code).

Once defined, you can call the stored procedure from any environment able to call stored procedures. Environments include:

■ T-SQL code, such as another stored procedure or trigger

■ Legacy environments, such as Visual Basic 6.0 and ASP

■ Any .NET language (Visual Basic.NET, C#.NET, J#.NET) from any .NET application type (such as ASP.NET or Microsoft ClickOnce)

This example calls the stored procedure from Visual Basic.NET code. This code is included in the sample files as \Ch09\InsertCitySP.vb.

```
Imports Microsoft.SqlServer.Server
Imports System.Data.SqlData

Function InsertCitySP(ByVal City As String, ByVal State As String) As Integer
    Dim RetVal = 0
    ' Create and open the connection
    Dim Cnx As New SqlConnection( _
        "Data Source=.;Initial Catalog=AdventureWorks;Integrated Security=True")
```

```
    Cnx.Open()
    Try
        ' Call the stored procedure
        Dim InsertCity As New SqlCommand("InsertCity", Cnx)
        InsertCity.CommandType = Data.CommandType.StoredProcedure
        InsertCity.Parameters.Add(New System.Data.SqlClient.SqlParameter( _
            "@RETURN_VALUE", System.Data.SqlDbType.Int, 4, _
            System.Data.ParameterDirection.ReturnValue, 10, 0, Nothing, _
            System.Data.DataRowVersion.Current, False, Nothing, "", "", ""))
        InsertCity.Parameters.Add("@STATE", Data.SqlDbType.Char).Value = State
        InsertCity.Parameters.Add("@CITY", Data.SqlDbType.Char).Value = City
        InsertCity.ExecuteScalar()
        RetVal = CInt(InsertCity.Parameters("@RETURN_VALUE").Value)
    Finally
        ' Close the connection
        Cnx.Close()
    End Try
    ' Return the primary key value
    Return RetVal
End Function
```

You can use stored procedures for almost any database operation. For instance, you could write a stored procedure to update the Cities table when given the primary key and modified city and state values.

```
CREATE PROCEDURE UpdateCity (@CITY_ID int, @STATE char(2), @CITY char(40))
AS
BEGIN
    UPDATE Cities SET STATE = @STATE, CITY_NAME = @CITY WHERE CITY_ID = @CITY_ID
END
```

You can execute this stored procedure using the following syntax:

```
EXEC UpdateCity 1, 'CA', 'Los Angeles'
```

This stored procedure deletes a line from the table when given its primary key.

```
CREATE PROCEDURE DeleteCity (@CITY_ID int)
AS
BEGIN
    DELETE FROM Cities WHERE CITY_ID = @CITY_ID
END
```

You can execute this stored procedure using the following syntax:

```
EXEC DeleteCity 1
```

You can use a stored procedure to wrap a SELECT statement, although generally you could also do the same by using a UDF. Since a stored procedure does not have an explicit return value, the trick is to place a SELECT query as the last statement so that it will become the stored procedure's result set.

The following stored procedure retrieves all of the cities in a specific state and returns the result set.

```
CREATE PROCEDURE GetCitiesFromState (@STATE char(2))
AS
BEGIN
   SELECT * FROM Cities WHERE @STATE = STATE
END
```

Using Stored Procedures and UDFs

Stored procedures and UDFs are programs that run in the database server. Both can be used to return values and result sets. However, this is where their similarities end. The main differences between the two types of server programs are detailed in Table 9-1.

Table 9-1 Database Server Programs

Stored Procedures	User-Defined Functions
Cannot be used as a function inside a query	Can be used as a function inside a query
Can change the database	Cannot change the database
Do not have an explicit return type, although they can return values and tables	Have an explicit return type through the RETURNS clause
Called without parentheses	Called with parentheses
Can call any function	Must be deterministic, must always return the same value for a given set of parameters, and must not have side effects

Note that stored procedures are analogous to Visual Basic subroutines; UDFs are analogous to Visual Basic functions.

Common Language Runtime UDFs and Procedures

You may choose not to write stored procedures and UDFs because the T-SQL language does not possess all of the bells and whistles of more developed languages, such as C# or Visual Basic.NET. T-SQL is constrained by the following limitations:

■ Limited ability to represent complex datatypes such as classes, arrays, and enumerations, or compositions of them

■ Lack of an extensive class library, such as the .NET Framework, which contains routines for tasks such as low-level disk access, TCP/IP and serial communication, and encryption

■ Limited performance due to its essentially interpreted nature compared with the compiled nature of other languages

■ A development environment that is not as powerful as other languages with capabilities such as automatic builds, unit testing, and powerful debugging

T-SQL works well as a language for data manipulation, but not for calculation or logic-intensive routines such as:

- Heavy numeric (mathematical) calculations
- Custom encryption
- Heavy text handling and formatting
- Complex financial calculations

The SQL Server functions and procedures written with a .NET Framework language, such as C# or Visual Basic.NET, are called common language runtime (CLR), which is the low-level layer of the .NET Framework.

> **Note**   A CLR UDF is not as restricted as a T-SQL UDF. One of its primary relaxed restrictions is that it does not need to be deterministic.

Working with Statistical Calculations

Assume that you have an application in which you must perform numerous statistical calculations over large batches of data. The *factorial function* is a building block for many probability calculations. A factorial (designated by the "!" notation) of integer N is defined as the product of the first N integers. For instance:

4! = 1 * 2 * 3 * 4 = 24

6! = 1 * 2 * 3 * 4 * 5 * 6 = 720

It is possible to write a factorial function using T-SQL, as shown below. You can access this sample code from the sample files as \Ch09\Samples06.sql.

```
CREATE FUNCTION CalcFact ( @N int )
    RETURNS float
AS
BEGIN
    DECLARE @R float
    SET @R = 1
    DECLARE @I int
    SET @I = 1
    WHILE @I <= @N
    BEGIN
        SET @R = @R * @I
        SET @I = @I + 1
    END
    RETURN @R
END
```

Obviously, the factorial function is calculation intensive. To obtain a ballpark idea of how expensive the algorithm is, you can write a procedure to time it. I tested the procedure by using an Athlon XP 3500 processor; although the results are not very scientific, they are sufficient for a ballpark figure.

```
-- Call Factorial of @Val a total of @N times and clock the execution
CREATE PROCEDURE TimeCalc (@Val int, @N int)
AS
BEGIN
    DECLARE @T0 datetime
    DECLARE @T1 datetime
    SET @T0 = GETDATE()
    DECLARE @I int
    SET @I = 1
    WHILE @I <= @N
    BEGIN
        DECLARE @F float
        SET @F = dbo.CalcFact( @Val )
        SET @I = @I + 1
    END
    SET @T1 = GETDATE()
    PRINT DATEDIFF(millisecond, @T0, @T1)
END
```

I calculated the factorial of 150 100,000 times and received this result:

```
TimeCalc 150, 100000

18616
```

Each calculation takes approximately 186 microseconds. Although this may seem fast, it may in fact be somewhat slow and become a bottleneck in your application if you must call this function millions of times in repetition.

All data that passes between SQL Server 2005 and CLR methods should be passed as some special type defined in the namespace *System.Data.SqlTypes*. Some of these special types are found in the middle column of Table 9-2.

Table 9-2   Types Used in CLR/SQL Functions

SQL Server Datatype	CLR/SQL Function Type	CLR Datatype
varbinary, binary	SqlBytes, SqlBinary	Byte[]
nvarchar	SqlChars, SqlString	String, Char[]
uniqueidentifier	SqlGuid	Guid
bit	SqlBoolean	Boolean
tinyint	SqlByte	Byte
smallint	SqlInt16	Int16
int	SqlInt32	Int32
bigint	SqlInt64	Int64
smallmoney, money	SqlMoney	Decimal
numeric, decimal	SqlDecimal	Decimal

Table 9-2   Types Used in CLR/SQL Functions

SQL Server Datatype	CLR/SQL Function Type	CLR Datatype
real	SqlSingle	Single
float	SqlDouble	Double
smalldatetime, datetime	SqlDateTime	DateTime

> **Tip**   SQLChars is a better match for data transfer and access, and SQLString is a better match for performing string operations.

All of the types in the middle column possess a read-only Value property that is used to retrieve its CLR data value. You can assign CLR datatypes to them directly.

> **Note**   Refer to "SQL Server Data Types and Their .NET Framework Equivalents" in SQL Server Books Online for a full list of types.

Another option exists, however. You can write the factorial function by using a .NET language, such as Visual Basic.NET.

Writing a Factorial Function Using Visual Basic.NET

1. Use any text editor, such as Notepad, to write the following code. You can cut and paste this code from \Ch09\Probability.vb in the sample files.

```
Imports Microsoft.SqlServer.Server
Imports System.Data.SqlTypes
Public Class Prob
    <SqlFunction(DataAccess:=DataAccessKind.Read, IsDeterministic:=True)> _
    Public Shared Function Fact(ByVal N As SqlInt32) As SqlDouble
        Dim R As Double = 1
        Dim I As Integer
        For I = 2 To N.Value
            R = R * I
        Next
        Return R
    End Function
End Class
```

> **Note**   Notice the use of the CLR SQL datatypes SqlInt32 and SqlDouble.

2. Create a new folder in the root of your C drive and name the folder **MyFunc**. Save the code as **Probability.vb** under the new folder.

3. Compile the code using the command prompt. The command prompt you use should have its PATH statement set to point to the .NET directory. You can simply use Start | All

Programs | Microsoft Visual Studio 2005 | Visual Studio Tools | Visual Studio 2005 Command Prompt.

4. Type **cd c:\MyFunc** to change to the directory in which you stored the Probability.vb file, then enter the following command at the c:\MyFunc> prompt:

```
C:\MyFunc>vbc /target:library Probability.vb
```

The term vbc is the Visual Basic compiler, and /target:library means that a .DLL instead of an .EXE file is being generated.

> **Caution** A CLR function may be deterministic or non-deterministic. It is your responsibility to supply the correct information in the *IsDeterministic* attribute. If you state that a deterministic function is not deterministic, you are restricting the situations in which it might be used, but no harm is actually done. On the other hand, if you state that a non-deterministic function is deterministic, you may end up with serious logical errors in your application.

5. After the compilation, load the assembly and make it callable from within SQL Server 2005. You can access this code from the sample files as \Ch09\Samples07.sql.

```
-- Load the assembly (DLL) into the database
CREATE ASSEMBLY Probability
FROM 'C:\MyFunc\Probability.dll'
go
-- Create a SQL Server function that calls the CLR function
CREATE FUNCTION CalcFactCLR( @N int )
RETURNS float
AS
EXTERNAL NAME Probability.Prob.Fact
GO
```

6. If this is the first time you are calling CLR functions, you must enable CLR code in the database.

```
-- Adjust SQL Server security to allow CLR functions
EXEC sp_configure 'clr enabled', '1';
GO
-- Required after calling sp_configure
RECONFIGURE
GO
-- Make the assemblies in the database callable without signing the code
ALTER DATABASE AdventureWorks SET TRUSTWORTHY ON
GO
```

You now have a new SQL Server UDF that will call the CLR function. You can easily call it by doing the following:

```
PRINT dbo.CalcFactCLR(6)
```

720

7. Create a timing procedure.

```
CREATE PROCEDURE TimeCalcCLR (@Val int, @N int)
AS
BEGIN
   DECLARE @T0 datetime
   DECLARE @T1 datetime
   SET @T0 = GETDATE()
   DECLARE @I int
   SET @I = 1
   WHILE @I <= @N
   BEGIN
      DECLARE @F float
      SET @F = dbo.CalcFactCLR( @Val )
      SET @I = @I + 1
   END
   SET @T1 = GETDATE()
   PRINT DATEDIFF(millisecond, @T0, @T1)
END
```

8. Complete the timing by calling the function 100,000 times.

```
EXEC TimeCalcCLR 150, 100000

1436
```

My test indicates approximately fourteen microseconds per calculation, which is about thirteen times faster than using T-SQL.

> **Note** This does not mean that CLR is thirteen times faster than T-SQL, for this timing is only valid for the current example. If a function is more database intensive, it is less advantageous to write a CLR function. Conversely, if a function is more calculation inten- sive, it is more advantageous to use a CLR function.

It is possible to write a CLR UDF that returns a table. Since the interest rate example is essen- tially a calculation-intensive function, it presents a good opportunity to rewrite it as a CLR function.

Using Table-Valued UDFs

A table-valued UDF is more complicated than a scalar UDF, and it will be defined as a static method in the CLR code. For the sake of the explanation below, it will be called the "root" method. This method should return either an *IEnumerator* or *IEnumerable* interface. Several CLR classes that deal with collections already implement the *IEnumerable* interface, so it is usually easy to use these classes. The *IEnumerable* interface has a single method called *Get Enumerator* that returns an *IEnumerator* interface. If you want to write your own class from scratch, you must implement the *IEnumerator* interface itself instead of implementing an *IEnu-*

merable interface, which returns the *IEnumerator* interface. To implement an *IEnumerator* interface, you must implement one property and two methods, as listed below.

- **Current property**   Returns the current row of the result set as an object
- *MoveNext* **method**   Moves the current position in the result set to the next row. By definition, the initial position of the cursor in the result set comes before the beginning record; therefore, the consumer (such as SQL Server 2005) will always call *MoveNext* before retrieving any data.
- *Reset* **method**   Resets the current position to fall before the first row

The root method should contain a *SqlFunctionAttribute* that indicates what the *FillRow* method is (typically, another static method in the same class as the root method). The *FillRow* method receives an object returned by a previous call to *IEnumerator.Current* and breaks it into multiple-column values using output parameters. Note that the first parameter is always of the type *Object*. The other parameters are *ByRef*, and their types correspond to a SQL Server type that is compatible with the *TableDefinition* attribute parameter.

Creating a Table-Valued UDF

1. Use any text editor, such as Notepad, to write the following code. You can cut and paste this code from \Ch09\Rates.vb in the sample files.

```vb
Imports Microsoft.SqlServer.Server
Imports System.Collections
Imports System.Data.SqlTypes

' Represents a table row in memory
Public Class TableRow
    Public N As Integer
    Public Rate As Double
    Sub New(ByVal N As Integer, ByVal Rate As Double)
        Me.N = N
        Me.Rate = Rate
    End Sub
End Class

' Main class that implements an IEnumerator
Public Class TblLoader
    Implements IEnumerator

    ' Current values of the IEnumerator
    Private CurrentIndex As Integer = 0
    Private CurrentFactor As Double = 1
    ' Stored constructor arguments
    Private NumPeriods As Integer
    Private PercentInterest As Double

    ' Constructor with the table's arguments
    Sub New(ByVal NumPeriods As Integer, ByVal PercentInterest As Double)
        ' Store as class variables
        Me.NumPeriods = NumPeriods
```

```vb
            Me.PercentInterest = PercentInterest
        End Sub


        ' Returns the current row
        Public ReadOnly Property Current() As Object _
            Implements IEnumerator.Current
            Get
                Return New TableRow(CurrentIndex, CurrentFactor)
            End Get
        End Property


        ' Get the next element in the enumeration
        Public Function MoveNext() As Boolean _
            Implements IEnumerator.MoveNext
            If CurrentIndex < NumPeriods Then
                ' Calculate next value
                CurrentIndex += 1
                CurrentFactor *= (1 + PercentInterest / 100)
                Return True
            Else
                Return False
            End If
        End Function


        ' Reset the enumeration
        Public Overridable Sub Reset() _
            Implements IEnumerator.Reset
            CurrentIndex = 0
            CurrentFactor = 1
        End Sub
    End Class

Public Class Interest
    ' Main function
    <SqlFunction(FillRowMethodName:="FillRow", _
        TableDefinition:="N int not null, Rate float not null")> _
    Public Shared Function AppreciationTbl(ByVal NumPeriods As Integer, _
        ByVal PercentInterest As Double) As IEnumerator
        Return New TblLoader(NumPeriods, PercentInterest)
    End Function

    ' Function called to retrieve each row
    Public Shared Sub FillRow(ByVal Obj As Object, ByRef N As SqlInt32, _
        ByRef Rate As SqlDouble)
        ' Check if the object is valid
        If Not (Obj Is Nothing) Then
            ' Retrieve the values
            Dim R As TableRow = CType(Obj, TableRow)
            N = R.N
            Rate = R.Rate
        Else
            ' Invalid object
            N = 0
            Rate = 1
        End If
```

```
End Sub

End Class
```

2.   Save the file as **Rates.vb** under the c:\MyFunc folder.

3.   Compile the code, as you did earlier with the Probability example, by using the Visual Studio 2005 command prompt.

```
C:\MyFunc>vbc /target:library Rates.vb
```

4.   Load the assembly within SQL Server 2005. You can access this sample code from the sample files as \Ch09\Samples08.sql.

```
CREATE ASSEMBLY Rates
FROM 'C:\MyFunc\rates.dll'
GO
CREATE FUNCTION IRate(@NumPeriods int, @PercentInterest float)
RETURNS TABLE(N int, Rate float)
AS
EXTERNAL NAME Rates.Interest.AppreciationTbl
GO
```

5.   Call the table function:

```
SELECT * FROM IRate(12, 1)
```

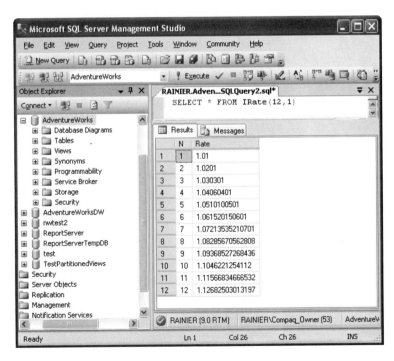

> **Note**   The difference between the results returned by the *GetInterest* function and the *IRate* function is due to different levels of precision in the variable used to calculate the result. *GetInterest* uses a money datatype, whereas *IRate* uses a double datatype.

Working with CLR Stored Procedures

CLR stored procedures can be created in a similar fashion as UDFs. The main difference between the two is that a stored procedure more closely resembles a basic subroutine instead of a function because it cannot return a value and must be called without parentheses. Since a CLR UDF does not need to be deterministic, there is nothing that a CLR stored procedure can do that a CLR UDF cannot also do.

Performing File Operations

You can write a stored procedure to perform simple file operations such as copying, moving, and deleting. This procedure can have several uses, such as managing an exported file created with a utility (e.g., BCP utility).

> **Note**   Stored procedures cannot be used to access opened files, such as the database files themselves.

Creating a CLR Stored Procedure

1. Write the following Visual Basic code. This code is included in the sample files as FileUtil.vb.

```
Imports System.IO
Imports System.Data.SqlTypes

Public Class FileUtil

    Public Shared Sub CopyFile(ByVal SourceFileName As SqlString, ByVal DestFileName A
s SqlString)
        File.Copy(SourceFileName, DestFileName)
    End Sub

    Public Shared Sub DeleteFile(ByVal FileName As SqlString)
        File.Delete(FileName)
    End Sub

    Public Shared Sub MoveFile(ByVal SourceFileName As SqlString, ByVal DestFileName A
s SqlString)
        File.Move(SourceFileName, DestFileName)
    End Sub

End Class
```

2. Save the code as **FileUtil.vb** in the c:\MyFunc folder.

3. Compile the code using the Visual Studio 2005 command prompt, as you did earlier with the Probability and Rates examples.

```
C:\MyFunc>vbc /target:library FileUtil.vb
```

4. Load the assembly inside SQL Server 2005. You can access this sample code from the sample files as \Ch09\Samples09.sql.

```
-- Load the assembly
CREATE ASSEMBLY FileUtil
FROM 'C:\MyFunc\FileUtil.dll'
WITH permission_set = external_access
GO
-- Create a SQL Server function that calls the CLR function
CREATE PROCEDURE CopyFile( @SourceFileName nvarchar(256), @DestFileName nvarchar(256) )
AS
EXTERNAL NAME FileUtil.FileUtil.CopyFile
GO
-- Create a SQL Server function that calls the CLR function
CREATE PROCEDURE MoveFile( @SourceFileName nvarchar(256), @DestFileName nvarchar(256) )
AS
EXTERNAL NAME FileUtil.FileUtil.MoveFile
GO
-- Create a SQL Server function that calls the CLR function
CREATE PROCEDURE DeleteFile( @FileName nvarchar(256) )
AS
EXTERNAL NAME FileUtil.FileUtil.DeleteFile
GO
```

Note   Notice that "with permission_set = external_access" is being used in the above code. This is necessary because the CLR assembly will access the external file system, which is beyond the control of SQL Server 2005. Even then, the account under which the methods will be called must contain enough privileges to access the files, meaning both ACL permission and CLR Code Access Security permission. These permissions may be necessary for both UDFs and stored procedures.

5. Call the procedure, as in the following example. (Make sure you have a file named Export.txt in the c:\Data folder and that you have a c:\Backup folder.)

```
EXEC CopyFile 'c:\Data\Export.txt', 'c:\Backup\Export.txt'
```

Conclusion

User-defined functions using the T-SQL language are a great way to extend the functionality of SQL Server 2005 when you want tight integration with queries, such as supplying conditions on a WHERE clause or creating a calculated column. T-SQL UDFs possess a major limitation: they must be deterministic and, as such, cannot alter the database.

To alter the database, you must use a T-SQL stored procedure. It's a good idea to use T-SQL stored procedures to update the database when your business logic needs tight integration with database operations. Using T-SQL stored procedures for updates has the added advantage of being parameterized by definition, thus making them less prone to a security issue known as SQL Injection.

Neither T-SQL UDFs nor stored procedures are the best alternative if your code contains little database manipulation and a great deal of unrelated logic, such as string handling and numeric calculation. In those situations, it is best to use your standard high-level language and run the code in a machine other than the database server such as the client, a Web server, or a component server, depending on your application architecture. If you want both tight database integration and logic-intensive operations, you may find that T-SQL is not well suited to the task due to poor performance or lack of some advanced programming features. In those cases, you can use a .NET language, such as Visual Basic.NET, C#, or C++, to write the logic-intensive code and call it from inside SQL Server 2005 itself using SQL Server CLR functions and procedures.

Chapter 9 Quick Reference

To	Do This
Create a T-SQL function that does not touch the database	Create a scalar UDF using the CREATE FUNCTION statement with a RETURNS clause.
Create a T-SQL function that returns the result set of a SQL SELECT statement	Create an in-line UDF using the CREATE FUNCTION statement with a RETURNS TABLE clause.
Create a T-SQL function that returns a result set involving more than a single SELECT statement that may use parameters and has programming logic	Create a table-valued UDF using the CREATE FUNCTION statement with a RETURNS @tablename TABLE clause.
Update data using T-SQL	Create a stored procedure using the CREATE PROCEDURE statement.
Create T-SQL-callable code that is CPU or calculation intensive rather than database intensive	Create a CLR UDF or CLR stored procedure.

Part IV
How to Modify Data in Microsoft SQL Server 2005

Chapter 10

Inserting Data in Microsoft SQL Server 2005

After completing this chapter, you will be able to:

■ Add information to your database

■ Secure information using view inserts instead of table inserts

■ Import data

■ Insert information asynchronously

You have already learned how to retrieve information from the database and handle other special considerations, such as transactions. In this chapter, you will learn how to add information that the user needs into the database from custom applications and other sources.

Using the INSERT Statement

The basis of adding information is the INSERT clause. This clause uses the following syntax:

```
INSERT INTO [<ServerName>.][<DataBaseName>.]<SchemaName>.<TableName>
        (<FieldName1>[,<FieldName2>...])
    VALUES
        (<Value1>[,<Value2>..])
```

If you execute the INSERT sentence with a connection to the current database, you can simply use the <SchemaName>.<TableName> form without including the server and database names.

When you want to insert a record, you must carefully consider some column limitations.

■ A column defined using the identity attribute cannot be inserted. You do not enlist the column in the field list and therefore do not assign a value for it.

■ Timestamp is not an assignable datatype.

■ Remember the constraints defined for each column.

■ Use CONVERT or CAST when necessary.

Creating an INSERT Sentence with SQL Server Management Studio

You can use Microsoft SQL Server Management Studio to help you create an INSERT sentence.

Creating an INSERT Sentence

1. From Object Explorer in SQL Server Management Studio, right-click the desired table.

2. Choose Script Table As, and then choose Insert To from the context menu.

3. Select New Query Editor Window. SQL Server Management Studio will create a template for you.

4. From the Query menu, select Specify Values For Template Parameters.

   You can now define your own values. The wizard takes care of such things as identity or timestamp fields, but allows you to define the rest of the values.

Look at the INSERT sentence generated for the Sales.SalesOrderHeader data table in the AdventureWorks database.

```
INSERT INTO [AdventureWorks].[Sales].[SalesOrderHeader]
           ([RevisionNumber]
           ,[OrderDate]
           ,[DueDate]
           ,[ShipDate]
           ,[Status]
           ,[OnlineOrderFlag]
           ,[PurchaseOrderNumber]
           ,[AccountNumber]
           ,[CustomerID]
           ,[ContactID]
           ,[SalesPersonID]
           ,[TerritoryID]
           ,[BillToAddressID]
           ,[ShipToAddressID]
           ,[ShipMethodID]
           ,[CreditCardID]
           ,[CreditCardApprovalCode]
           ,[CurrencyRateID]
           ,[SubTotal]
           ,[TaxAmt]
           ,[Freight]
           ,[Comment]
           ,[rowguid]
           ,[ModifiedDate])
     VALUES
           (<RevisionNumber, tinyint,>
           ,<OrderDate, datetime,>
           ,<DueDate, datetime,>
           ,<ShipDate, datetime,>
           ,<Status, tinyint,>
           ,<OnlineOrderFlag, Flag,>
           ,<PurchaseOrderNumber, OrderNumber,>
           ,<AccountNumber, AccountNumber,>
           ,<CustomerID, int,>
           ,<ContactID, int,>
           ,<SalesPersonID, int,>
           ,<TerritoryID, int,>
```

```
,<BillToAddressID, int,>
,<ShipToAddressID, int,>
,<ShipMethodID, int,>
,<CreditCardID, int,>
,<CreditCardApprovalCode, varchar(15),>
,<CurrencyRateID, int,>
,<SubTotal, money,>
,<TaxAmt, money,>
,<Freight, money,>
,<Comment, nvarchar(128),>
,<rowguid, uniqueidentifier,>
,<ModifiedDate, datetime,>)
```

Using Special Values for Row Insertion

You may want to use special values when inserting a row. In the SalesOrderHeader example, the rowguid column requires a value of uniqueidentifier as the datatype. In that case, you can use the *NEWID()* function. DueDate is another good example. If you want to assign the actual date and time to this column, you can use the *GETDATE()* function. If a column allows NULL and you do not want to specify a value, you can use the NULL keyword. Finally, if you look at the data definition language for this table, the ModifiedDate column has an assigned default value that refers to the *GETDATE()* function. You can simply use the DEFAULT keyword to assign the default value.

 Note   You can find all of the script samples for this chapter in \Ch10\Sample Codes\Chapter 10 Scripts in the sample files.

The following code sample (Insert Special Values.sql) demonstrates how to use these special values.

```
INSERT INTO [AdventureWorks].[Sales].[SalesOrderHeader]
        ([RevisionNumber]
        ,[OrderDate]
        ,[DueDate]
        ,[ShipDate]
        ,[Status]
        ,[OnlineOrderFlag]
        ,[PurchaseOrderNumber]
        ,[AccountNumber]
        ,[CustomerID]
        ,[ContactID]
        ,[SalesPersonID]
        ,[TerritoryID]
        ,[BillToAddressID]
        ,[ShipToAddressID]
        ,[ShipMethodID]
        ,[CreditCardID]
        ,[CreditCardApprovalCode]
        ,[CurrencyRateID]
```

```
        ,[SubTotal]
        ,[TaxAmt]
        ,[Freight]
        ,[Comment]
        ,[rowguid]
        ,[ModifiedDate])
    VALUES
        (0 --RevisionNumber
        ,GETDATE() -- Actual date
        ,DATEADD(day,5,GETDATE()) -- five days from now
        ,null -- ShipDate is not yet known
        ,1
        ,1
        ,null -- order number
        ,null -- AccountNumber
        ,1 -- CustomerID
        ,1 -- ContactID
        ,1 -- SalesPersonID
        ,1 -- TerritoryID
        ,1 -- BillToAddressID
        ,1 -- ShipToAddressID
        ,1 -- ShipMethodID
        ,1 -- CreditCardID
        ,'ok' -- CreditCardApprovalCode
        ,1 -- CurrencyRateID
        ,100 -- SubTotal
        ,5 -- TaxAmt
        ,0 -- Freight
        ,null -- Comment
        ,NEWID() -- rowguid
        ,DEFAULT -- ModifiedDate
    )
```

Using Other Forms of the INSERT Statement

There may be times when you merely want to insert a row into a table. If all of the columns have defined default values or allow NULLs, you can insert a row using the following syntax:

```
INSERT INTO <TableName> DEFAULT VALUES
```

If you want to keep summarized information in a separate table for the purpose of results analysis, you can use code to derive that data from the detailed table. You may instead want to increase the performance of your queries by executing a process to accumulate the information in another database.

The following code sample (Create TestTable.sql) adds a data table to the AdventureWorks database.

```
USE [AdventureWorks]
GO
CREATE TABLE [Sales].[TotalSales](
    [TotalSalesId] [int] IDENTITY(1,1) NOT NULL,
    [Period] [char](7)  NOT NULL,
```

```
    [CustomerID] int  NOT NULL,
    [Total] [money] NOT NULL,
 CONSTRAINT [PK_TotalSales] PRIMARY KEY CLUSTERED
(
    [TotalSalesId] ASC
)WITH (IGNORE_DUP_KEY = OFF) ON [PRIMARY]
) ON [PRIMARY]
GO
```

The data needed to fill this table can be obtained from the following sentence.

```
SELECT   CONVERT(varchar(7), OrderDate, 120) AS OrderMonth,
      CustomerID,
      SUM(TotalDue) AS TotalDue
FROM   Sales.SalesOrderHeader
GROUP BY
   CustomerID,
   CONVERT(varchar(7), OrderDate, 120)
```

In addition, you can insert the results into the new table with a simple Transact-SQL (T-SQL) statement, such as the following:

```
INSERT INTO Sales.TotalSales (Period,CustomerID,Total)
SELECT   CONVERT(varchar(7), OrderDate, 120) AS OrderMonth,
      CustomerID,
      SUM(TotalDue) AS TotalDue
FROM   Sales.SalesOrderHeader
GROUP BY
   CustomerID,
   CONVERT(varchar(7), OrderDate, 120)
```

Notice that the values to be inserted must match the datatypes of the destination columns. Also, because the TotalSalesId column contains the identity attribute, it is not managed by the script and will be updated automatically.

Inserting Data through Views

You can insert values into views in the same way that you insert values into tables. However, you must be careful to only insert values for columns that belong to a single table. If a view includes several tables, the insert values can only manage columns from one of the tables. For example, the CategoryName column cannot be updated in the following view.

Inserting a Value into a View

1. Open SQL Server Management Studio and connect to your server.

2. Click the New Query button and type the following:

   ```
   USE [Adventureworks]
   GO
   CREATE VIEW [dbo].[vProductFullCategories]
   AS
   ```

```
SELECT
    Production.ProductSubcategory.ProductSubcategoryID,
    Production.ProductCategory.Name AS CategoryName,
     Production.ProductSubcategory.Name
FROM
    Production.ProductSubcategory
INNER JOIN
    Production.ProductCategory
        ON Production.ProductSubcategory.ProductCategoryID
        = Production.ProductCategory.ProductCategoryID

GO
```

3. Try to insert a row by using the following sentence:

```
INSERT INTO [AdventureWorks].[Production].[vProductFullCategories]
            ([ProductSubcategoryID]
            ,[CategoryName]
            ,[Name])
        VALUES
            (1
            ,'Bikes'
            ,'My New Subcategory')
```

You will receive the following error:

```
Msg 4405, Level 16, State 1, Line 1
View or function 'AdventureWorks.Production.vProductFullCategories' is not
updatable because the modification affects multiple base tables.
```

Using the WITH Clause

You can use a WITH clause to obtain recursive information to insert into another table. This is a good way to reconstruct multilevel relational information into a single table.

Consider the following example: The managers at Adventure Works want to send a special Christmas e-mail to all employees. They decide that each manager should send the e-mail to his own employees. You can create a table containing information about each manager's employees and the sender's e-mail address.

The table can be constructed as follows:

```
CREATE TABLE [Person].[ChristmasMails](
    [EMailID] [int],
    [FirstName] [dbo].[Name] NOT NULL,
    [LastName] [dbo].[Name] NOT NULL,
    [EmailAddress] [nvarchar](50)  NULL,
    [EmailSender] [nvarchar](50)  NULL
)
GO
```

Using a common table expression, you can then build the entire list of destinations, with the sender's e-mail address included as one of the columns in the query. Since one of the employees is the top manager, that person will not receive an e-mail and the sender's address will be an empty string.

```
WITH MailDestinations(EmployeeID, FirstName, LastName,
    EmailAddress, EMailSender)
AS
(
    SELECT   HumanResources.Employee.EmployeeID,
        Person.Contact.FirstName,
        Person.Contact.LastName,
        Person.Contact.EmailAddress,
        CONVERT(nvarchar(50),'') AS EMailSender
    FROM HumanResources.Employee
        INNER JOIN Person.Contact
            ON HumanResources.Employee.ContactID = Person.Contact.ContactID
        WHERE     (HumanResources.Employee.ManagerID IS NULL)
    UNION ALL
    SELECT   e.EmployeeID,
        Person.Contact.FirstName,
        Person.Contact.LastName,
        Person.Contact.EmailAddress,
        d.EmailAddress AS EmailSender
    FROM HumanResources.Employee AS e
        INNER JOIN Person.Contact
            ON e.ContactID = Person.Contact.ContactID
        JOIN MailDestinations AS d
            ON e.ManagerID = d.EmployeeID
)
INSERT INTO [Person].[ChristmasMails]
    SELECT * FROM MailDestinations
```

The first SELECT statement selects the information about the top manager who has no assigned Manager ID. The second section makes recursive queries to obtain information about those employees who are supervised by the top manager. The query then recurses to obtain information about the employees of those who are already in the common table expression until no more employees are found. The execution of this query will add 290 records to the [Person].[ChristmasMails] table.

Using INSTEAD OF INSERT Triggers on Views

Suppose that you use the vProductFullCategories statement to give users the opportunity to obtain information from an Office application, such as Excel. However, the user tries to use the same view from Microsoft Access, assuming he has no rights to insert information into the tables. In fact, the user *can* do that if he has insert rights on the view. Access tries to insert values for all of the columns, including those belonging to other tables.

You can use an INSTEAD OF INSERT trigger on the view to discard those values. Moreover, you can manage the insertion in several related tables inside a view. The trigger, like any trigger, uses a special table named "inserted" that receives the values defined by the user. The trigger can select from this table to insert the appropriate values in one or more tables.

Adding the following INSTEAD Of INSERT trigger allows you to manage the insertion properly.

```
CREATE TRIGGER [Production].[vProductFullCategoriesInsertTrigger]
   on [Production].[vProductFullCategories]
INSTEAD OF INSERT
AS
BEGIN
   DECLARE @idCategory INT
-- Retrieve the id from the ProductCategory table
   SET @idCategory=
      (SELECT ProductCategoryID
         FROM Production.ProductCategory
         WHERE     (Name =
            (SELECT CategoryName FROM inserted)
         )
      )
-- Insert the proper values
INSERT INTO [AdventureWorks].[Production].[ProductSubcategory]
         ([ProductCategoryID]
         ,[Name]
         ,[rowguid]
         ,[ModifiedDate])
      SELECT @IdCategory
         ,inserted.name
         ,newid()
         ,getdate() FROM inserted
END
```

Importing Data into SQL Server 2005

You may need to add information from legacy systems or databases into your database. There are several tools available for this purpose. In each situation, choosing the appropriate tool depends on the source, the amount of information, and occasionally on security considerations.

Using the BCP Utility

This command line utility allows you to import or export large amounts of data. As a command line utility, BCP can be used to initialize the database for an application during the application setup process. BCP can be used to fill some tables in your database with certain information according to user selections. As with any command line utility, you must understand the different switches and command options.

> **Note**   Refer to SQL Server Books Online for a complete list of options.

BCP requires the names of the source/destination database and table (or view), an action identifier such as *in* or *out*, and the name of the external data file. You may need to specify the server and instance name (if it is not the default instance), plus the username and password if you need to specify information other than the ID of the current user.

The basic BCP syntax is:

```
BCP <Database>.<Schema>.<TableName>/<ViewName>
        <in/out>
<ExternalFileName>
<SecurityModifier>
<FormatModifier>
```

The following example exports the records from the Product data table to a comma-separated values file.

```
bcp AdventureWorks.Production.Product out "Products.txt" -T -c
```

With that flat file, you can import the information into another database.

If you execute the following script (located in the sample files as CREATE Production2 Table.sql), you will create a new Product table named Product2 in the AdventureWorks database.

```
CREATE TABLE [Production].[Product2](
    [ProductID] [int] IDENTITY(1,1) NOT NULL,
    [Name] [dbo].[Name] NOT NULL,
    [ProductNumber] [nvarchar](25) COLLATE SQL_Latin1_General_CP1_CI_AS NOT NULL,
    [MakeFlag] [dbo].[Flag] NOT NULL CONSTRAINT [DF_Product_MakeFlag2]  DEFAULT ((1)),
    [FinishedGoodsFlag] [dbo].[Flag] NOT NULL CONSTRAINT [DF_Product_FinishedGoodsFlag2]
 DEFAULT ((1)),
    [Color] [nvarchar](15) COLLATE SQL_Latin1_General_CP1_CI_AS NULL,
    [SafetyStockLevel] [smallint] NOT NULL,
    [ReorderPoint] [smallint] NOT NULL,
    [StandardCost] [money] NOT NULL,
    [ListPrice] [money] NOT NULL,
    [Size] [nvarchar](5) COLLATE SQL_Latin1_General_CP1_CI_AS NULL,
    [SizeUnitMeasureCode] [nchar](3) COLLATE SQL_Latin1_General_CP1_CI_AS NULL,
    [WeightUnitMeasureCode] [nchar](3) COLLATE SQL_Latin1_General_CP1_CI_AS NULL,
    [Weight] [decimal](8, 2) NULL,
    [DaysToManufacture] [int] NOT NULL,
    [ProductLine] [nchar](2) COLLATE SQL_Latin1_General_CP1_CI_AS NULL,
    [Class] [nchar](2) COLLATE SQL_Latin1_General_CP1_CI_AS NULL,
    [Style] [nchar](2) COLLATE SQL_Latin1_General_CP1_CI_AS NULL,
    [ProductSubcategoryID] [int] NULL,
    [ProductModelID] [int] NULL,
    [SellStartDate] [datetime] NOT NULL,
    [SellEndDate] [datetime] NULL,
    [DiscontinuedDate] [datetime] NULL,
    [rowguid] [uniqueidentifier] ROWGUIDCOL  NOT NULL CONSTRAINT [DF_Product_rowguid2]
 DEFAULT (newid()),
    [ModifiedDate] [datetime] NOT NULL CONSTRAINT [DF_Product_ModifiedDate2]
        DEFAULT (getdate()),
```

```
    CONSTRAINT [PK_Product_ProductID2] PRIMARY KEY CLUSTERED
    (
        [ProductID] ASC
    )WITH (IGNORE_DUP_KEY = OFF) ON [PRIMARY]
    ) ON [PRIMARY]

    GO
```

You can then import the data by using the following syntax:

```
bcp AdventureWorks.Production.Product2 in "Products.txt" -T -c
```

When importing or exporting complex data table structures, it is advisable to precisely define what structure your flat file will have. You can do this by using the format modifier instead of *in* or *out*, using *nul* as the output file, and specifying a format file name as follows:

```
bcp AdventureWorks.Production.ProductCategory format nul  -T  -f categories.fmt -c
```

The categories.fmt file in this example contains descriptors for each file. Since the −c modifier instructs the BCP utility to export or import as a character, all of the columns are defined as characters.

1	SQLCHAR	0	12	"\t"	1	ProductCategoryID	""
2	SQLCHAR	0	100	"\t"	2	NameSQL_Latin1_General_CP1_CI_AS	

However, if you want to use native SQL datatypes, you must use the −N modifier instead of the −c modifier.

Using the BULK INSERT Command

You need to import information into a database, but you find that you cannot use the BCP tool because security constraints in the user's environment do not allow the user to open a command prompt window. There is a T-SQL sentence available to solve this problem. The BULK INSERT command requires arguments similar to the BCP command. At a minimum, it requires the name of the destination table and the file name for the source.

```
BULK INSERT
    [AdventureWorks].[Production].[Product2]
    FROM 'C:\Products.txt'
```

In addition, you can specify modifiers to set the row delimiter and column delimiter, to use a format file, and so on.

Using Integration Services to Insert Data

In the real world, things are not always as easy as expected. Try to migrate an application based on an Access database or on .dbf files created with dBase or Fox and you will see how difficult it can be. Occasionally, you may need to obtain information from other sources, such as mainframes or other database or legacy systems. You may also need to create a new application based on an existing one and enhance the database while users continue to use the legacy application during your development process.

These three examples demonstrate the need to understand the features of Integration Services. You will initially address Integration Services by creating a simple export package using a wizard.

Creating an Export Package

1. In SQL Server Management Studio, right-click the AdventureWorks database in Object Explorer and select Tasks | Export Data. This will start the SQL Server Import And Export Data Wizard.

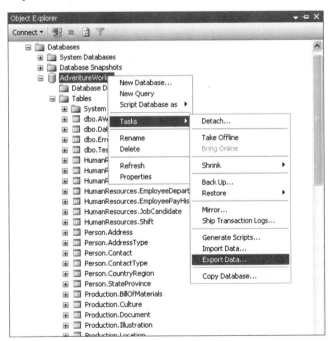

2.   After the welcome page appears, your server and database will already be selected in the
     Choose A Data Source page.

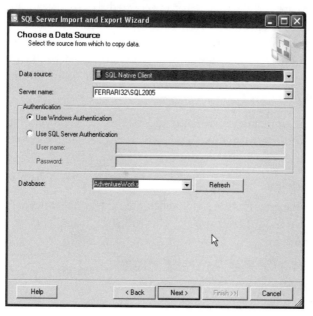

3.   On the Choose A Destination page, select Flat File Destination from the Destination
     drop-down list and enter a filename.

4.   Check the Column Names In The First Data Row checkbox to add column names at the
     beginning of the text file.

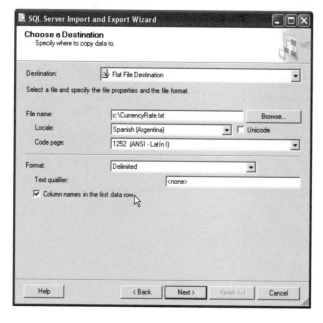

5. On the Specify Table Copy Or Query page, keep the Copy Data From One Or More Tables Or Views option selected.

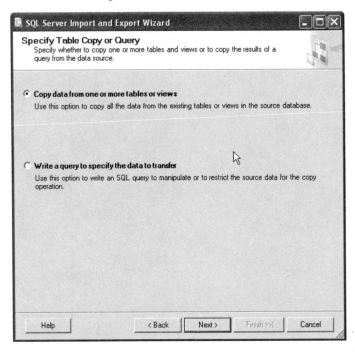

6. On the Configure Flat File Destination page, select [AdventureWorks].[Sales].[CurrencyRate].

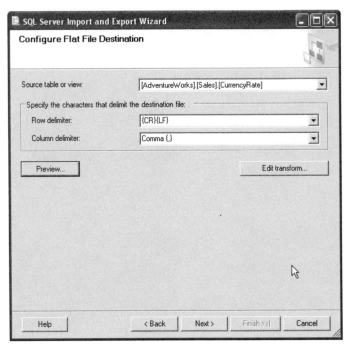

7. On the Save And Execute Package page, uncheck the Execute Immediately checkbox. Check the Save SSIS Package option and select the File System option.

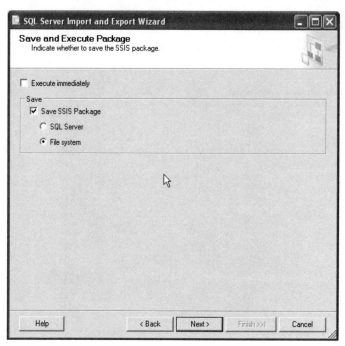

8. In the Package Protection Level dialog box, select Do Not Save Sensitive Data from the drop-down list.

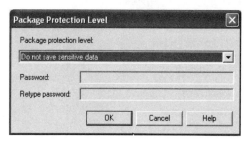

9. Finally, in the Save SSIS Package dialog box, assign a name and filename to your package.

Editing the Package

1. Open Visual Studio 2005.

2. On the File menu, point to Open and then click File...

3. Navigate to your package file (with the .dtsx extension) and open it. You will see something similar to the following figure.

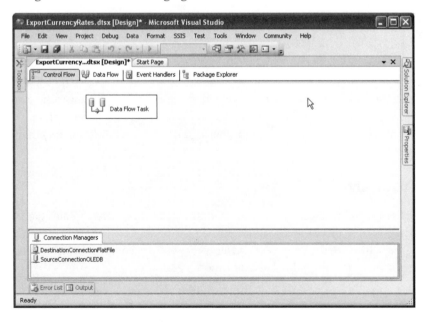

The Package editor displays four tabs.

- Control Flow

- Data Flow

- Event Handlers

- Package Explorer

The Data Flow tab displays the exporting process from a database connection to a flat file.

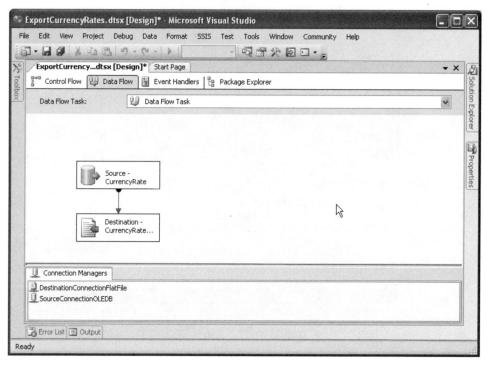

4. Right-click each element, the connections, and the green arrow to view how the package stores all of the information needed to execute the task. Moreover, move your mouse pointer over the Toolbox tab to view a variety of tasks and elements that are available to use in a package.

Creating Your Own Package

Consider the following scenario: You need to update the CurrencyRates table with new information provided in an Excel worksheet. The requirements state that you must assign the datetime fields with the dates of the insert process. To accomplish this, you must intercept the import process to assign the date and time.

Creating a New Project

1. Open Visual Studio 2005.

2. From the File menu, select New | Project, then select the Business Intelligence Projects type and the Integration Services Project template.

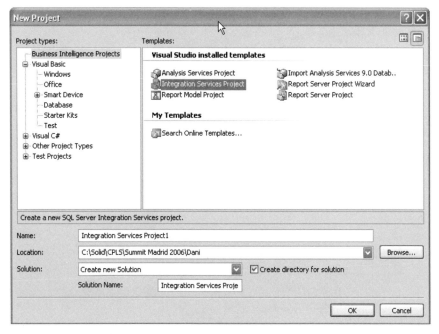

3. Enter a name for your project. When you click OK in the dialog box, you will view the same environment that is seen when you open the package created by the wizard (as in Step 3 in the previous procedure).

Defining the Source

1. Select the Data Flow tab. From the Data Flow Sources section in the Toolbox, drag an Excel Source to the designer.

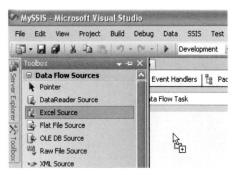

2. Right-click it (at the bottom of the designer) and select Edit.

3. Click the New button to the right of the OLE DB Connection Manager drop-down list.

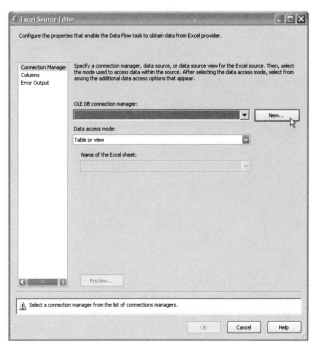

4. Browse to the \Ch10\SSIS\CurrencyRate200602.xls file in the sample files, click the Open button, and then click OK.

5. From the Name Of The Excel Sheet drop-down list, select CurrencyRate$ and click OK. This completes the source configuration.

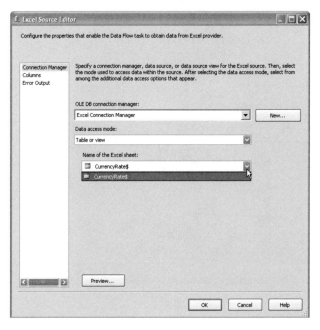

Defining the Destination

1. From the Data Flow Destinations section in the Toolbox, drag a SQL Server Destination.

2. Right-click it and select Edit. You will receive a message that there is no connection.

3. To the right of the OLE DB Connection Manager drop-down list, click the New button and define the connection to AdventureWorks in your database.

4. Select [Sales].[CurrencyRate] from the Use A Table Or View drop-down list and click Cancel. You must follow additional steps to complete the definition of this destination, which you will perform later.

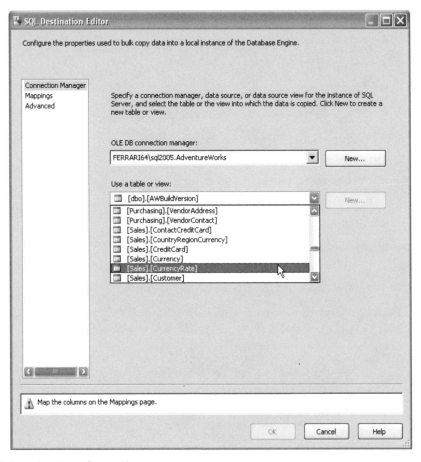

Defining the Transformation

1. From the Data Flow Transformations section in the Toolbox, drag a Script Component. When you do this, a dialog box will appear.

2. Select Transformation and click OK.

Defining the Process

1. Right-click the Script Component and select Add Path.

2. In the dialog box, select Excel Source in the From drop-down list and Script Component in the To drop-down list. When you click the OK button, a new dialog box appears. Select Excel Source Output from the Output drop-down list and click OK.

3. Right-click and again select Add Path on the Script Component. Choose SQL Server Destination from the To drop-down list.

4. Right-click the Script Component and select Edit.

5. In the Input Columns step, check the following fields:

   - FromCurrencyCode

   - ToCurrencyCode

   - AverageRate

   - EndOfDayRate

6. Click the Inputs And Outputs step, expand the Output node, click the Output Columns folder, and then click the Add Column button.

7. Enter **ThisDate** as the name of the column, and select Date [DT_DATE] as the datatype.

8. Using the same datatype, add another column with **ThisDate2** as the name. (You need one output column for each destination column.)

9. Add two additional columns named **AvgRate** and **EODRate**, and select Currency [DT_CY] as the datatype.

10. In the Script step, click the Design Script button.

11. Add the following code in the *Input0_ProcessInputRow* method. You can find the code at \Ch10\SSIS\ScriptMain.vb in the sample files.

```vb
Public Overrides Sub Input0_ProcessInputRow(ByVal Row As Input0Buffer)
    'Get the date and time from the system
    Dim ActualDate As Date = System.DateTime.Now
    'Assign the same value to both columns
    With Row
        .ThisDate = ActualDate
        .ThisDate2 = ActualDate
        'Convert types to currency destination
        .AvgRate = CDec(.AverageRate)
        .EODRate = CDec(.EndOfDayRate)
    End With
End Sub
```

12. Close the Script Editor and click OK in the Edit Script Component dialog box.

13. Right-click the SQL Server Destination and select Edit.

14. Select [Sales].[CurrencyRate] from the Use A Table Or View drop-down list.

15. In the Mapping step, assign <ignore> to the CurrencyRateID column (it is an identity column). Assign ThisDate to CurrencyRateDate and ThisDate2 to ModifiedDate. Assign AvgRate to AverageRate and EODRate to EndOfDayRate.

16. Save the package.

> **Note**   You will see an alert icon in the SQL Server Destination component. This alert appears because the Script Component manages a string without any length control. Since the destination field has a specific size for the From and To Currency codes, the alert informs you that some data may be truncated.

Encapsulating Insert Operations in Stored Procedures

Creating INSERT sentences can be difficult if you must deal with all of the datatype conversions and differences between the globalization configuration in the database and the client workstation. A good example is evidenced when using the datetime datatype. Typically, the database server uses the U.S. date/time format; yet, in our global environment, the user could be in Latin America or Japan. Even though the database expects dates in the mm-dd-yyyy format, the Latin American user will send dates in the dd-mm-yyyy format and the Japanese user will send dates in the yyyy.mm.dd format.

However, more importantly, you must secure your database. Creating insert sentences dynamically can be a security risk. Therefore, a database administrator would prefer to secure data tables by denying write permissions on the tables. These are two good reasons to manage insert operations through stored procedures.

The syntax used to insert data through stored procedures is similar to the syntax used in a simple script. You merely have to use parameters instead of values.

```
CREATE PROCEDURE ProductCategory_Insert
    @Name nvarchar(50)
AS

INSERT INTO [AdventureWorks].[Production].[ProductCategory]
(
    [Name]
)
    VALUES
(
    @Name
)
```

Notice that you must specify the datatype for the parameters as well as the length in some situations. In addition, you can manage some value replacement inside the stored procedure.

Since the parameters for stored procedures can accept NULL values, you can replace them with the values you want or apply some basic business rules inside the stored procedure.

```
CREATE PROCEDURE ProductCategory_Insert
    @Name nvarchar(50),
    @ModifiedDate datetime =null
AS
-- If the @modifiedDate parameter receives a null value
-- it is replaced with the actual date in the database server
SET @ModifiedDate=isnull(@ModifiedDate,getdate())
INSERT INTO [AdventureWorks].[Production].[ProductCategory]
(
    [Name],
    [ModifiedDate]
)
    VALUES
(
    @Name,
    @ModifiedDate
)
```

Moreover, you can encapsulate several insert operations to different tables in the same stored procedure to accomplish business rule requirements.

```
CREATE PROCEDURE CategorySubCategory_Insert
    @CategoryName nvarchar(50),
    @SubCategoryName nvarchar(50)
AS
-- Insert the new category
INSERT INTO [AdventureWorks].[Production].[ProductCategory]
(
    [Name]
)
    VALUES
(
    @Name
)
DECLARE @CategoryID INT
-- Get the CategoryId for the recent inserted row
SET @CategoryId=IDENT_CURRENT('Production.ProductCategory')
-- Insert the SubCategory
INSERT INTO [AdventureWorks].[Production].[ProductSubcategory]
    (
        [ProductCategoryID]
         ,[Name]
    )
VALUES
    (
        @CategoryInd
        ,@SubCategoryName
    )
```

> **Note**   *IDENT_CURRENT* is a SQL function that retrieves the newest value for an identity column in the table that you use as an argument. You can obtain the same value using *@@IDENTITY*, but this function returns the last identity generated, which can come from some other table. This can occur if the insert operation executes an INSTEAD OF trigger.

Because some columns in your table can have default values, you can retrieve the final values stored in your record by using parameters to obtain the results. You must define the parameters as output and assign values to them from the newly inserted record before you complete the execution of the stored procedure.

```
CREATE PROCEDURE ProductCategory_Insert2
    @CategoryId int=null OUTPUT
    ,@Name nvarchar(50)=null OUTPUT
    ,@RowGuid uniqueidentifier=null OUTPUT
    ,@ModifiedDate datetime=null OUTPUT
AS
-- Insert a new row
INSERT INTO [AdventureWorks].[Production].[ProductCategory]
          ([Name]
)
    VALUES
          (@Name
)
-- Retrieve the values for the inserted row
SELECT @CategoryID=CategoryId
    ,@Name=Name
    ,@RowGuid=rowguid
    ,@ModifiedDate=ModifiedDate
FROM Production.ProductCategory
WHERE CategoryId=IDENT_CURRENT('Production.ProductCategory')
```

Triggering Actions Automatically when Inserting Data

You may need to perform some actions when a new row is to be inserted. Of course, you can make those actions inside a stored procedure, but what if you need to have full control over any insertion or if other applications will insert into your data table in the future? Although you are the developer of your application, your customer is the real owner of the data. In that case, you can manage those changes inside the database by adding an INSERT trigger to your table.

For auditing purposes, suppose that any change in the Product table must be recorded with the date, time, and user. To do this, you add a new ProductHistory table to the database.

```
CREATE TABLE [Production].[ProductHistory](
    [ProductID] [int] NOT NULL,
    [Name] [dbo].[Name] NOT NULL,
    [ProductNumber] [nvarchar](25) COLLATE SQL_Latin1_General_CP1_CI_AS NOT NULL,
    [MakeFlag] [dbo].[Flag] NOT NULL CONSTRAINT [DF_Product_MakeFlagH] DEFAULT ((1)),
```

```
    [FinishedGoodsFlag] [dbo].[Flag] NOT NULL CONSTRAINT
        [DF_Product_FinishedGoodsFlagH]  DEFAULT ((1)),
    [Color] [nvarchar](15) COLLATE SQL_Latin1_General_CP1_CI_AS NULL,
    [SafetyStockLevel] [smallint] NOT NULL,
    [ReorderPoint] [smallint] NOT NULL,
    [StandardCost] [money] NOT NULL,
    [ListPrice] [money] NOT NULL,
    [Size] [nvarchar](5) COLLATE SQL_Latin1_General_CP1_CI_AS NULL,
    [SizeUnitMeasureCode] [nchar](3) COLLATE SQL_Latin1_General_CP1_CI_AS NULL,
    [WeightUnitMeasureCode] [nchar](3) COLLATE SQL_Latin1_General_CP1_CI_AS NULL,
    [Weight] [decimal](8, 2) NULL,
    [DaysToManufacture] [int] NOT NULL,
    [ProductLine] [nchar](2) COLLATE SQL_Latin1_General_CP1_CI_AS NULL,
    [Class] [nchar](2) COLLATE SQL_Latin1_General_CP1_CI_AS NULL,
    [Style] [nchar](2) COLLATE SQL_Latin1_General_CP1_CI_AS NULL,
    [ProductSubcategoryID] [int] NULL,
    [ProductModelID] [int] NULL,
    [SellStartDate] [datetime] NOT NULL,
    [SellEndDate] [datetime] NULL,
    [DiscontinuedDate] [datetime] NULL,
    [rowguid] [uniqueidentifier] ROWGUIDCOL  NULL,
    [ModifiedDate] [datetime] NOT NULL CONSTRAINT [DF_Product_ModifiedDateH]
        DEFAULT (getdate()),
    [Action] [nchar](1) COLLATE SQL_Latin1_General_CP1_CI_AS NULL,
    [UserName] [nvarchar](100) COLLATE SQL_Latin1_General_CP1_CI_AS NOT NULL
        CONSTRAINT [DF_Product_UserNameH]  DEFAULT (user_name()),
 CONSTRAINT [PK_ProductHistory] PRIMARY KEY CLUSTERED
(
    [ProductID] ASC,
    [ModifiedDate] ASC
)WITH (IGNORE_DUP_KEY = OFF) ON [PRIMARY]
) ON [PRIMARY]

GO
USE [AdventureWorks]
GO
ALTER TABLE [Production].[ProductHistory]  WITH CHECK
    ADD CONSTRAINT [CK_ProductHistory] CHECK  (([Action] like '[I,M,D]'))
```

> **Note**   The final part of the script modifies the table by adding a CONSTRAINT to the Action column. The CONSTRAINT admits only three letters for the column, which indicate whether the action was an insertion, modification, or deletion.

After adding the ProductHistory table, you can add a trigger on the Product table to add the row into the ProductHistory table.

```
CREATE TRIGGER Production.Product_InsertTrigger
    ON  Production.Product
    AFTER INSERT
AS
BEGIN
    SET NOCOUNT ON;
```

```
INSERT INTO [AdventureWorks].[Production].[ProductHistory]
        ([ProductID],[Name],[ProductNumber],[MakeFlag]
        ,[FinishedGoodsFlag],[Color],[SafetyStockLevel]
        ,[ReorderPoint],[StandardCost],[ListPrice]
        ,[Size],[SizeUnitMeasureCode],[WeightUnitMeasureCode]
        ,[Weight],[DaysToManufacture],[ProductLine]
        ,[Class],[Style],[ProductSubcategoryID]
        ,[ProductModelID],[SellStartDate],[SellEndDate]
        ,[DiscontinuedDate],[rowguid],[ModifiedDate]
        ,[Action],[UserName])
    SELECT [ProductID],[Name],[ProductNumber],[MakeFlag]
        ,[FinishedGoodsFlag],[Color],[SafetyStockLevel]
        ,[ReorderPoint],[StandardCost],[ListPrice]
        ,[Size],[SizeUnitMeasureCode],[WeightUnitMeasureCode]
        ,[Weight],[DaysToManufacture],[ProductLine]
        ,[Class],[Style],[ProductSubcategoryID]
        ,[ProductModelID],[SellStartDate],[SellEndDate]
        ,[DiscontinuedDate],[rowguid],GetDate(),'I',USER_NAME()
    FROM inserted
END
```

> **Note**   This is an AFTER trigger, which executes just after the insertion is completed. An INSTEAD OF trigger is responsible for inserting the appropriate data into the table. In the above scenario, data has already been inserted when the trigger code starts its execution.

Dealing with Errors when Inserting Data

You can receive error messages during insert operations. Moreover, they can be of different types.

Try to execute the following code:

```
INSERT INTO [AdventureWorks].[Sales].[Currency]
        ([CurrencyCode]
        ,[Name]
        ,[ModifiedDate])
    VALUES
        ('NEW'
        ,'New currency')
```

You will find that the following error appears:

```
Msg 109, Level 15, State 1, Line 1
There are more columns in the INSERT statement than values specified in the VALUES clause.
The number of values in the VALUES clause must match the number of columns specified in the
INSERT statement.
```

This is obvious, for you are supplying fewer values than the specified columns. However, the message title provides various information besides the text itself. It appears that the messages are numbered (e.g., 109), and they contain levels (15) and states (1).

If you execute the following sentence, you can view the complete list of error messages defined in SQL Server 2005, which is stored in the sys.messages table.

```
select * from sys.messages
```

The table contains 7549 error messages in nine different languages.

The level value supplies information about the type of message. Some errors are not true errors, but are merely warnings. However, any of them will be raised to the application. It is sometimes necessary to know the exact level of the received message to decide whether it deserves to be managed in your application.

You can use the following table as a guideline.

Table 10-1   Severity Levels

Level	Meaning
0	Succeed
1 to 9	Information only; no real error
10	Information or not severe error
11 to16	Errors that can be corrected by the user
17 to 19	Software errors to be reported to the system administrator
20 to 25	Severe error; execution will be canceled

When inserting data, you may receive the previous missing values error or other errors, as demonstrated by executing the following invalid SQL Server sentences.

You cannot insert a string value in a datetime column, as in the following code.

```
INSERT INTO [AdventureWorks].[Sales].[Currency]
           ([CurrencyCode]
           ,[Name]
           ,[ModifiedDate])
     VALUES
           ('NEW'
           ,'New currency'
           ,'Today')
```

The following error is the result:

```
Msg 241, Level 16, State 1, Line 1
Conversion failed when converting datetime from character string.
```

The CurrencyCode column has a defined size that is less than the text you are trying to insert in the following example.

```
INSERT INTO [AdventureWorks].[Sales].[Currency]
           ([CurrencyCode]
           ,[Name]
           ,[ModifiedDate])
```

```
VALUES
        ('NEW CURRENCY TO ADD IN THE CURRENCY TABLE'
        ,'New currency'
        ,getdate())
```

The following error is the result:

```
Msg 8152, Level 16, State 4, Line 1
String or binary data would be truncated.
The statement has been terminated.
```

The CurrencyRate table has a foreign key restriction with the CurrencyCode table. The 'NEW' code is not found in the CurrencyRate table in the following code.

```
INSERT INTO [AdventureWorks].[Sales].[CurrencyRate]
        ([CurrencyRateDate]
        ,[FromCurrencyCode]
        ,[ToCurrencyCode]
        ,[AverageRate]
        ,[EndOfDayRate]
        ,[ModifiedDate])
    VALUES
        (getdate()
        ,'NEW'
        ,'USD'
        ,1
        ,1
        ,getdate())
```

The following error is the result:

```
Msg 547, Level 16, State 0, Line 1
The INSERT statement conflicted with the FOREIGN KEY constraint "FK_CurrencyRate_Currency_
FromCurrencyCode". The conflict occurred in database "AdventureWorks", table "Sales.Currency
", column 'CurrencyCode'.
The statement has been terminated.
```

Managing the Error

In SQL Server 2000 and previous versions, you can determine whether an error occurs using the @@ERROR system variable. This variable only provides the error number; you can check whether an error occurs by checking the variable immediately after executing a sentence.

```
DECLARE @ErrVar INT
INSERT INTO [AdventureWorks].[Sales].[CurrencyRate]
        ([CurrencyRateDate]
        ,[FromCurrencyCode]
        ,[ToCurrencyCode]
        ,[AverageRate]
        ,[EndOfDayRate]
        ,[ModifiedDate])
    VALUES
```

```
                 (getdate()
                 ,'NEW'
                 ,'USD'
                 ,1
                 ,1
                 ,getdate())
     SET @ErrVar=@@ERROR
     IF @ErrVar<>0
         PRINT 'error: '+ cast(@ErrVar AS nvarchar(8))
```

SQL Server 2005 helps you manage errors more efficiently by implementing the *TRY...CATCH* structure, which is similar to that used in .NET languages. Using *TRY*, you can obtain more information about the error by using the following functions.

Table 10-2   Error Functions

ERROR_NUMBER()
ERROR_SEVERITY()
ERROR_STATE()
ERROR_LINE()
ERROR_PROCEDURE()
ERROR_MESSAGE()

If an error occurs in the following example, the query returns a row with complete information about the error.

```
BEGIN TRY
INSERT INTO [AdventureWorks].[Sales].[CurrencyRate]
            ([CurrencyRateDate]
            ,[FromCurrencyCode]
            ,[ToCurrencyCode]
            ,[AverageRate]
            ,[EndOfDayRate]
            ,[ModifiedDate])
    VALUES
            (getdate()
            ,'NEW'
            ,'USD'
            ,1
            ,1
            ,getdate())
END TRY
BEGIN CATCH
SELECT
        ERROR_NUMBER() AS [Error Number],
        ERROR_SEVERITY() AS Severity,
        ERROR_STATE()AS State,
        ERROR_LINE ()AS Line,
        ERROR_PROCEDURE()AS [Procedure],
        ERROR_MESSAGE()AS Message;
END CATCH
```

Inserting Data from ADO.NET

Whatever method you use in T-SQL to insert information into your tables, you need similar code in your application to execute the insertion. In an insert operation, you need two ADO.NET objects to accomplish the operation:

- ADO.NET *Connection* object
- ADO.NET *Command* object

The *Connection* object establishing the connection to the database defines the context in which to execute the insert such as which user, which access rights, and occasionally which transaction. The *Command* object contains your T-SQL sentence or the stored procedure's name to be executed.

> **Note**   The following examples use a new AdventureWorks table named TestTable. The script to create the new table is included in the sample files in the SQL Server Management Studio Solution in the \Ch10\Sample Codes\Chapter 10 Scripts folder.

Using ADO.NET Objects

1. Open Visual Studio 2005 and create a new Windows Application Project.

2. You need a *Command* object:

    ```
    Dim myCommand As New SqlClient.SqlCommand()
    ```

    If you want to use a T-SQL sentence, you must assign the sentence to the CommandText property and assign CommandType.Text to the CommandType property. Since this is the default configuration, you may skip setting the CommandType. In the following example, the T-SQL sentence is inside the *txtTSQL* textbox.

    ```
    With myCommand
        .CommandText = txtTSQL.Text
        .CommandType = CommandType.Text
    ```

3. You must then assign the connection and call the *ExecuteNonQuery* method. Because you are not retrieving information in this chapter, this method uses fewer resources during execution.

    ```
            .Connection = myConnection
            Try
                myConnection.Open()
                .ExecuteNonQuery()
                myConnection.Close()
            Catch ex As Exception
                MsgBox(ex.Message)
            End Try
        End With
    ```

4. When you want to use a stored procedure, you must assign the stored procedure's name to the CommandText property and change the CommandType property to StoredProcedure.

    However, you must add additional steps. If you intend to use a stored procedure, you must define its parameters and add them one by one with at least their names and datatypes.

5. You then assign the values to the parameters and finally execute the command with the *ExecuteNonQuery* method.

```
With myCommand
    .CommandText = "TestTable_Insert"
    .CommandType = CommandType.StoredProcedure
    .Connection = myConnection
    .Parameters.Add("@Name", SqlDbType.NVarChar)
    .Parameters.Add("@Description", SqlDbType.NVarChar)
    .Parameters("@Name").Value = txtName.Text
    .Parameters("@Description").Value = txtDescription.Text
    Try
        myConnection.Open()
        .ExecuteNonQuery()
        myConnection.Close()
    Catch ex As Exception
        MsgBox(ex.Message)
    End Try
End With
```

Conclusion

In this chapter, you learned different ways to insert information into your databases. Depending on the source, you can choose different tools for inserting information. You also learned how to use T-SQL sentences to insert information from known applications and from your own applications by using ADO.NET.

Chapter 10 Quick Reference

To	Do This
Create an INSERT statement in SQL Server Management Studio	Right-click the desired table.
	Select Script Table As...
	Select Insert To...
	Choose the desired destination.
Insert a blank row	Ensure that you have default values for all of the columns.
	Execute INSERT INTO <*Table_Name*> DEFAULT VALUES.

To	Do This
Insert values from another table	Execute INSERT INTO *<Table_Name>* (*<columnlist>*) SELECT *<Matching_column_List>* from *<Source_Table_name>*.
Insert values using views	Ensure that you are only inserting values for columns in a single table.
Insert values using views to more than one table	Implement an INSTEAD OF trigger on the view to insert the values in the different tables appropriately.
Import data from files	Use the BCP utility.
	Use Integration Services to fine-tune your import process.
Enhance control and security in insert operations	Encapsulate the insert commands in stored procedures.
Perform other actions while inserting data	Implement an AFTER trigger on the table.
Control errors during database actions	Use *TRY ... CATCH* blocks to obtain information from the *ERROR_x* functions.
Insert data from an ADO.NET application	Use the ADO.NET *Connection* and *Command* objects.

Chapter 11

Deleting Data from Microsoft SQL Server 2005

After completing this chapter, you will be able to:

- Delete information from your database
- Manage deletions and control row deletions
- Delete data using ADO.NET

Using the DELETE Statement

There will be occasions when you need to delete some or all of the information in your database. You may need to remove a record inserted by error, or you may decide to delete information physically from a table when the user wants to delete some records. Alternatively, you may need to remove old information from an historical table. In all of these cases, you will use the DELETE statement.

The basic DELETE sentence is:

```
DELETE FROM [<ServerName>.][<DataBseName>.]<SchemaName>.<TableName>
    WHERE <Conditions>
```

If you execute the DELETE sentence with a connection to the current database, you can simply use the <SchemaName>.<TableName> form without including the server and database names. You can use the DELETE statement without a WHERE condition, but typically you do not want to remove all of the content from a table.

> **Tip** If you want to remove all of the rows from a table, you can use the TRUNCATE TABLE statement instead of the DELETE statement. It will perform the task quickly, but you must be sure that there are no relationships from or to the table.

Creating a DELETE Sentence with SQL Server Management Studio

To create a DELETE sentence using SQL Server Management Studio, perform the following steps.

Creating a DELETE Sentence

1. Right-click on the desired table in Object Explorer.

2. Choose Script Table As.

3. Choose Delete To.

4. Choose New Query Editor Window. SQL Server Management Studio will create a template for you.

> **Important**   If you work through the procedures in this chapter using the AdventureWorks database, it is important to back up your database first.

Defining the WHERE Condition

You can use any or all columns of a table to create the WHERE condition. You can enhance the performance of the WHERE condition by using the following guidelines.

- Use the Primary.Key column/s in the condition.

- Use columns that are part of an index.

These are suggestions only, for you can delete rows by using any column of a table in the WHERE condition. It is also not necessary to use a column from an index.

The following is an example of a simple DELETE sentence:

```
DELETE FROM [AdventureWorks].[Person].[Address]
    WHERE AddressID=1
```

The WHERE condition can be used with any of the conditional arguments it accepts to delete information, including those that establish ranges of data, or with logical combinations of AND, OR, and NOT.

> **Tip**   If you need to delete a set of records that depends on several conditions, it is better to write a SELECT query with the same filters first to check that you will be deleting only the necessary records.

Review the following example (included in the sample files as \Ch11\AdvWorks\Queries\Sample01.sql) in which different WHERE filtering operators are utilized.

```
DELETE
FROM          Production.Product
WHERE (MakeFlag = 1)
      AND
       (ReorderPoint BETWEEN 200 AND 600)
      AND
       (SellStartDate < CONVERT(DATETIME, '2000-01-01 00:00:00', 102))
```

You may need to remove rows from one table depending on conditions applied to another table or tables. The best way to accomplish this is to use the IN clause, which is applied over a field included on one index. The following example removes the history information about those products matching the same conditions we used in the previous sample (included in the sample files as \Ch11\AdvWorks\Queries\Sample02.sql).

```
DELETE FROM [AdventureWorks].[Production].[ProductInventory]
     WHERE ProductID in
  ( SELECT      ProductID
    FROM        Production.Product
    WHERE       (MakeFlag = 1)
    AND (ReorderPoint BETWEEN 200 AND 600)
    AND (SellStartDate < CONVERT(DATETIME, '2000-01-01 00:00:00', 102))
  )
```

Another way to remove these rows is to create a WHERE condition that is applied over relationships between the tables, but to specify the table from which you want to delete the rows. This code is included in the sample files as \Ch11\AdvWorks\Queries\Sample03.sql.

```
DELETE Production.ProductInventory
   FROM Production.ProductInventory
      INNER JOIN Production. Product
   ON Production.ProductInventory.ProductID =
      Production. Product .ProductID
   WHERE (Production. Product .MakeFlag = 1)
     AND (Production. Product .ReorderPoint BETWEEN 200 AND 600)
     AND (Production. Product .SellStartDate <
       CONVERT(DATETIME, '2000-01-01 00:00:00', 102))
```

Using Relationships to Perform Deletions

When you design a database, you can establish rules about how the deletion process occurs. In a relationship between tables, you can configure the relationship to delete in cascade during the deletion process of a row.

Assume that the Purchase Order business rule establishes that it is possible to delete cancelled purchase orders. In this scenario, you can use data definition language (DDL) to define that when some process deletes a row from the PurchaseOrderHeader table, the corresponding rows in the PurchaseOrderDetails table will automatically be deleted as well. The DDL would look something like the following (included in the sample files as \Ch11\Adv-Works\Queries\Sample04.sql):

```
ALTER TABLE Purchasing.PurchaseOrderDetail ADD CONSTRAINT
   FK_PurchaseOrderDetail_PurchaseOrderHeader_PurchaseOrderID FOREIGN KEY
   (
   PurchaseOrderID
   ) REFERENCES Purchasing.PurchaseOrderHeader
   (
   PurchaseOrderID
   ) ON UPDATE  NO ACTION
    ON DELETE  CASCADE

GO
```

If you use SQL Server Management Studio to create your database objects, pay attention to the Insert And Update Specification option when creating a relationship, as shown in Figure 11-1.

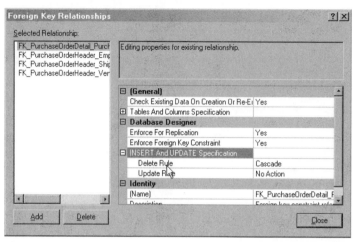

Figure 11-1   Specifying properties of foreign key relationhips.

> **Important**   Be careful when using the Cascade feature. Deleting rows with a dependency on other tables can be dangerous, and important information can be lost. Referential integrity will prevent you from losing the rows that you need. When you enable the Cascade Delete feature, you must be sure that none of your essential data will be lost.

Deleting Data through Views

You can also delete rows from tables by using views. However, the following restrictions apply.

- You can delete rows from only one table.

  Consider the following view (included in the sample files as \Ch11\AdvWorks\Queries\Sample05.sql):

```
USE [AdventureWorks]
GO
CREATE VIEW [dbo].[vProductFullCategories]
AS
SELECT
    Production.ProductSubcategory.ProductSubcategoryID,
    Production.ProductCategory.Name AS CategoryName,
    Production.ProductSubcategory.Name
FROM
    Production.ProductSubcategory
INNER JOIN
    Production.ProductCategory
        ON Production.ProductSubcategory.ProductCategoryID
        = Production.ProductCategory.ProductCategoryID
```

```
GO
```

Delete one row by using the following sentence:

```
DELETE TOP (1) FROM vProductFullCategories
```

You will receive the following error:

```
Msg 4405, Level 16, State 1, Line 1
View or function 'vProductFullCategories' is not updatable because the modification
affects multiple base tables.
```

■ The connected user must have delete rights over the view in question.

Assume that a user has read-only rights over a view. The following code is included in the sample files as \Ch11\AdvWorks\Queries\Sample06.sql.

```
USE [master]
GO
CREATE LOGIN [ReadOnlyUser] WITH PASSWORD=N'ReadOnlyUser' MUST_CHANGE, DEFAULT_DATABAS
E=[master], CHECK_EXPIRATION=ON, CHECK_POLICY=ON
GO
USE [AdventureWorks]
GO
EXEC sp_addrolemember N'db_datawriter', N'ReadOnlyUser'
GO
use [AdventureWorks]
GO
DENY DELETE ON [dbo].[vProductFullCategories] TO [ReadOnlyUser]
GO
```

The ReadOnlyUser will not be allowed to delete anything from the view.

■ The view's creator must have delete rights over the table.

Using INSTEAD OF DELETE Triggers on Views

There are ways to get around the limitations placed on deleting information by using a view. To delete a subcategory from a view, you can create an INSTEAD OF trigger to process the request and perform the delete action over the subcategory's data table only.

As with any other trigger, the table named deleted contains the row or rows intended to be deleted when the trigger is fired. Using that table, you can retrieve the ProductSubcategoryID and use it to delete the row in the ProductSubcategory table. The following code is included in the sample files as \Ch11\AdvWorks\Queries\Sample07.sql.

```
Use AdventureWorks
GO
CREATE TRIGGER [dbo].[vProductFullCategoriesInsertDeleteTrigger]
   ON [dbo].[vProductFullCategories]
INSTEAD OF DELETE
AS
BEGIN
   DECLARE @Id int
```

```
    SET @Id=(SELECT [ProductSubcategoryID] FROM deleted)
    DELETE FROM Production.ProductSubcategory WHERE ProductSubcategoryID = @Id
END
GO
```

However, a problem exists with this trigger. Try to execute the following sentence:

```
DELETE TOP (10) FROM vProductFullCategories
```

You will receive the following error:

```
Msg 512, Level 16, State 1, Procedure vProductFullCategoriesInsertDeleteTrigger, Line 7
Subquery returned more than 1 value. This is not permitted when the subquery follows =, !=,
<, <= , >, >= or when the subquery is used as an expression.
The statement has been terminated.
```

When the trigger attempts to assign the @Id variable, an error is raised because the SELECT statement returns more than one row!

When creating a trigger, you must keep in mind that the trigger will be fired when a delete action is performed and not when a single row is to be deleted. The correct syntax for the trigger must establish a relationship between the table to be deleted and the table named deleted. The following code is included in the sample files as \Ch11\AdvWorks\Queries\ Sample08.sql.

> **Tip**   Any object used in a SQL Server sentence must be part of the FORM clause. In the fol-
> lowing second version, having the table named deleted linked to ProductSubcategory through
> the INNER JOIN operation allows you to use the ProductSubcategory in the trigger code.

```
ALTER TRIGGER [dbo].[vProductFullCategoriesInsertDeleteTrigger]
    ON [dbo].[vProductFullCategories]
INSTEAD OF DELETE
AS
BEGIN
    DELETE Production.ProductSubcategory
        FROM Production.ProductSubcategory
        INNER JOIN deleted
        ON Production.ProductSubcategory.ProductSubcategoryID =
            deleted.ProductSubcategoryID
END
GO
```

Encapsulating Delete Operations in Stored Procedures

You will obtain the best control over database operations if you use stored procedures to per-form any operation. Implementing this encapsulation is similar to implementing other actions inside stored procedures. It is most important to control which rows will be deleted by defin-ing the parameter to be used in the WHERE clause.

> **Tip**   Remember, the fastest operations will be performed if the WHERE clause uses columns belonging to indexes, especially if the columns are from the primary key.

The simplest example is to use a stored procedure to delete just one row. This code is included in the sample files as \Ch11\AdvWorks\Queries\Sample09.sql.

```
CREATE PROCEDURE [Sales].[CurrencyRate_Delete]
    @Id int
AS
DELETE FROM [AdventureWorks].[Sales].[CurrencyRate]
      WHERE CurrencyRateID=@id
GO
```

Inside a stored procedure, you may use any DELETE sentence you need, including those that filter by using an IN clause or related tables. Moreover, you can include several Delete instructions inside a stored procedure. The last Delete instruction in the example above was used in SQL Server versions prior to 2000 because the database engine did not include Cascade Delete relationships. When using those versions, if you needed to delete rows in a hierarchical structure, you had to delete them from bottom to top in the hierarchy.

It is a good practice to encapsulate actions performed against the database, thereby isolating them from the application. A stored procedure should have a representative name that states the action it will perform, such as EntirePurchaseOrder_Remove, which will be the only one a developer will call to remove an order. However, the stored procedure can perform several actions, such as removing records from different tables or inserting rows in history tables.

Implementing Pessimistic Concurrency for Delete Operations

The above examples assume that your sentences are the only ones being executed against a database in a given time period. However, in real life, this is a very uncommon situation, for there are often several users connected to a database at the same time.

In a real-life scenario, it is possible that you might want to delete a row that was modified by another user just seconds earlier. If you perform the deletion, you will destroy the other user's work. A worst-case scenario could be that changes were made to a table by another user that affect some of the primary key columns that you are using to filter the delete operation. In this situation, you will not be able to delete a row because the primary key that you are looking for no longer exists.

Assume that you have an application to manage the SalesPersonQuotaHistory table. You want to delete an old entry within that table for a sales person. The application may execute the following sentence to retrieve the first entry for "sales person id equals 268." This code is included in the sample files as \Ch11\AdvWorks\Queries\Sample10.sql.

```
SELECT   TOP (1)  SalesPersonID, QuotaDate
FROM        Sales.SalesPersonQuotaHistory
WHERE    (SalesPersonID = 268)
```

The application obtains the following information:

SalesPersonID	QuotaDate
268	2001-07-01 00:00:00.000

Meanwhile, another user changes the row because the month in this specific entry is wrong. The following procedure illustrates what may occur when you try to delete your sales person entry.

Changing Row Information in a Table

1. In SQL Server Management Studio, right-click the Sales.SalesPersonQuotaHistory table and select Open Table.

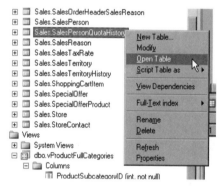

2. Change the month of the date in the first row in the first column to 08, and move the cursor to the next row to update the information.

3. In a Query window, execute the following sentence to delete the row based on the information previously retrieved. This code is included in the sample files as \Ch11\Adv-Works\Queries\Sample11.sql.

```
DELETE FROM Sales.SalesPersonQuotaHistory
WHERE (SalesPersonID = 268)
    AND
    (QuotaDate = CONVERT(DATETIME, '2001-07-01 00:00:00', 102))
```

You will receive the following message:

```
(0 row(s) affected)
```

As you can see, it is important to retrieve the rows affected by a DELETE query to ensure that the deletion occurs since no error is generated when attempting to delete something that no longer exists. Deleting rows after another user has made changes is something you must monitor to keep consistency in your database.

Implementing Optimistic Concurrency for Delete Operations

You can implement several methods to ensure that you are deleting the exact row that you retrieved previously and that no changes have been made to the row during the interim period.

Method 1. Comparing All Columns

You can create a stored procedure that receives parameters for each column in the table and use them in the WHERE clause, as shown in the following example. This code is included in the sample files as \Ch11\AdvWorks\Queries\Sample12.sql.

```
CREATE PROCEDURE Sales.SalesReason_Delete
    @SalesReasonID int,
    @Name nvarchar(50),
    @ReasonType nvarchar(50),
    @ModifiedDate datetime
AS
BEGIN
    DELETE
    FROM         Sales.SalesReason
    WHERE      (SalesReasonID = @SalesReasonID)
      AND (Name = @Name)
      AND (ReasonType = @ReasonType)
      AND (ModifiedDate = @ModifiedDate)
END
```

However, this method may be expensive when working with tables that have several columns, such as Production.Product and Person.Contact.

Method 2. Using the ModifiedDate Column

In the sample above, the table contains a ModifiedDate column. If that column contains date and time information, you can use it with the primary key to ensure that you are deleting only the row you want (because the primary key identifies it), and you can verify that there have been no changes because the ModifiedDate information remains the same as that which was viewed earlier.

However, you depend on the fact that any update process must update the ModifiedDate column. If another user modifies information outside of your application, you cannot control the update on the ModifiedDate column.

Method 3. Using a Timestamp Column

The timestamp datatype contains special behavior. The SQL Server engine updates it automatically any time a row is updated. If you add a Timestamp column to your table, you can use it as part of your WHERE clause when deleting a row. The following example adds a Timestamp column to a table.

```
ALTER TABLE Sales.SalesReason ADD
    LastVersion timestamp NULL
GO
```

Make sure that you obtain the Timestamp value when receiving information from the row.

Using a Timestamp column from .NET   When retrieving information from a Timestamp column in Visual Basic, C#, or any other .NET-compatible language, you must deal with arrays of bytes. You can simply manage the byte-to-byte comparison, or you can transform the value you receive to another datatype that is easier to manage in .NET.

Consider the following SELECT statement (included in the sample files as \Ch11\Adv-Works\Queries\Sample13.sql):

```
SELECT  SalesReasonID,
     Name,
     ReasonType,
     ModifiedDate,
     cast(Lastversion as bigint) AS EasyLastVersion
FROM    Sales.SalesReason
```

It converts the Timestamp value to a bigint datatype. This value is much easier to manage in a .NET language, and you can use the same conversion when you want to delete a row.

The following script adds a new row to the table. This code is included in the sample files as \Ch11\AdvWorks\Queries\Sample14.sql.

```
INSERT INTO [AdventureWorks].[Sales].[SalesReason]
           ([Name]
           ,[ReasonType]
           ,[ModifiedDate])
     VALUES
           ('Test reason'
           ,'Just for Test'
           ,getdate())
```

Now, retrieve the primary key and the Timestamp column just as your application would when it is about to delete a row.

```
SELECT  SalesReasonID,
     cast(Lastversion AS bigint) AS EasyLastVersion
FROM    Sales.SalesReason
where    name='Test reason'
```

This script returns results similar to those shown below:

```
SalesReasonID EasyLastVersion
------------- --------------------
11            3001

(1 row(s) affected)
```

A stored procedure for deleting the row using both values can be similar to the following script (included in the sample files as \Ch11\AdvWorks\Queries\Sample15.sql).

```
CREATE PROCEDURE Sales.SalesReason_DeleteChecked
    @SalesReasonId int,
    @CheckStamp bigint,
    @DeletedRecords int=null OUTPUT
AS
BEGIN
    DELETE Sales.SalesReason
        WHERE SalesReasonID=@SalesReasonId
        AND cast(LastVersion as bigint)=@CheckStamp
    SET @DeletedRecords=@@ROWCOUNT
END
```

You can now test the stored procedure.

Testing a Stored Procedure

1. Under the AdventureWorks database, expand the Programmability node.

2. On the Stored Procedures node, right-click and select Refresh.

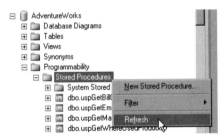

3. On the Sales.SalesReason_DeleteChecked stored procedure, right-click and select Execute Stored Procedure...

4. A new window will appear that asks for the stored procedure's parameters. Check the Pass Null Value box for the @DeletedRecords parameter, and enter the appropriate values for the others.

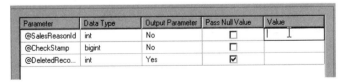

Parameter	Data Type	Output Parameter	Pass Null Value	Value
@SalesReasonId	int	No	☐	1
@CheckStamp	bigint	No	☐	
@DeletedReco...	int	Yes	☑	

5. A script will be created similar to the following (included in the sample files as \Ch11\AdvWorks\Queries\Sample16.sql):

```
USE [Adventureworks]
GO

DECLARE   @return_value int,
       @DeletedRecords int

EXEC   @return_value = [Sales].[SalesReason_DeleteChecked]
       @SalesReasonId = 11,
       @CheckStamp = 3001,
       @DeletedRecords = @DeletedRecords OUTPUT

SELECT   @DeletedRecords AS N'@DeletedRecords'

SELECT   'Return Value' = @return_value

GO
```

The script will return the following results:

6. Execute the insert script to insert the "Test reason" again and retrieve the new values. Note these values for use in Step 12 below.

7. On the Sales.SalesReason table, right-click and select Open Table.

8. Locate the last row just added and change the ReasonType value. Move the cursor to update the row.

9. Execute the stored procedure with the new Id and Timestamp that you previously obtained in Step 9 from this new row. Do not retrieve the values once the row has been modified.

10. You will obtain a zero value in @DeletedRecords since the row was updated after you received the Timestamp value. The Timestamp column is updated automatically each time a row is modified.

Method 4. Using a Unique Identifier Column

Starting with SQL Server© 2000, a new datatype is available to manage optimistic concurrency. The unique identifier column contains a global unique identifier (GUID), and this column is very useful when synchronizing information with the same structure between different databases and even different servers.

If two different rows in two different databases or servers are updated at exactly the same time, there is a chance that both of them will contain the same Timestamp, which can be a problem during the synchronization process. The unique identifier is guaranteed to be unique no matter where it is generated. However, the GUID value will not be updated automatically during every change as is done with the Timestamp value. As with the *ModifiedDate* method discussed earlier, you are responsible for ensuring that the unique identifier is updated consistently so that it can be used as a concurrency check.

You can define a unique identifier as follows. This code is included in the sample files as \Ch11\AdvWorks\Queries\Sample17.sql.

```
ALTER TABLE Production.Culture ADD
    RowId uniqueidentifier NOT NULL CONSTRAINT DF_Culture_RowId DEFAULT newid()
GO
```

Each time you need to ensure a deletion, include the unique identifier in your select statement and use it as a parameter in the stored procedure to delete the row in the same manner explained earlier.

Triggering Actions Automatically when Deleting Data

Chapter 10, Inserting Data in Microsoft SQL Server 2005, discussed reasons why it may be necessary to control what happens when a process or application inserts a row. When triggering actions automatically in delete operations, the main difference is which virtual table to use. Since you are about to delete rows, the table containing the changes is named deleted.

Using the same Production.ProductHistory table that was used in the previous chapter, it is possible to keep a log concerning the deletions in the Production table. This code is included in the sample files as \Ch11\AdvWorks\Queries\Sample18.sql.

```
CREATE TRIGGER Production.Product_DeleteTrigger
    ON  Production.Product
    AFTER DELETE
AS
BEGIN
    SET NOCOUNT ON;
    INSERT INTO [AdventureWorks].[Production].[ProductHistory]
            ([ProductID],[Name],[ProductNumber],[MakeFlag]
            ,[FinishedGoodsFlag],[Color],[SafetyStockLevel]
            ,[ReorderPoint],[StandardCost],[ListPrice]
            ,[Size],[SizeUnitMeasureCode],[WeightUnitMeasureCode]
            ,[Weight],[DaysToManufacture],[ProductLine]
            ,[Class],[Style],[ProductSubcategoryID]
            ,[ProductModelID],[SellStartDate],[SellEndDate]
            ,[DiscontinuedDate],[rowguid],[ModifiedDate]
            ,[Action],[UserName])
        SELECT [ProductID],[Name],[ProductNumber],[MakeFlag]
            ,[FinishedGoodsFlag],[Color],[SafetyStockLevel]
            ,[ReorderPoint],[StandardCost],[ListPrice]
            ,[Size],[SizeUnitMeasureCode],[WeightUnitMeasureCode]
            ,[Weight],[DaysToManufacture],[ProductLine]
            ,[Class],[Style],[ProductSubcategoryID]
```

```
    ,[ProductModelID],[SellStartDate],[SellEndDate]
    ,[DiscontinuedDate],[rowguid],GetDate(),'D',USER_NAME()
FROM deleted
END
```

> **Note**   The above code involves an AFTER trigger. The row is deleted before any action takes place in your trigger code. However, you can cancel the deletion if you raise an error from inside the trigger.

Dealing with Errors

As with any other action against a database, deleting rows may end with errors. An error may range from a simple "can't delete" announcement to a catastrophic server failure. The level and severity values for errors have been discussed previously. The following information involves the specifics of delete actions.

Data Does Not Exist

Based on a discussion earlier in this chapter, you are familiar with what happens when you try to delete data using a WHERE clause that has no matches within the table: absolutely nothing happens. The delete instruction performs the action, but the command has nothing to do because there are no rows that match the WHERE clause. However, this fact might go unnoticed because Microsoft SQL Server 2005 does not interpret it as an error.

Execute the sentence that follows:

```
DELETE FROM [AdventureWorks].[Sales].[SalesReason]
    WHERE SalesReasonID=100
```

You will receive the message below because there is no row in the SalesReason table with Id equal to 100.

```
(0 row(s) affected)
```

If you base your application development on trapping errors in your database actions, you must add your own error for this action. You can add your own error and error messages to SQL Server 2005 to raise specific information by using the sp_addmessage stored procedure.

Sp_addmessage takes the following parameters shown in Table 11-1.

Table 11-1   Parameters for the sp_addmessage Stored Procedure

Name	Content
@msgnum	Integer identifying your message. This value must be between 50,001 and 2,147,483,647. It is a good practice to use values in a defined range for each application.
@severity	Severity level. If you create your own error for something that your code or the user can solve, you should specify a value between 11 and 16.
@msgtext	Text to display when this error is raised
@lang	Language used in the msgtext. This allows you to add multiple messages for the same error, depending on the user's language. If this value is NULL, then the default language of your actual connection session will be used.
@with_log	If TRUE, the error will be written into the Application log when it is raised.

The following example uses a number greater than 50,001 for the message.

```
sp_addmessage 51001,16,'No rows deleted','us_english',FALSE
```

You should always use stored procedures to delete rows and raise the error when nothing has been deleted.

```
ALTER PROCEDURE [Sales].[SalesReason_DeleteChecked]
    @SalesReasonId int,
    @CheckStamp bigint,
    @DeletedRecords int=null OUTPUT
AS
BEGIN
    DELETE Sales.SalesReason
        WHERE SalesReasonID=@SalesReasonId
        AND cast(Lastversion AS bigint)=@CheckStamp
    SET @DeletedRecords=@@ROWCOUNT
-- Raise an error when no row was deleted
IF @DeletedRecords=0
    RAISERROR (51001,16,1)
END
```

Data to Be Deleted Is Related to Other Tables

This is probably the most common error you will encounter during the life of your applications. You must therefore trap the error to manage it appropriately.

Execute the following code:

```
DELETE FROM [AdventureWorks].[Sales].[SalesTerritory]
    WHERE territoryId=1
```

You will receive the following error:

```
Msg 547, Level 16, State 0, Line 1
The DELETE statement conflicted with the REFERENCE constraint "FK_SalesOrderHeader_Sales
Territory_TerritoryID". The conflict occurred in database "AdventureWorks", table
"Sales.SalesOrderHeader", column 'TerritoryID'.
The statement has been terminated.
```

Notice that this is a Level 16 error, indicating that the user can solve the problem. With this level, you can trap the error in your own application code. Because the user needs to understand the mistake, you can provide clearer information than the information provided by SQL Server 2005 (which is more technical information).

Other Errors

As in any SQL Server sentence, you may receive other errors, such as syntax or system failure errors. You must manage each error properly. Syntax errors will be a Level 16 error, which is the same level as referential integrity errors or the errors you created for DELETE sentences that do not affect any records.

Deleting Data from ADO.NET

To delete rows using ADO.NET, you use the same objects that you used in the insert process: *Connection* and *Command* objects.

> **Note**   The following examples use the same new AdventureWorks: TestTable file that you used for your insert samples. The script to create the table is included in the sample files in the SQL Server Management Studio Solution in the Ch10\Sample Codes\Chapter 10 Scripts folder.

Deleting Rows Using ADO.NET

1. Open the Ch11.sln file from the \Ch11 folder in the sample files. (A completed version of this application is included in the sample files in the \Ch11-completed folder.)

2. In the AdvWorks project under the Change Scripts folder, right-click the Add Rows to Test Table.sql file and select Run On, then select the connection on which to run the script. This will fill the table with information.

3. In the Ch11 project, double-click Form1.

4. In the menu bar, click TestTable Actions and then double-click the Get Rows menu.

5. Review the code in the LoadData procedure to load the rows into the data grid.

6. Return to the design view of Form1. Go to the TestTable Actions menu, click the Delete Selected menu, and double-click the T-SQL menu.

7. Add the following code. This code is included in the sample files as \Ch11\Codes\Sample19.vb.

```
Const SQLSentence As String = _
    "DELETE FROM [AdventureWorks].[dbo].[TestTable] WHERE id={0}"
Dim Count As Integer = 0
For Each r As DataGridViewRow In DataGridView1.SelectedRows
    Dim com As New SqlClient.SqlCommand( _
        String.Format(SQLSentence, r.Cells(0).Value))
    With com
        .Connection = App.Connection
        Count += .ExecuteNonQuery
    End With
Next
MsgBox(String.Format("{0} rows deleted", Count))
LoadData()
```

8. Run the application. Use the Database | Change Connection menu as necessary, and then connect to the database. Load the information using the Test Table Actions | Get Rows menu.

9. Select one or more rows. Click Test Table Actions | Delete Selected | T-SQL menu to remove them from the table.

10. Stop the execution.

11. Under the AdvWorks project, right-click the CREATE PROCEDURE TestTable_Delete.sql file in the Create Scripts folder, and click Run On to create the stored procedure.

12. Go to the Ch11 project and, in the design view of Form1, click the Delete Selected menu, click the TestTable Actions menu, and then double-click the Stored Procedure menu.

13. Add the following code. This code is included in the sample files as \Ch11\Codes\Sample20.vb.

```
Dim Com As New SqlClient.SqlCommand("TestTable_Delete")
Dim Count As Integer = 0
With Com
    .Connection = App.Connection
    .CommandType = CommandType.StoredProcedure
    .Parameters.Add("@Id", SqlDbType.Int)
    For Each r As DataGridViewRow In DataGridView1.SelectedRows
        .Parameters(0).Value = r.Cells(0).Value
        count += .ExecuteNonQuery
    Next
    MsgBox(String.Format("{0} rows deleted", Count))
    LoadData()
End With
```

14. Run the application and test the code.

Managing Errors during the Delete Process

There are more opportunities to receive an error when deleting a row than when inserting one. Issues such as referential integrity and other business-related rules must be properly managed.

To evaluate how to manage errors, perform the following steps.

Evaluating Errors in ADO.NET

1. In the AdvWorks project, right-click the CREATE PROCEDURE
    Sales.SalesReason_DeleteChecked.sql file and click Run On to create the stored procedure.

2. In the Ch11 project, go to the design view of Form1. Double-click the Delete Selected
    (SP) menu under the Sales Reason Actions menu.

3. Add the following code. This code is included in the sample files as
    \Ch11\Codes\Sample21.vb.

```
Dim Com As New _
    SqlClient.SqlCommand("Sales.SalesReason_DeleteChecked")
Dim Count As Integer = 0
With Com
    .Connection = App.Connection
    .CommandType = CommandType.StoredProcedure
    .Parameters.Add("@SalesReasonId", SqlDbType.Int)
    .Parameters.Add("@CheckStamp", SqlDbType.BigInt)
    With .Parameters.Add("@DeletedRecords", SqlDbType.Int)
        .Direction = ParameterDirection.Output
    End With
    For Each r As DataGridViewRow In DataGridView1.SelectedRows
        .Parameters(0).Value = r.Cells(0).Value
        .Parameters(1).Value = r.Cells("LastVersion").Value
        Try
            .ExecuteNonQuery()
            Count += CInt(.Parameters(2).Value)
        Catch ex As SqlClient.SqlException
            MsgBox(ex.Number)
        Catch ex As Exception
            MsgBox(ex.Message)
        End Try
    Next
    MsgBox(String.Format("{0} rows deleted", Count))
    LoadSales()
End With
```

The try... catch block allows you to trap any error during the delete process. Inside the block, the Catch ex as SqlClient.SqlException section provides specific information about the error from the database.

4. Run the application.

5. After loading the SalesReason information, try to delete the Price row (SalesReasonID equal to 1).

   You will receive a message containing the error number (in this case, 547), which is the same number you will receive if you try to remove the row using SQL Server Management Studio.

6. By modifying the *catch* portion, you can implement a case selector to manage every error code of your choice and give the user a more adequate message, including different action choices, depending on the kind of error the code receives. In the following example, replace the *MsgBox(ex.Number)* line of code with this new block of code. This code is included in the sample files as \Ch11\Codes\Sample22.vb.

```
Select Case ex.Number
    Case 547 'Referential integrity
        MsgBox("This information has other related pieces of information." & _
            "You can't remove it", MsgBoxStyle.Exclamation)
        'Continue adding your own control actions here
    Case Else
        MsgBox("Unspecified error. Can't delete", MsgBoxStyle.Critical)
End Select
```

7. Build and test the code as before.

Conclusion

In this chapter, you learned how to perform record deletions in your data tables. You also learned how to administer the deletion process to obtain more control of what happens to your records. Lastly, the process necessary to perform deletion operations using ADO.NET objects, T-SQL sentences, and stored procedures was discussed.

Chapter 11 Quick Reference

To	Do This
Create a DELETE statement in SQL Server Management Studio	Right-click the desired table.
	Select Script Table As.
	Select Delete To.
	Choose your destination.
Remove all rows in a table	Use TRUNCATE TABLE <*Table_Name*>.
Automatically delete rows from related tables	Add the ON DELETE CASCADE modifier to the relationship definition by selecting the CASCADE modifier in the DELETE rule.
Delete rows from a view	Make sure you remove rows from only one table.
Delete rows from several tables using a view	Implement an INSTEAD OF trigger.
Enhance control and security in delete operations	Encapsulate the DELETE statements in stored procedures.
Perform other actions while deleting data	Implement AFTER triggers on the table.
Control errors during database actions	Use *try... catch* blocks to obtain information from the *ERROR_xxx* functions.
Delete data from an ADO.NET application	Use the ADO.NET *Connection* and *Command* objects.
Control the information displayed to the user when an error occurs	Catch the *SqlClient.SqlException* class and evaluate the Number value.

Chapter 12

Updating Data from Microsoft SQL Server 2005

After completing this chapter, you will be able to:

- Update information in your databases
- Manage update issues by using triggers
- Use ADO.NET components to perform update operations

Using the UPDATE Statement

You use the UPDATE statement to modify information in your data tables. The basic syntax for updates is the following:

```
UPDATE [<ServerName>].[<Database>].[<Schema>].[<TableName>]
    SET [<ColumnName>] = <NewValue>>
        ,....
 WHERE <Search Conditions,,>
```

As usual, if you execute the UPDATE sentence with a connection to the current database, you can simply use the <SchemaName>.<TableName> form without including the server and database names.

You can use the UPDATE sentence without a WHERE condition. A developer uses this option to modify the entire table with some calculation, such as incrementing or decrementing the product's prices, or with any other massive change. If you want to update specific information, you must include the WHERE condition in your sentence. Moreover, the WHERE condition must be specific enough to update just one row.

Creating an UPDATE Sentence with SQL Server Management Studio

To create an UPDATE sentence using SQL Server Management Studio, perform the following steps.

Creating an UPDATE Sentence

1. Right-click the desired table.
2. Choose Script Table As.
3. Choose Update To.

4. Choose New Query Editor Window. SQL Server Management Studio will create a template for you.

> **Important**   If you work through the procedures in this chapter using the AdventureWorks database, it is important to back up your database first.

Defining the WHERE Condition

Similar to the DELETE statement, you can use any or all columns of a table to create the WHERE condition. You can enhance the performance of the UPDATE statement by using the following guidelines:

- Use the Primary.Key column/s in the condition.
- Use columns that are part of an index.

Assigning New Values to Columns

The values assigned to columns must match the datatype. You can assign various types of values to a column.

- **NULL**   Can be used when the column accepts NULLs
- **DEFAULT**   Can be used when the column has a default value defined
- **SQL Functions**   You must use a function that returns the same datatype accepted by the column. Some examples include:
  - **GetDate()**   Used to assign the actual server-side date and time values
  - **NEWID()**   Used to assign a new Id to a unique identifier column
  - **user_name()**   Used to assign the current username, which is useful for auditing purposes
- **Your own values**   You can supply any valid value.

During any column update, you must match the datatype and stay within the max values that the column accepts. In the following sentence, the ModifiedDate receives a valid date.

```
UPDATE [AdventureWorks].[Sales].[SalesReason]
   SET [ModifiedDate] = 01/01/2006
 WHERE SalesReasonID=1
```

However, if you look at the row content, you notice that the column in that row contains 01/01/1900 12:00:00 a.m. Microsoft SQL Server 2005 assumes that the date you enter is an arithmetic operation: 1 divided by 1 divided by 2006. The query analyzer executes the operation and converts the result into a new date, which results in day 0 since the calculated value is less than 1.

You cannot use Visual Basic syntax, such as the following:

```
UPDATE [AdventureWorks].[Sales].[SalesReason]
   SET [ModifiedDate] = #01/01/2006#
WHERE SalesReasonID=1
```

The above code generates the following syntax error message:

```
Msg 102, Level 15, State 1, Line 2
Incorrect syntax near '#'.
```

You must enter the date as a string and cast it to a datetime value.

```
UPDATE [AdventureWorks].[Sales].[SalesReason]
   SET [ModifiedDate] = cast('01/01/2006'as datetime)
WHERE SalesReasonID=1
```

However, the issue has futher complications. The following sentence changes the modified date to Oct 31, 2006.

```
UPDATE [AdventureWorks].[Sales].[SalesReason]
   SET [ModifiedDate] = cast('10/31/2006'as datetime)
WHERE SalesReasonID=1
```

The code above is valid if you are from the United States or any country that uses the mm/dd/yyyy date format. In other countries, the format might be different. For example, it might be dd/mm/yyyy, as in all Spanish-speaking countries, or yyyy.mm.dd, as in Japan.

The SQL Server engine assumes the date to be formatted according to its own language. If you have installed the English version of SQL Server 2005, it will interpret dates in the US or UK format. Nowadays, increasing numbers of applications are Web enabled and have clients from around the world. Each user will enter a date in a Web page using his customary format. Thus, if you use input from Japan, you will receive many conversion errors.

To avoid this problem, you can use the *CONVERT* function instead of the *CAST* function. *CONVERT* accepts another argument or style to define the format to use in the datatype conversion.

> **Tip**   Search for the *CAST* and *CONVERT* functions in SQL Server Books Online to review the complete list of style values.

Using Arithmetic to Update Information

You can update a group of rows or the entire content of a table by adjusting the WHERE condition. This is typically done when you need to update the same column by applying a differential value such as incrementing or decrementing a discount, adding or subtracting amounts, and so on.

You do not need to use a variable to perform the calculation. You can use the calculus directly as the right part of the assignment, as follows:

```
UPDATE [AdventureWorks].[Production].[Product]
   SET [ListPrice] = [ListPrice] * 0.9
 WHERE ProductSubcategoryID=1
```

Changing the Content of a Large (MAX) Column

If you need to modify part of the content of a large field, such as a column with a varchar(MAX), nvarchar(MAX), or nvarbinary(MAX) datatype, you can simply change that part instead of modifying the entire content. You can apply the following modifier to the UPDATE sentence:

```
UPDATE <table_Name>
   SET <Column_Name>.WRITE(<New_Value>,<Offset>,<Length>)
```

> **Note**   The offset value starts with zero.

> **Tip**   To enhance performance, try to use .WRITE with 8040-byte chunks.

Changing the Content of a Large (BLOB) Column

Changing the content of a text or ntext column may need a different approach. If you want to change the entire content, you need to use the WRITETEXT sentence, which was the only way to accomplish this until the arrival of SQL Server 2005. If you want to partially change the content, you can use UPDATETEXT. Using these sentences requires that you obtain a pointer to the column before executing them. You will use the pointer to implement the UPDATE-TEXT or WRITETEXT sentences. For more information, search for UPDATETEXT in SQL Server Books Online.

> **Important**   Starting with SQL Server 2005, avoid using the WRITETEXT or UPDATETEXT sentences, for they are not guaranteed to exist in future versions of SQL Server. Using the MAX modifier for any long blocks of content allows you to enhance the database. You should always use the .WRITE modifier.

Updating Data through Views

You can perform update actions by using views in the same way that you create insert or delete actions. However, the following limitations apply.

- Updates are only allowed on columns from a single table.
- The connected user must have write access to the view.

■ The view creator must have write access to the table.

Using INSTEAD OF UPDATE Triggers on Views

Just as you can personalize certain actions involving views, you can manage and change the behavior of update actions on views by using INSTEAD OF UPDATE triggers. In this case, the update action will respond like any other trigger by using a double-phase action: the engine deletes the old row and then adds a new one.

Although this last statement is not precisely accurate, it does reflect the representation you obtain with the trigger procedure. According to this, you will use both a virtual table named deleted and a virtual table named inserted. The first table will contain the old version of the row, and the second table will contain the new version of the row as it will look when the update procedure is completed. To understand this concept, consider the following scenario.

Understanding the INSTEAD OF UPDATE Trigger

1. Call an UPDATE statement.

2. The engine copies the old row into a virtual table named deleted.

3. The engine copies the old row again into another virtual table named inserted.

4. The engine performs the changes in the row inside the table named inserted with the values you pass to the UPDATE statement.

5. The engine calls your INSTEAD OF trigger and passes it to both the table named deleted and the table named inserted.

6. If your INSTEAD OF trigger is successful, the engine calls the AFTER trigger–if one exists–in the table named deleted and also in the table named inserted with the changes you made in the INSTEAD OF trigger.

7. If this last trigger is successful or if no AFTER trigger exists, the transaction ends and all of the changes commit to the database.

The syntax is similar to that used for the other INSTEAD OF triggers. This code is included in the sample files as \Ch12\AdvWorks\Queries\Sample01.sql.

```
Use AdventureWorks
GO
CREATE TRIGGER [dbo].[vProductFullCategoriesUpdateTrigger]
   ON [dbo].[vProductFullCategories]
INSTEAD OF UPDATE
AS
BEGIN
   UPDATE Production.ProductSubcategory
   SET Name=inserted.Name
   FROM
   Production.ProductSubcategory
     INNER JOIN inserted
     ON Production.ProductSubcategory.ProductSubcategoryID=
```

```
                    inserted.ProductSubcategoryID
END
```

Detecting Changes in a View

In the previous trigger sample, you assumed that the user will change the subcategory's name. However, the view shows the category name, which the user can also change. To determine exactly what columns have been changed, you can use the *UPDATE(<column>)* function. This function returns true if the specified column has been changed in the update process.

Using the *UPDATE(<column>)* function, the trigger can decide which table to update by using the following syntax. This code is included in the sample files as \Ch12\AdvWorks\Queries\Sample02.sql.

```
Use AdventureWorks
GO
ALTER TRIGGER [dbo].[vProductFullCategoriesUpdateTrigger]
    ON [dbo].[vProductFullCategories]
INSTEAD OF UPDATE
AS
BEGIN
    IF UPDATE(Name)
        BEGIN
            UPDATE Production.ProductSubcategory
            SET Name=inserted.Name
            FROM
            Production.ProductSubcategory
                INNER JOIN inserted
                ON Production.ProductSubcategory.ProductSubcategoryID
                    =inserted.ProductSubcategoryID
        END
    IF UPDATE(CategoryName)
        BEGIN
            UPDATE Production.Productcategory
            SET Name=inserted.Name
            FROM
            Production.ProductSubcategory
                INNER JOIN inserted
                ON Production.ProductSubcategory.ProductSubcategoryID
                    =inserted.ProductSubcategoryID
            INNER JOIN Production.ProductCategory
                ON Production.ProductCategory.ProductCategoryID
                    =Production.ProductSubcategory.ProductCategoryID
        END
END
```

> **Note**   Transact-SQL (T-SQL) supports the *COLUMNS_UPDATED* function to test several updated columns at the same time. This function returns a varbinary datatype with one or more bytes with the bitwise results of the updated columns. That is, if the update changes the first column, the rightmost bit of the byte is turned on, and so forth. To check the value, you must use bitwise operations. Search for COLUMNS_UPDATED in SQL Server Books Online for more information and examples.

Encapsulating Update Operations in Stored Procedures

It is best to encapsulate your updates within stored procedures to improve both performance and security. Furthermore, you can implement several actions against different objects inside the database in the same procedure. Using stored procedures is an easy way to standardize procedures and calls from applications. The developer does not need to know how many tables to update because the process involves only a "call this procedure" action, thus passing the appropriate parameters.

To better understand how to implement stored procedure update operations, refer to the following considerations.

- Stored procedures execute "near the data," which means directly inside the database. This translates into better performance.

- Stored procedures are compiled and contain the best query plan for their execution. This also translates into better performance.

- Performing several calls to the same or different stored procedures from an application can increase network traffic, which could result in a bottleneck.

- Implementing business logic inside stored procedures can be problematic. There are richer language elements in ADO.NET than in T-SQL. Moreover, a great deal of logic and calculation processing can be performed only by using cursors or temporary tables. Both require tremendous resources and decrease performance.

- More resource utilization (mainly processor resources) implies more time expended, and more time implies more risk of losing the transaction and increasing timeout errors.

The following stored procedure updates a row in the HumanResources.Department table according to its primary key. This code is included in the sample files as \Ch12\Adv-Works\Queries\Sample03.sql.

```
CREATE PROCEDURE [HumanResources].[DepartmentUpdate]
    @DepartmentID int,
    @Name nvarchar(50),
    @GroupName nvarchar(50),
    @ModifiedDate datetime
AS
BEGIN
UPDATE [AdventureWorks].[HumanResources].[Department]
    SET [Name] = @Name
       ,[GroupName] = @GroupName
       ,[ModifiedDate] = @ModifiedDate
 WHERE DepartmentID=@DepartmentID
END
```

You can implement updates for changing the values for one or more columns in one or more tables. In the following example, the procedure accepts values for the subcategory and category names. If the procedure receives a value for the category name, it updates the column in the Category table. This code is included in the sample files as \Ch12\AdvWorks\Queries\Sample04.sql.

```
CREATE PROCEDURE [Production].[SubcategoryUpdate]
    @SubcategoryID int,
    @Name nvarchar(50),
    @CategoryName nvarchar(50)=null
AS
BEGIN
    UPDATE [AdventureWorks].[Production].[ProductSubcategory]
      SET
       [Name] = @Name
      ,[ModifiedDate] = GETDATE()
      WHERE ProductSubcategoryID=@SubcategoryID
    -- Check if we receive a Category Name
    IF NOT @CategoryName IS NULL
        -- Update the Category Name
        UPDATE [AdventureWorks].[Production].[ProductCategory]
          SET
              [Name] = @CategoryName
             ,[rowguid] = NEWID()
             ,[ModifiedDate] = GETDATE()
          WHERE
          ProductCategoryID=
           (
              SELECT ProductCategoryID
              FROM Production.ProductSubcategory
              WHERE (ProductSubcategoryID = @SubCategoryID)
           )
END
```

In the following example, the ListPrice of the products will be changed by a percentage depending on the subcategory Id. The same procedure can be used to apply the percentage to all of the products if the second parameter is not passed during the procedure's execution. This code is included in the sample files as \Ch12\AdvWorks\Queries\Sample05.sql.

```
CREATE PROCEDURE [Production].[Product_ChangePrices]
    @Percent decimal,
    @ProductSubcategoryID int=null
AS
BEGIN
    UPDATE [AdventureWorks].[Production].[Product]
      SET [ListPrice] = [ListPrice] * @Percent
     WHERE ([ProductSubcategoryID]=@ProductSubcategoryID)
        -- If the second argument is null the percent applies to all the products
        OR (@ProductSubcategoryID IS NULL)
END
```

Finally, the next example demonstrates how to use the same procedure to update or insert a row in a table, receiving values from the application in the parameters. This is a common scenario used in object-oriented programming to send the most updated information into the object once again. This code is included in the sample files as \Ch12\AdvWorks\Queries\Sample06.sql.

```
CREATE PROCEDURE [Person].[AddressTypeFullUpdate]
    @AddressTypeID int OUTPUT,
    @Name nvarchar(50) OUTPUT,
    @rowguid uniqueidentifier=null OUTPUT,
    @ModifiedDate datetime=null OUTPUT
AS
-- Check if a row exists with the same AddressTypeID
IF exists(
        SELECT AddressTypeID
        FROM Person.AddressType
        WHERE (AddressTypeID = @AddressTypeID)
    )
    BEGIN -- Update the existing row
        UPDATE [AdventureWorks].[Person].[AddressType]
            SET [Name] = @Name
             ,[rowguid] = NEWID()
             ,[ModifiedDate] = GETDATE()
          WHERE AddressTypeID = @AddressTypeID
    END
ELSE
    BEGIN -- Insert a new row
        INSERT INTO [AdventureWorks].[Person].[AddressType]
                ([Name]
                ,[rowguid]
                ,[ModifiedDate])
            VALUES
                (@Name
                ,NEWID(),
                ,@GETDATE())
    -- Retrieve the new AddressTypeID
    SET @AddressTypeID=IDENT_CURRENT('Person.AddressType')
    END
-- Assign the actual values from the row to the parameters
SELECT    @AddressTypeID=AddressTypeID,
        @Name=Name,
        @rowguid=rowguid,
        @ModifiedDate=ModifiedDate
FROM [AdventureWorks].[Person].[AddressType]
WHERE (AddressTypeID = @AddressTypeID)
```

Implementing Pessimistic and Optimistic Concurrency for Update Operations

The same issues exist for update operations as for delete operations. Refer to Chapter 11, Deleting Data from Microsoft SQL Server 2005, to refresh your knowledge about the management of pessimistic and optimistic concurrency.

Triggering Actions Automatically when Updating Data

The previous chapter discussed the occasional need to control what happens when any process or application inserts or deletes a row. The main difference when updating data is the virtual tables that are used. When updating rows, there are two tables that contain the changes: the table named deleted and the table named inserted.

Using the same Production.ProductHistory table that was used in Chapter 11, it is possible to keep a log detailing the updates in the Production table. This code is included in the sample files as \Ch12\AdvWorks\Queries\Sample07.sql.

```
CREATE TRIGGER Production.Product_UpdateTrigger
   ON  Production.Product
   AFTER UPDATE
AS
BEGIN
   SET NOCOUNT ON;
    INSERT INTO [AdventureWorks].[Production].[ProductHistory]
           ([ProductID],[Name],[ProductNumber],[MakeFlag]
           ,[FinishedGoodsFlag],[Color],[SafetyStockLevel]
           ,[ReorderPoint],[StandardCost],[ListPrice]
           ,[Size],[SizeUnitMeasureCode],[WeightUnitMeasureCode]
           ,[Weight],[DaysToManufacture],[ProductLine]
           ,[Class],[Style],[ProductSubcategoryID]
           ,[ProductModelID],[SellStartDate],[SellEndDate]
           ,[DiscontinuedDate],[rowguid],[ModifiedDate]
           ,[Action],[UserName])
      SELECT [ProductID],[Name],[ProductNumber],[MakeFlag]
           ,[FinishedGoodsFlag],[Color],[SafetyStockLevel]
           ,[ReorderPoint],[StandardCost],[ListPrice]
           ,[Size],[SizeUnitMeasureCode],[WeightUnitMeasureCode]
           ,[Weight],[DaysToManufacture],[ProductLine]
           ,[Class],[Style],[ProductSubcategoryID]
           ,[ProductModelID],[SellStartDate],[SellEndDate]
           ,[DiscontinuedDate],[rowguid],GetDate(),'M',USER_NAME()
         FROM inserted
END
```

If you want to track both the old and new versions, you can insert two rows in the History table, with one containing the old version from the table named deleted and the other containing the new version from the table named inserted. This code is included in the sample files as \Ch12\AdvWorks\Queries\Sample08.sql.

```
CREATE TRIGGER Production.Product_UpdateTrigger
   ON  Production.Product
   AFTER UPDATE
AS
BEGIN
   SET NOCOUNT ON;
   DECLARE @Stamp datetime;
   SET @Stamp=getdate();
-- Add the old row to the History table
```

```
  INSERT INTO [AdventureWorks].[Production].[ProductHistory]
          ([ProductID],[Name],[ProductNumber],[MakeFlag]
          ,[FinishedGoodsFlag],[Color],[SafetyStockLevel]
          ,[ReorderPoint],[StandardCost],[ListPrice]
          ,[Size],[SizeUnitMeasureCode],[WeightUnitMeasureCode]
          ,[Weight],[DaysToManufacture],[ProductLine]
          ,[Class],[Style],[ProductSubcategoryID]
          ,[ProductModelID],[SellStartDate],[SellEndDate]
          ,[DiscontinuedDate],[rowguid],[ModifiedDate]
          ,[Action],[UserName])
      SELECT [ProductID],[Name],[ProductNumber],[MakeFlag]
          ,[FinishedGoodsFlag],[Color],[SafetyStockLevel]
          ,[ReorderPoint],[StandardCost],[ListPrice]
          ,[Size],[SizeUnitMeasureCode],[WeightUnitMeasureCode]
          ,[Weight],[DaysToManufacture],[ProductLine]
          ,[Class],[Style],[ProductSubcategoryID]
          ,[ProductModelID],[SellStartDate],[SellEndDate]
          ,[DiscontinuedDate],[rowguid],@Stamp,'O',USER_NAME()
        FROM deleted
-- Add the new version to the History table
      INSERT INTO [AdventureWorks].[Production].[ProductHistory]
          ([ProductID],[Name],[ProductNumber],[MakeFlag]
          ,[FinishedGoodsFlag],[Color],[SafetyStockLevel]
          ,[ReorderPoint],[StandardCost],[ListPrice]
          ,[Size],[SizeUnitMeasureCode],[WeightUnitMeasureCode]
          ,[Weight],[DaysToManufacture],[ProductLine]
          ,[Class],[Style],[ProductSubcategoryID]
          ,[ProductModelID],[SellStartDate],[SellEndDate]
          ,[DiscontinuedDate],[rowguid],[ModifiedDate]
          ,[Action],[UserName])
      SELECT [ProductID],[Name],[ProductNumber],[MakeFlag]
          ,[FinishedGoodsFlag],[Color],[SafetyStockLevel]
          ,[ReorderPoint],[StandardCost],[ListPrice]
          ,[Size],[SizeUnitMeasureCode],[WeightUnitMeasureCode]
          ,[Weight],[DaysToManufacture],[ProductLine]
          ,[Class],[Style],[ProductSubcategoryID]
          ,[ProductModelID],[SellStartDate],[SellEndDate]
          ,[DiscontinuedDate],[rowguid],@Stamp,'N',USER_NAME()
        FROM inserted
END
```

Dealing with Errors

The update process involves the same errors as those explained in previous chapters. You might try to update a row that no longer exists. This will not be considered an error from the database engine point of view; it will simply return a "0 rows affected" message. Refer to Chapter 11 for more details on how to handle this situation.

Some special errors that occur during update operations are detailed in the following section.

Assigned Value Is Higher than the Field Datatype Limit

This error may appear when you update rows with calculations. Using stored procedures can protect you from this error. A stored procedure receives the values through parameters, which have their own datatypes. The overflow will occur as soon as you try to assign a datatype that could contain a higher value to a parameter.

Execute the following update. This code is included in the sample files as \Ch12\Adv-Works\Queries\Sample09.sql.

```
UPDATE [AdventureWorks].[Production].[Product]
   SET [ReorderPoint] = ReorderPoint *2^128
```

You obtain an overflow error similar to the following message:

```
Msg 220, Level 16, State 1, Line 1
Arithmetic overflow error for data type smallint, value = 48128.
The statement has been terminated.
```

Column Value Violates Referential Integrity

An application usually allows the user to choose from the actual values to update a column that uses referential integrity. However, it is possible for another user to remove one of these choices between the read and the update calls. That is why you must check the integrity error each time you update a row. You can obtain the error by executing the following code. This code is included in the sample files as \Ch12\AdvWorks\Queries\Sample10.sql.

```
UPDATE [AdventureWorks].[Production].[Product]
   SET [ProductSubcategoryID] = 0
 WHERE ProductID=1
```

You will receive an error similar to the following message:

```
Msg 547, Level 16, State 0, Line 1
The UPDATE statement conflicted with the FOREIGN KEY constraint "FK_Product_ProductSubcatego
ry_ProductSubcategoryID". The conflict occurred in database "AdventureWorks", table "Product
ion.ProductSubcategory", column 'ProductSubcategoryID'.
The statement has been terminated.
```

Updating Data from ADO.NET

To perform updates using ADO.NET, you use the same objects utilized in the insert and delete actions: *Connection* and *Command* objects. The *Command* object may contain a T-SQL sentence or the name of a stored procedure in its CommandText property.

Note   Remember: It is better to use stored procedures in all database operations.

To update a row using a stored procedure, perform the following steps.

Updating a Row Using a Stored Procedure in ADO.NET

1. Create a *Connection* object with a valid connection string.

2. Create a *Command* object with the stored procedure name in its CommandText property and *Stored Procedure* in its CommandType property.

3. Assign the *Connection* object to the *Command* object's Connection property.

4. Add parameters for the stored procedure to the *Parameters* collection in the *Command* object.

5. Open the connection.

6. Call the *Command* object's *ExecuteNonQuery* method.

7. Close the connection.

Using Datasets and Table Adapters

You can use datasets to bind and manage data in your applications. ADO.NET 2.0 adds new objects to the dataset implementation, allowing you to encapsulate the actions inside the dataset.

You can graphically create the infrastructure to use this feature, which is a quick way to implement Create Read Update Delete (CRUD) applications. However, keep in mind this is not the best way to build complex, reliable applications.

Creating a Dataset and Table Adapter

1. Open Visual Studio 2005, and create a new Windows application.

2. In the Solution Explorer, right-click the Project node and choose Add | New Item.

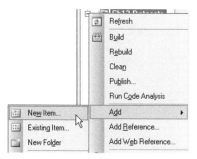

3. In the dialog box that appears, choose DataSet and give the dataset the **AdvWorks** name.

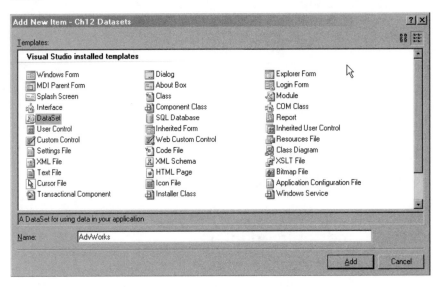

4. Choose Server Explorer from the View menu, or press Ctrl+Alt+S to show the Server Explorer window.

5. Expand Data Connections and your AdventureWorks connection, then expand Tables.

6. Drag the TestTable and drop it over the Dataset Designer.

In the designer surface, you will see the table structure.

7. Right-click the table structure, choose Configure, and then click the Advanced Options button. You will see that the DataTable implements INSERT, UPDATE, and DELETE SQL sentences, manages optimistic concurrency, and retrieves the new values after the execution of any update or insert action.

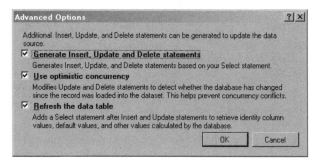

8. Close the Dataset Designer and save the changes.

9. Choose Build Solution from the Build menu, or press Ctrl+Shift+B to build the entire solution.

10. Open the form in design view. Expand the Toolbox window. You will see the DataSet and TestTableTableAdapter available at the top.

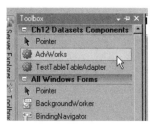

11. Drag the DataSet and TestTableTableAdapter and drop them over Form1. By doing this, you will obtain automatically created instances of these objects that are ready for you to use.

Creating a User Interface

1. Drag a ToolStrip over Form1.

2. Right-click it on the tray below the form, and choose Insert Standard Items.

3. Drag a DataGridView over the form.

4. If necessary, open the DataGridView Tasks window by clicking the black arrow in the upper-right corner of the control. From the Choose Data Source drop-down list in the DataGridView Tasks window, expand the Other Data Sources node, then the Project Data Sources node, and then select AdvWorks1.

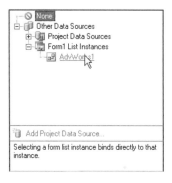

5. Right-click DataGridView1 and choose Properties, or press F4 to display the Properties window.

6. In the DataMember property, choose TestTable. The grid will display the columns' names.

7. In the Dock property, choose Fill by clicking the larger button in the middle of the pane.

8. In the ToolStrip, double-click the Open button (the folder icon).

9. Add the following code. This code is included in the sample files as \Ch12\Codes\Sample11.vb.

```
TestTableTableAdapter1.Fill(AdvWorks1.TestTable)
```

10. Return to the Form1 designer and double-click the Save button on the toolbar.

11. Add the following code to perform the update. This code is included in the sample files as \Ch12\Codes\Sample12.vb.

```
Try
    TestTableTableAdapter1.Update(AdvWorks1.TestTable)
Catch ex As Exception
    MsgBox(ex.Message)
End Try
```

12. Run the application and test the update actions (click the Open button on the toolbar, modify some records, and then click the Save button on the toolbar).

> **Tip**   After editing a row, move to another row before clicking the Save button. This is the only way that the data grid can update the information to the data table.

Pay attention to what is happening behind the scenes. For example, double-click the AdvWorks.xsd node in the Solution Explorer to bring up the DataSet Designer. Right-click TestTableTableAdapter and choose Properties from the context menu. In the Properties window, expand the Update Command node.

Observe the Update command for the AdvWorks dataset in the TestTableTable-Adapter's CommandText property. You will see the UPDATE sentence that follows, in which each column has two parameter definitions: one for the new value and one for the original value. Moreover, the WHERE clause is built with conditions for every column in the table. This code is included in the sample files as \Ch12\AdvWorks\Queries\Sample13.sql.

```
UPDATE TestTable
SET   Name = @Name,
   Description = @Description,
   ActiveDate = @ActiveDate,
   IsActive = @IsActive
WHERE
   (Id = @Original_Id)
AND (@IsNull_Name = 1)
AND (Name IS NULL)
AND (ActiveDate = @Original_ActiveDate)
AND (IsActive = @Original_IsActive)
OR
   (Id = @Original_Id)
AND (Name = @Original_Name)
AND (ActiveDate = @Original_ActiveDate)
AND (IsActive = @Original_IsActive)
```

This example creates only a small table, but imagine what would occur with the Production.Product table, which would produce twenty-five WHERE conditions. It is inefficient to perform numerous WHERE conditions. Refer to the Implementing Optimistic Concurrency for Delete Operations section in Chapter 11 to see alternatives to this method.

Using Stored Procedures with Table Adapters

You can use your own stored procedures to manage update actions in a Table Adapter.

Creating Stored Procedures for Table Adapters

1. Create the following stored procedure to obtain the complete SubCategories list with the associated Category name. This code is included in the sample files as \Ch12\AdvWorks\Queries\Sample14.sql.

```
CREATE Procedure SubCategories_GetAll
AS
SELECT   Production.ProductSubcategory.ProductSubcategoryID,
      Production.ProductCategory.Name AS Category,
      Production.ProductSubcategory.Name
FROM   Production.ProductSubcategory
INNER JOIN
   Production.ProductCategory
ON
   Production.ProductSubcategory.ProductCategoryID =
      Production.ProductCategory.ProductCategoryID
ORDER BY   Category,
         Production.ProductSubcategory.Name
GO
```

2. Add the following stored procedure to retrieve the values for just one row. This code is included in the sample files as \Ch12\AdvWorks\Queries\Sample15.sql.

```
CREATE Procedure SubCategories_GetOne
    @ProductSubcategoryID int
AS
SELECT   ProductSubcategoryID,
         ProductCategoryID,
      Name,
      rowguid,
      ModifiedDate
FROM   Production.ProductSubcategory
WHERE
    (ProductSubcategoryID = @ProductSubcategoryID)
GO
```

3. Add a stored procedure for the insert operation. This code is included in the sample files as \Ch12\AdvWorks\Queries\Sample16.sql.

```
CREATE Procedure SubCategory_Insert
    @ProductCategoryID int,
    @Name nvarchar(50),
    @rowguid uniqueidentifier,
    @ModifiedDate datetime
AS
INSERT INTO [AdventureWorks].[Production].[ProductSubcategory]
            ([ProductCategoryID]
            ,[Name]
            ,[rowguid]
            ,[ModifiedDate])
     VALUES
            (@ProductCategoryID
            ,@Name
            ,NEWID()
            ,GETDATE())
GO
```

4. Add a stored procedure for the update operation. This code is included in the sample files as \Ch12\AdvWorks\Queries\Sample17.sql.

```
CREATE Procedure SubCategory_Update
    @ProductSubCategoryID int,
    @ProductCategoryID int,
     @Name nvarchar(50),
    @rowguid uniqueidentifier,
    @ModifiedDate datetime
AS
UPDATE [AdventureWorks].[Production].[ProductSubcategory]
    SET [ProductCategoryID] = @ProductCategoryID
        ,[Name] = @Name
        ,[rowguid] = NEWID()
        ,[ModifiedDate] = GETDATE()
  WHERE ProductSubCategoryId=@ProductSubCategoryId
   AND [rowguid] = @rowguid
GO
```

5. Add a stored procedure for the delete operation. This code is included in the sample files as \Ch12\AdvWorks\Queries\Sample18.sql.

```
CREATE Procedure SubCategory_Delete
   @ProductSubCategoryID int,
   @rowguid uniqueidentifier
AS
DELETE FROM [AdventureWorks].[Production].[ProductSubcategory]
 WHERE ProductSubCategoryId=@ProductSubCategoryId
   AND [rowguid] = @rowguid
GO
```

> **Important**   In the update and delete stored procedures, you use the rowguid field to locate the same row that you retrieved previously.

6. In Visual Studio, edit the AdvWorks.xsd dataset in the new project you built in the procedure titled "Creating a Dataset and Table Adapter."

7. From the View menu, select Server Explorer.

8. Expand the Database Connections node, expand your AdventureWorks connection, and then expand the Stored Procedures folder.

9. In Design view, drag the SubCategories_GetAll stored procedure and drop it over the Design view of the dataset.

10. Repeat this action for the SubCategories_GetOne stored procedure.

11. Right-click the SubCategories_GetOne table and choose Configure.

12. Assign the appropiate stored procedures for each action as shown below and click Finish.

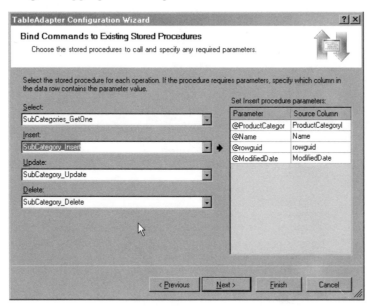

Creating an Editor

1. Drag the Production.ProductCategory table to the dataset.

2. Build the solution.

3. Add a new Windows form to your Windows application by using the Project | Add Windows Form menu and name it **SubCategories.vb**.

4. From the Toolbox, drag the SubCategories_GetAllTableAdapter, the SubCategories_GetOneTableAdapter, the ProductCategoryTableAdapter, and the AdvWorks dataset to the form.

5. Add a ToolStrip to the form.

6. Drag a SplitContainer from the Toolbox and change the orientation to Horizontal.

7. Drag a DataGridView to the upper SplitContainer panel. Drag two Labels, one ComboBox, one Textbox, and one Button to the lower SplitContainer panel.

8. Assign the AdvWorks dataset as the Data Source in the Properties window of the DataGridView, and assign SubCategories_GetAll as the DataMember in the DataGridView. The form will look like the following:

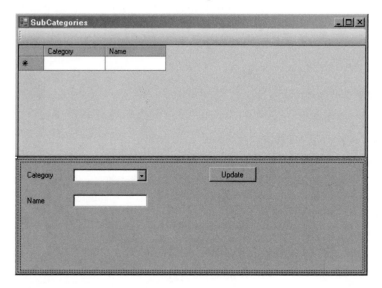

9. Enable the Use Data Bound Items option in the DropDownList's Tasks window and assign the properties as follows:

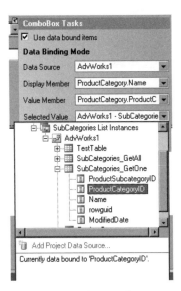

10.   Select the textbox and press F4 to display the Properties window.

11.   In the Properties window, expand the DataBindings section and change the Text prop-
      erty data bindings to point to the Name field of the SubCategories_GetOne table in
      AdvWorks1.

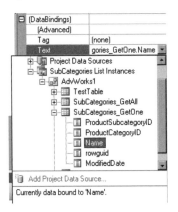

12.   Choose Code from the View menu to display the code editor.

13.   Add the following code to load the DataGridView when the form starts. This code is
      included in the sample files as \Ch12\Codes\Sample19.vb.

```vb
Private Sub SubCategories_Load( _
    ByVal sender As System.Object, _
    ByVal e As System.EventArgs) Handles MyBase.Load
    SubCategories_GetAllTableAdapter1.Fill(AdvWorks1.SubCategories_GetAll)
    ProductCategoryTableAdapter1.Fill(AdvWorks1.ProductCategory)
End Sub
```

14. View the form again, select DataGridView, and press F4 to display the Properties window.

15. Click the Events toolbar button in the Properties window (the button with the lightning bolt), scroll down to the *rowEnter* event, and double-click it.

16. Add code in the DataGridView's *RowEnter* event to fill the SubCategories_GetOne table when a row is selected. This code is included in the sample files as \Ch12\Codes\Sample20.vb.

```
With SubCategories_GetOneTableAdapter1
    .Fill( _
        AdvWorks1.SubCategories_GetOne, _
        AdvWorks1.SubCategories_GetAll.Rows(e.RowIndex).Item(0))
End With
```

17. Add code for the button's *Click* event to update the changes to the database. This code is included in the sample files as \Ch12\Codes\Sample21.vb.

```
Try
    AdvWorks1.SubCategories_GetOne.Rows(0).EndEdit()
    SubCategories_GetOneTableAdapter1.Update( _
        AdvWorks1.SubCategories_GetOne)
    SubCategories_GetAllTableAdapter1.Fill( _
        AdvWorks1.SubCategories_GetAll)
Catch ex As Exception

End Try
```

18. Add a button to the ToolStrip by clicking the small black down arrow and selecting Button.

19. Assign New as the Text property, and change the DisplayStyle to Text.

20. Double-click the New button and add the following code to insert a new row. This code is included in the sample files as \Ch12\Codes\Sample22.vb.

```
With AdvWorks1.SubCategories_GetOne
    .Clear() 'remove any previous row
    'Create a new row
    Dim r As AdvWorks.SubCategories_GetOneRow = _
        .NewSubCategories_GetOneRow
    'Assign default values to each column
    r.ProductCategoryID = 0
    r.Name = ""
    r.rowguid = Guid.NewGuid
    r.ModifiedDate = System.DateTime.Now
    'Add the row to the table
    .AddSubCategories_GetOneRow(r)
End With
```

21. Add code that explains what to do when a category is not selected. In the *Button_Click* event, catch the *SQLException* to manage the Number property. (Add this code right after the END WITH statement.) This code is included in the sample files as \Ch12\Codes\Sample23.vb.

```
Catch ex As SqlClient.SqlException
    Select Case ex.Number
        Case 547
            MsgBox("Please, select one of the categories")
            ComboBox1.Focus()
        Case Else
            MsgBox(ex.Message)
    End Select
End Try
```

22. Remember to add a TRY statement before the WITH statement.

23. Add a button to the ToolStrip, change the text to Delete, and set the DisplayStyle as Text.

24. Double-click the Delete button and add code to delete a subcategory. Remember to manage the referential error. This code is included in the sample files as \Ch12\Codes\Sample24.vb.

```
If MsgBox("Do you want to delete the selected sub category?", _
    MsgBoxStyle.Question Or MsgBoxStyle.YesNo) = MsgBoxResult.Yes Then
    Try
'Get the row depending on the selected cell in the Gridview
        With SubCategories_GetOneTableAdapter1
            .Fill( _
                AdvWorks1.SubCategories_GetOne, _
                AdvWorks1.SubCategories_GetAll.Rows( _
                DataGridView1.SelectedCells(0).RowIndex).Item(0))
'Delete the row in the DataTable
            AdvWorks1.SubCategories_GetOne.Rows(0).Delete()
'Update the changes to the database
            .Update(AdvWorks1.SubCategories_GetOne)
        End With
'reload the Datagrid rows
        SubCategories_GetAllTableAdapter1.Fill( _
            AdvWorks1.SubCategories_GetAll)
    Catch ex As SqlClient.SqlException
        Select Case ex.Number
            Case 547 'Referential error.
'In this case, the row has related rows in other tables
                MsgBox("Cannot delete. The subcategory is in use in some Products")
            Case Else
                MsgBox(ex.Message)
        End Select

    Catch ex As Exception
        MsgBox(ex.Message)
    End Try
End If
```

When you run the application, you will observe what happens when you try to delete a row on which other rows in other tables depend.

> **Note**   To run the application using the SubCategories form, right-click the project in the Solution Explorer, select Properties from the context menu, and then set the Startup form to SubCategories. Rebuild and run the application.

Conclusion

In this chapter, you learned how to update existing rows with new or modified information. Moreover, you learned new procedures to ensure referential integrity plus how to manage the update process by using triggers. By combining the information contained in the last three chapters, you can now create complete applications by applying the best practices when using SQL Server 2005.

Chapter 12 Quick Reference

To	Do This
Create an UPDATE statement in SQL Server Management Studio	Right-click the desired table.
	Choose Script Table As.
	Choose Update To.
	Choose your destination.
Update rows from a view	Make sure to update rows from only one table.
Update rows in several tables using a view	Implement an INSTEAD OF trigger.
Enhance control and security in update operations	Encapsulate the UPDATE commands into stored procedures.
Perform other actions while updating data	Implement AFTER triggers on the table.
Control errors during database actions	Use *try ... catch...* blocks to obtain information from the *ERROR_x* functions.
Update data from .NET	Use ADO.NET objects: *Connection* and *Command*
Update data from .NET (2)	Use the Table Adapter as well as your own stored procedures in the Table Adapter.
Control user information when errors occur	Catch the *SqlClient.SqlException* class and evaluate the Number value.

Index

Additional SQL Server Resources for Developers

Published and Forthcoming Titles from Microsoft Press

Microsoft® SQL Server™ 2005 Express Edition
Step by Step
Jackie Goldstein • ISBN 0-7356-2184-5

Teach yourself how to get data-base projects up and running quickly with SQL Server Express Edition—a free, easy-to-use database product that is based on SQL Server 2005 technology. It's designed for building simple, dynamic applications, with all the rich functionality of the SQL Server database engine and using the same data access APIs, such as Microsoft ADO.NET, SQL Native Client, and T-SQL. Whether you're new to database programming or new to SQL Server, you'll learn how, when, and why to use specific features of this simple but powerful data-base development environment. Each chapter puts you to work, building your knowledge of core capabilities and guiding you as you create actual components and working applications.

Microsoft SQL Server 2005 Programming
Step by Step
Fernando Guerrero • ISBN 0-7356-2207-8

SQL Server 2005 is Microsoft's next-generation data manage-ment and analysis solution that delivers enhanced scalability, availability, and security features to enterprise data and analytical applications while making them easier to create, deploy, and manage. Now you can teach yourself how to design, build, test, deploy, and maintain SQL Server databases—one step at a time. Instead of merely focusing on describing new features, this book shows new database programmers and administrators how to use specific features within typical business scenarios. Each chapter provides a highly practical learning experience that demonstrates how to build database solutions to solve common business problems.

Microsoft SQL Server 2005 Analysis Services
Step by Step
Hitachi Consulting Services • ISBN 0-7356-2199-3

One of the key features of SQL Server 2005 is SQL Server Analysis Services—Microsoft's customizable analysis solution for business data modeling and interpretation. Just compare SQL Server Analysis Services to its competition to understand the great value of its enhanced features. One of the keys to harnessing the full functionality of SQL Server will be leveraging Analysis Services for the powerful tool that it is—including creating a cube, and deploying, customizing, and extending the basic calcula-tions. This step-by-step tutorial discusses how to get started, how to build scalable analytical applications, and how to use and ad-minister advanced features. Interactivity (enhanced in SQL Server 2005), data translation, and security are also covered in detail.

Microsoft SQL Server 2005 Reporting Services
Step by Step
Hitachi Consulting Services • ISBN 0-7356-2250-7

SQL Server Reporting Services (SRS) is Microsoft's customizable reporting solution for business data analysis. It is one of the key value features of SQL Server 2005: functionality more advanced and much less expensive than its competition. SRS is powerful, so an understanding of how to architect a report, as well as how to install and program SRS, is key to harnessing the full functional-ity of SQL Server. This procedural tutorial shows how to use the Report Project Wizard, how to think about and access data, and how to build queries. It also walks through the creation of charts and visual layouts for maximum visual understanding of data analysis. Interactivity (enhanced in SQL Server 2005) and security are also covered in detail.

Programming Microsoft SQL Server 2005
Andrew J. Brust, Stephen Forte, and William H. Zack
ISBN 0-7356-1923-9

This thorough, hands-on reference for developers and database administrators teaches the basics of programming custom appli-cations with SQL Server 2005. You will learn the fundamentals of creating database applications—including coverage of T-SQL, Microsoft .NET Framework, and Microsoft ADO.NET. In addition to practical guidance on database architecture and design, application development, and reporting and data analysis, this essential reference guide covers performance, tuning, and availability of SQL Server 2005.

Inside Microsoft SQL Server 2005:
The Storage Engine
Kalen Delaney • ISBN 0-7356-2105-5

Inside Microsoft SQL Server 2005:
T-SQL Programming
Itzik Ben-Gan • ISBN 0-7356-2197-7

Inside Microsoft SQL Server 2005:
Query Processing and Optimization
Kalen Delaney • ISBN 0-7356-2196-9

Programming Microsoft ADO.NET 2.0 Core Reference
David Sceppa • ISBN 0-7356-2206-X

Additional Resources for Developers: Advanced Topics and Best Practices

Published and Forthcoming Titles from Microsoft Press

Code Complete, Second Edition
Steve McConnell • ISBN 0-7356-1967-0

For more than a decade, Steve McConnell, one of the premier authors and voices in the software community, has helped change the way developers write code—and produce better software. Now his classic book, *Code Complete*, has been fully updated and revised with best practices in the art and science of constructing software. Topics include design, applying good techniques to construction, eliminating errors, planning, managing construction activities, and relating personal character to superior software. This new edition features fully updated information on programming techniques, including the emergence of Web-style programming, and integrated coverage of object-oriented design. You'll also find new code examples—both good and bad—in C++, Microsoft® Visual Basic®, C#, and Java, although the focus is squarely on techniques and practices.

More About Software Requirements: Thorny Issues and Practical Advice
Karl E. Wiegers • ISBN 0-7356-2267-1

Have you ever delivered software that satisfied all of the project specifications, but failed to meet any of the customers expectations? Without formal, verifiable requirements—and a system for managing them—the result is often a gap between what developers think they're supposed to build and what customers think they're going to get. Too often, lessons about software requirements engineering processes are formal or academic, and not of value to real-world, professional development teams. In this follow-up guide to *Software Requirements*, Second Edition, you will discover even more practical techniques for gathering and managing software requirements that help you deliver software that meets project and customer specifications. Succinct and immediately useful, this book is a must-have for developers and architects.

Software Estimation: Demystifying the Black Art
Steve McConnell • ISBN 0-7356-0535-1

Often referred to as the "black art" because of its complexity and uncertainty, software estimation is not as hard or mysterious as people think. However, the art of how to create effective cost and schedule estimates has not been very well publicized. *Software Estimation* provides a proven set of procedures and heuristics that software developers, technical leads, and project managers can apply to their projects. Instead of arcane treatises and rigid modeling techniques, award-winning author Steve McConnell gives practical guidance to help organizations achieve basic estimation proficiency and lay the groundwork to continue improving project cost estimates. This book does not avoid the more complex mathematical estimation approaches, but the non-mathematical reader will find plenty of useful guidelines without getting bogged down in complex formulas.

Debugging, Tuning, and Testing Microsoft .NET 2.0 Applications
John Robbins • ISBN 0-7356-2202-7

Making an application the best it can be has long been a time-consuming task best accomplished with specialized and costly tools. With Microsoft Visual Studio® 2005, developers have available a new range of built-in functionality that enables them to debug their code quickly and efficiently, tune it to optimum performance, and test applications to ensure compatibility and trouble-free operation. In this accessible and hands-on book, debugging expert John Robbins shows developers how to use the tools and functions in Visual Studio to their full advantage to ensure high-quality applications.

The Security Development Lifecycle
Michael Howard and Steve Lipner • ISBN 0-7356-2214-0

Adapted from Microsoft's standard development process, the Security Development Lifecycle (SDL) is a methodology that helps reduce the number of security defects in code at every stage of the development process, from design to release. This book details each stage of the SDL methodology and discusses its implementation across a range of Microsoft software, including Microsoft Windows Server™ 2003, Microsoft SQL Server™ 2000 Service Pack 3, and Microsoft Exchange Server 2003 Service Pack 1, to help measurably improve security features. You get direct access to insights from Microsoft's security team and lessons that are applicable to software development processes worldwide, whether on a small-scale or a large-scale. This book includes a CD featuring videos of developer training classes.

Software Requirements, Second Edition
Karl E. Wiegers • ISBN 0-7356-1879-8

Writing Secure Code, Second Edition
Michael Howard and David LeBlanc • ISBN 0-7356-1722-8

CLR via C#, Second Edition
Jeffrey Richter • ISBN 0-7356-2163-2

For more information about Microsoft Press® books and other learning products,
visit: **www.microsoft.com/mspress** *and* **www.microsoft.com/learning**

Microsoft®
Press

Additional Resources for C# Developers

Published and Forthcoming Titles from Microsoft Press

Microsoft® Visual C#® 2005 Express Edition: Build a Program Now!
Patrice Pelland • ISBN 0-7356-2229-9

In this lively, eye-opening, and hands-on book, all you need is a computer and the desire to learn how to program with Visual C# 2005 Express Edition. Featuring a full working edition of the software, this fun and highly visual guide walks you through a complete programming project—a desktop weather-reporting application—from start to finish. You'll get an unintimidating introduction to the Microsoft Visual Studio® development environment and learn how to put the lightweight, easy-to-use tools in Visual C# Express to work right away—creating, compiling, testing, and delivering your first, ready-to-use program. You'll get expert tips, coaching, and visual examples at each step of the way, along with pointers to additional learning resources.

Microsoft Visual C# 2005 *Step by Step*
John Sharp • ISBN 0-7356-2129-2

Visual C#, a feature of Visual Studio 2005, is a modern programming language designed to deliver a productive environment for creating business frameworks and reusable object-oriented components. Now you can teach yourself essential techniques with Visual C#—and start building components and Microsoft Windows®–based applications—one step at a time. With *Step by Step*, you work at your own pace through hands-on, learn-by-doing exercises. Whether you're a beginning programmer or new to this particular language, you'll learn how, when, and why to use specific features of Visual C# 2005. Each chapter puts you to work, building your knowledge of core capabilities and guiding you as you create your first C#-based applications for Windows, data management, and the Web.

Programming Microsoft Visual C# 2005 Framework Reference
Francesco Balena • ISBN 0-7356-2182-9

Complementing *Programming Microsoft Visual C# 2005 Core Reference*, this book covers a wide range of additional topics and information critical to Visual C# developers, including Windows Forms, working with Microsoft ADO.NET 2.0 and Microsoft ASP.NET 2.0, Web services, security, remoting, and much more. Packed with sample code and real-world examples, this book will help developers move from understanding to mastery.

Programming Microsoft Visual C# 2005 *Core Reference*
Donis Marshall • ISBN 0-7356-2181-0

Get the in-depth reference and pragmatic, real-world insights you need to exploit the enhanced language features and core capabilities in Visual C# 2005. Programming expert Donis Marshall deftly builds your proficiency with classes, structs, and other fundamentals, and advances your expertise with more advanced topics such as debugging, threading, and memory management. Combining incisive  reference with hands-on coding examples and best practices, this *Core Reference* focuses on mastering the C# skills you need to build innovative solutions for smart clients and the Web.

CLR via C#, Second Edition
Jeffrey Richter • ISBN 0-7356-2163-2

In this new edition of Jeffrey Richter's popular book, you get focused, pragmatic guidance on how to exploit the common language runtime (CLR) functionality in Microsoft .NET Framework 2.0 for applications of all types— from Web Forms, Windows Forms, and Web services to solutions for Microsoft SQL Server™, Microsoft code names "Avalon" and "Indigo," consoles, Microsoft Windows NT® Service,  and more. Targeted to advanced developers and software designers, this book takes you under the covers of .NET for an in-depth understanding of its structure, functions, and operational components, demonstrating the most practical ways to apply this knowledge to your own development efforts. You'll master fundamental design tenets for .NET and get hands-on insights for creating high-performance applications more easily and efficiently. The book features extensive code examples in Visual C# 2005.

Programming Microsoft Windows Forms
Charles Petzold • ISBN 0-7356-2153-5

CLR via C++
Jeffrey Richter with Stanley B. Lippman
ISBN 0-7356-2248-5

Programming Microsoft Web Forms
Douglas J. Reilly • ISBN 0-7356-2179-9

Debugging, Tuning, and Testing Microsoft .NET 2.0 Applications
John Robbins • ISBN 0-7356-2202-7

For more information about Microsoft Press® books and other learning products, visit: **www.microsoft.com/books** *and* **www.microsoft.com/learning**

Additional Resources for Visual Basic Developers

Published and Forthcoming Titles from Microsoft Press

Microsoft® Visual Basic® 2005 Express Edition: Build a Program Now!
Patrice Pelland • ISBN 0-7356-2213-2

Featuring a full working edition of the software, this fun and highly visual guide walks you through a complete programming project—a desktop weather-reporting application—from start to finish. You'll get an introduction to the Microsoft Visual Studio® development environment and learn how to put the lightweight, easy-to-use tools in Visual Basic Express to work right away—creating, compiling, testing, and delivering your first ready-to-use program. You'll get expert tips, coaching, and visual examples each step of the way, along with pointers to additional learning resources.

Microsoft Visual Basic 2005 *Step by Step*
Michael Halvorson • ISBN 0-7356-2131-4

With enhancements across its visual designers, code editor, language, and debugger that help accelerate the development and deployment of robust, elegant applications across the Web, a business group, or an enterprise, Visual Basic 2005 focuses on enabling developers to rapidly build applications. Now you can teach yourself the essentials of working with Visual Studio 2005 and the new features of the Visual Basic language—one step at a time. Each chapter puts you to work, showing you how, when, and why to use specific features of Visual Basic and guiding as you create actual components and working applications for Microsoft Windows®. You'll also explore data management and Web-based development topics.

Programming Microsoft Visual Basic 2005 *Core Reference*
Francesco Balena • ISBN 0-7356-2183-7

Get the expert insights, indispensable reference, and practical instruction needed to exploit the core language features and capabilities in Visual Basic 2005. Well-known Visual Basic programming author Francesco Balena expertly guides you through the fundamentals, including modules, keywords, and inheritance, and builds your mastery of more advanced topics such as delegates, assemblies, and My Namespace. Combining in-depth reference with extensive, hands-on code examples and best-practices advice, this *Core Reference* delivers the key resources that you need to develop professional-level programming skills for smart clients and the Web.

Programming Microsoft Visual Basic 2005 Framework Reference
Francesco Balena • ISBN 0-7356-2175-6

Complementing *Programming Microsoft Visual Basic 2005 Core Reference*, this book covers a wide range of additional topics and information critical to Visual Basic developers, including Windows Forms, working with Microsoft ADO.NET 2.0 and ASP.NET 2.0, Web services, security, remoting, and much more. Packed with sample code and real-world examples, this book will help developers move from understanding to mastery.

Programming Microsoft Windows Forms
Charles Petzold • ISBN 0-7356-2153-5

Programming Microsoft Web Forms
Douglas J. Reilly • ISBN 0-7356-2179-9

Debugging, Tuning, and Testing Microsoft .NET 2.0 Applications
John Robbins • ISBN 0-7356-2202-7

Microsoft ASP.NET 2.0 *Step by Step*
George Shepherd • ISBN 0-7356-2201-9

Microsoft ADO.NET 2.0 *Step by Step*
Rebecca Riordan • ISBN 0-7356-2164-0

Programming Microsoft ASP.NET 2.0 *Core Reference*
Dino Esposito • ISBN 0-7356-2176-4

For more information about Microsoft Press® books and other learning products,
visit: **www.microsoft.com/books** *and* **www.microsoft.com/learning**

What do you think of this book? We want to hear from you!

Do you have a few minutes to participate in a brief online survey? Microsoft is interested in hearing your feedback about this publication so that we can continually improve our books and learning resources for you.

To participate in our survey, please visit:

www.microsoft.com/learning/booksurvey

And enter this book's ISBN, 0-7356-2207-8. As a thank-you to survey participants in the United States and Canada, each month we'll randomly select five respondents to win one of five $100 gift certificates from a leading online merchant.* At the conclusion of the survey, you can enter the drawing by providing your e-mail address, which will be used for prize notification *only*.

Thanks in advance for your input. Your opinion counts!

Sincerely,

Microsoft Learning

Learn More. Go Further.